THIS BOOK
BELONGS TO

_____

A
LITTLE
GOD
TIME

FOR
COUPLES

BroadStreet
PUBLISHING

BroadStreet Publishing Group, LLC.
Savage, Minnesota, USA
Broadstreetpublishing.com

A LITTLE GOD TIME FOR COUPLES

© 2020 by BroadStreet Publishing®

978-1-4245-6015-8 (faux)
978-1-4245-5369-3 (ebook)

Devotional entries composed by Janelle Anthony Breckell, Michelle Cox, Diane Dahlen, Nedra Dugan, Shawn Dugan, Linda Gilden, Mike & Sharon Harris, Carol Hatcher, and Brenda Scott.

Design by Chris Garborg | garborgdesign.com
Compiled and edited by Michelle Winger

Printed in China.

20 21 22 23 24 25 26   7 6 5 4 3 2 1

MANY WATERS CANNOT QUENCH LOVE; RIVERS CANNOT SWEEP IT AWAY.

SONG OF SONGS 8:7 NIV

INTRODUCTION

One of the best ways to strengthen your relationship and fill your day with hope and joy is to spend time together with God.

Engage with God and each other as you ponder the words and Scripture in each devotion. Use the questions for healthy reflection and encouragement toward positive change. Closing prayers will help you submit your hearts and day to God.

May your marriage be blessed as you spend a little God time together each day!

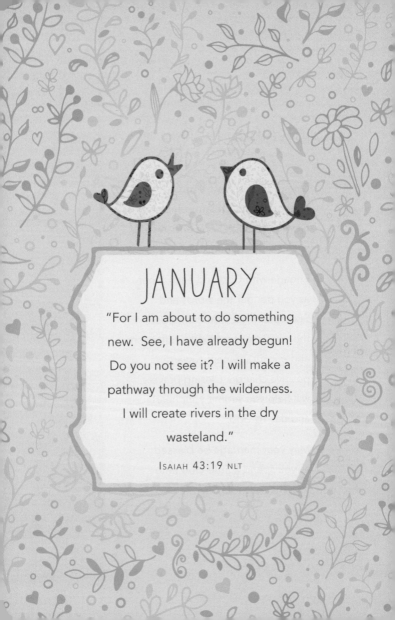

JANUARY

"For I am about to do something new. See, I have already begun! Do you not see it? I will make a pathway through the wilderness. I will create rivers in the dry wasteland."

ISAIAH 43:19 NLT

RESOLUTIONS

I will give heed to the blameless way.
When will you come to me?
I will walk within my house in the integrity of my heart.
I will set no worthless thing before my eyes;
I hate the work of those who fall away;
It shall not fasten its grip on me.

PSALM 101:2-3 NASB

Many of us make annual New Year's resolutions, only to abandon them while the year is still young. The resolutions are usually great goals, but we lack the willpower to keep them. In Psalm 101, King David speaks boldly about his resolve to govern his kingdom and his home with integrity and righteousness.

Have you considered making the same declarations for your home and your marriage? Would your behavior, attitudes, words, and choice of movies and entertainment change? Would you be more mindful of keeping your word and be less influenced by the world? We know that determination alone cannot carry us, but David knew that too. He could make these bold statements because he knew that God was loving, kind, fair, and dependable. God is the real power behind resolutions.

Are the two of you willing to make David's resolutions your own? How can you walk with integrity in every area of your life?

Lord, we know that all the good intentions in the world are not enough. We want our lives and our home to be free of sin and filled with your righteousness.

TRUE WEALTH

Be still before the Lord and wait patiently for him;
fret not yourself over the one who prospers in his way,
over the man who carries out evil devices!

PSALM 37:7 ESV

Have you and your spouse ever been in a situation where it seems like everyone else is prospering more than you? You've watched your friends wear their stilettos or power suits as they climbed the corporate ladder. You've seen photos from their exotic trips. And you've visited their gorgeous homes complete with fancy cars and gleaming boats in the garage. Meanwhile at your house, you're stretching the budget by eating beans and rice. Your cheap car is falling apart, and your home needs repairs.

Sometimes it's hard not to be envious. It's often difficult to understand when you're trying to serve God and your friends aren't. That's when we're wise to be still before God and to share our hearts with him. When we stop to think about it, we realize that we're the ones who are truly blessed. Our homes might be humble, but they're happy. Our trips might not be expensive, but they're filled with laughter and love. Our riches aren't in our possessions—they're in each other.

What makes you truly wealthy? When's the last time you thought about how rich you are to have each other?

Lord, help us to realize our true wealth lies in each other.
Thank you for blessing us.

BEING QUIET

Be angry, and do not sin;
ponder in your own hearts on your beds,
and be silent.
PSALM 4:4 ESV

It's easy to get mad at our spouses. They hurt us and make us more mad than anyone else—because they're the closest to our hearts. It's a gift of love when we bite back the angry words and stay quiet instead. And it's an even bigger gift when we take the time to look inside the hearts of our spouses and think about ways we can love them more.

We come to marriage with suitcases packed with all the baggage of our pasts. Scars of our past carry into our marriage and affect us in many ways. A wise husband or wife will ponder those things, looking for ways to help heal old hurts and gaining a better understanding of why their spouses react as they do.

What scars did you bring to your marriage? Have you discussed them with your spouse?

Lord, help us to be kind and loving. Keep anger from our relationship, and help us work to understand each other better.

JUST FOR ME

You are worthy, our Lord and God, to receive glory and honor and
power, for you created all things, and by your will they were created
and have their being.
REVELATION 4:11 NIV

When you wake up and look at your spouse do you see
bed head or smell morning breath and think, *What have I done?*
Or do you thank God for making your spouse just for you.
God created each individual, and even though we are different
and flawed, the greatest thing about our mates is they are
uniquely ours by God's design.

Respecting God's creation for you is essential. You may
have a few choice things to say about bed head, fingernail-
biting, snoring, stinky feet, and more, but because you love
and respect your spouse, you never say those things outside
of the home. In public, you should respect and praise your
mate openly. When you do, you are honoring God as well.
Keep the jokes and jibes about flaws between the two of you.

When was the last time you told your spouse you loved him
or her despite any flaws or shortcomings?

Lord, teach us to love each other as you love us. Help us to
cover each other's flaws by keeping them to ourselves.

OVERFLOW OF KINDNESS

Show respect for all people: Love the brothers and sisters of God's family, respect God, honor the king.
1 PETER 2:17 NCV

Nancy watched Gary pull off the road. She knew he spotted the car ahead. An elderly lady was in the driver's seat. She was crying. "Ma'am," said Gary, "do you need help?" She looked at him and nodded. She was too upset to speak. Nancy looked at her husband of five years. She loved his tender side so much. He was always looking out for others. If he saw someone in need, he was the first to stop and offer help.

Nancy felt blessed to have a man who loved and respected others. That part of his character transferred to their marriage. He was such a gentleman and respected her in every way. She had friends who weren't as lucky. Every time she saw those friends with their husbands she said an extra prayer of thanks for Gary. His relationship with God was what drew her to him. Because his relationship with God was strong, God's love flowed through him in everything.

Can your spouse say that your relationship with God overflows in all you do?

Lord, thank you that your love is the greatest love. Show us how to let your love flow through us.

LEARN FROM THE EXPERIENCED

Stand up in the presence of the aged, show respect for the elderly and revere your God. I am the Lord.
LEVITICUS 19:32 NIV

One of the greatest blessings about extended family is the opportunity to learn from those who have more experience than you. Many young couples are fortunate enough to have parents or grandparents who have been married fifty years or longer. Being in the presence of those enduring marriages gives others a chance to learn the secrets of making marriage last. Looking at couples who have been married a long time, you can see the love on their faces accompanied by the lines and wrinkles of experience.

As you build your marriage, draw from the tried and true wisdom of others. Copy the good things you see. Visit with those you respect and make note of their wisdom. God will bless your marriage and strengthen it when you do.

Are there those in your family who have been married a long time? Take them out to dinner and soak up their wisdom.

Lord, thank you that we can learn from others who have gone before us.

HONORING PARENTS

"Honor your father and your mother, so that you may live long in the land the Lord your God is giving you."

EXODUS 20:12 NIV

God set up marriage as an institution where a man and a woman would leave their parents and start their own families. That doesn't mean that God wants us to forget about our parents—and he promises there are big benefits in honoring them. A smart couple will avail themselves of the wisdom their parents have accumulated over the years. They'll ask for and listen to sage advice that will keep them from making mistakes they don't have to make.

A wise couple will set aside time to go see their parents, to call them, or to lend a helping hand whenever needed. As the years go by and their parents begin to need assistance, husbands and wives should honor the lifetime of love and care their parents gave them by returning the favor. God says that if we'll honor our parents, we'll live long in the land. Let's determine that we'll look back with sweet memories instead of regrets.

How can you honor your mother and father? Do you carve time out of your schedule to be with them?

Lord, give us hearts of compassion for our parents. Help us to honor them.

NOT ALL ABOUT ME

Each one of you also must love his wife as he loves himself, and the wife must respect her husband.
EPHESIANS 5:33 NIV

I don't think any of us would argue with the fact that we love ourselves. We plan what makes us happy. We buy our favorite foods. We head for the most comfortable chair and turn the television stations to our favorite shows. Loving ourselves is easy. We say that we love our spouses and other people, but if we don't watch it, that all-about-me mindset will creep in and take over.

What if we put as much effort into loving our spouses? True love gives up the comfortable chair—and the (gasp!) remote. True love picks the restaurant our spouse loves even though we don't really like the food there. True love says, "You are the most important thing in the world to me—even more important than me." And something special happens as a result of that. The love that's given away returns to us in a bigger portion, and it's wrapped in respect from a spouse who feels loved and valued.

How does it make you feel when you do something special for your spouse? How long has it been since you've done that?

Lord, help me to put my spouse's interests before my own. I acknowledge that life isn't all about me, and I want my spouse to see that reflected in my words and actions.

WORK ETHIC

In all the work you are doing, work the best you can. Work as if you were doing it for the Lord, not for people.
COLOSSIANS 3:23 NCV

Even though we don't begrudge working to support our families because we love them, it's easy to become weary along the way. And sometimes when the drudgery of life piles on us, we end up not doing our best. We have a responsibility to do our very best. Little eyes are watching us, and it's especially important that we set a good example.

A good work ethic will make a huge difference in our homes and at our work places. Our attitudes make the biggest difference, especially if we work as if we are doing it for God. If he is pleased with our efforts, it's guaranteed that our spouses and bosses will be as well. There's a special joy that is experienced when we work to please God. Can you imagine how different our homes would be if that were the standard for all of our responsibilities?

How can our attitudes affect our work? What difference does it make when we do things as to the Lord?

Lord, help us to do our best for you. Help us to fulfill the responsibilities that you have for us to accomplish, and cause us to do so joyfully.

BEARING FRUIT

We continually ask God to fill you with the knowledge of his will through all the wisdom and understanding that the Spirit gives, so that you may live a life worthy of the Lord and please him in every way: bearing fruit in every good work, growing in the knowledge of God.

COLOSSIANS 1:9-10 NIV

There's something beautiful about an apple orchard when the fruit grows and ripens on the trees. Bright green leaves and branches laden with glossy red fruit present a charming vignette and the hope of apple pies, jelly, and fresh applesauce. There's also something beautiful about our lives and marriages when we bear fruit spiritually, continuing to grow in the knowledge of God.

A wise couple will ask the Lord for wisdom and understanding. They'll listen to the whispers of God, and their goal will be to please him in every way. It's a goal for each of us personally, but when we have the opportunity to observe our spouses as they grow more like Jesus, it's inspiring. And that provides a sweet hope for the future.

What can you do as a couple to help each other grow in Christ? How does it make you feel to see your spouse serving God?

Father, we want to grow in you so that we can serve you more as a couple. Help us to accept and nurture that responsibility.

A CLEAR GUIDE

The Lord has told you what is good,
and this is what he requires of you:
to do what is right, to love mercy,
and to walk humbly with your God.
MICAH 6:8 NLT

Fortunately, as Christians, we don't have to question what God requires of us. He has written it in the Bible. We have a plan book that shows us the way and gives us specific instructions on how to live right, love mercy, and walk with God. Any time we question the right thing for us to do, we can search the Scriptures and find the answer.

That same principle applies to marriage. When we must make a decision, we need to search the Bible and pray and ask God for answers. Responsibilities increase with the marriage vows. But the source of knowledge remains unchanging. God always has the answers if we will just turn to him to find them.

Do you have a big decision looming? Have you asked God what to do about it?

Father, thank you that you are always available to give us wisdom. Help us put our trust in you.

TENDER HEARTS

This is how we know that we belong to the truth and how we set our hearts at rest in his presence.
1 JOHN 3:19 NIV

Love is how we set our hearts at rest in God's presence. In the same way that Jesus gave his life for us, we should be willing to do likewise for our spouses. When God blesses us with material possessions, that's awesome, but we should also have hearts that are tender toward others who are in need. One unexpected benefit about having a generous heart is that when our spouses see our love in action, it makes them love us even more.

It's great to express our love with words—and that's vital in a marriage—but when we put that love into action, it's powerful. We can't out-give God. It seems that the more we give away, the more we love each other, and the more God blesses us and our homes. Determine as a couple to love others and to help whenever you can. You'll never regret it.

How can you put your love into action? How does it make you feel when you see your spouse being loving and kind to someone else?

Lord, help us to love like you do. Give us hearts that are loving and generous.

WAITING QUIETLY

Let all that I am wait quietly before God,
for my hope is in him.

PSALM 62:5 NLT

This verse sounds so simple, but most of us have trouble actually putting it into action. When hard times come, we try to fix things ourselves. When our spouse is hurting, we try to ease the pain. We want instant replies to our prayers. We want answers. But sometimes God says, "Wait." Ouch. That's so hard for all of us "I want it now!" folks.

A wise husband or wife will learn the art of waiting quietly before God. Set aside a block of time. Go outside in God's creation if that's a possibility. Play some praise music. Spend some time in God's Word, and then have some "be still" time where you pray, "Father, I'm here and I want to hear from you. Whisper to my heart what you want to say to me." There's something special about worship, about taking time to spend with God. And even though the tough times often don't change, there's hope in him and rest for our souls. And that's a good thing.

Do you have a hard time waiting quietly on God? How can you and your spouse spend more time with God in this manner?

Lord, help us to rest in you. Bless our marriage and help us to wait quietly before you.

OUR FORTRESS

Truly my soul finds rest in God;
my salvation comes from him.
Truly he is my rock and my salvation;
he is my fortress, I will never be shaken.
PSALM 62:1-2 NIV

When we were children, many of us had a play fort where we took refuge from the bad guys who were after us. Usually, we'd be under attack, and then just as things were going south, a hero would sweep in and save the day. Wouldn't it be nice to have a similar option as married couples: a fortress where we could take refuge from all the hard times in our lives? Sounds great, doesn't it? If we pause to think about it, we really do have a fortress—the best fortress ever—Jesus.

Jesus loved us so much he gave his life for us. He promises rest for our souls. He's our rock and our strong shield, and when we commit our lives and our marriages to him, we won't be shaken by life. So next time difficult or scary circumstances arrive, let's remember to head to our fortress.

What does it mean to you to know that you have a fortress in God? How can that impact your marriage?

Lord, thank you for giving us rest for our souls and for being our fortress during difficult times.

LOVE COVERS US

Above all, love each other deeply, because love covers over a multitude of sins.
1 PETER 4:8 NIV

Stuart looked up at the ceiling. *How long am I going to lay here listening to Brigit snore?* he thought. It was the same thing every night. Brigit's head hit the pillow and she was asleep. Asleep and snoring. Some nights Stuart lay in the bed for hours fussing to himself about her snoring that was keeping him awake. Tonight was different. Stuart decided that instead of focusing on Brigit's snoring, he was going to count his blessings and spend whatever time he was awake thanking God for his beautiful wife.

Snoring is only one of the things husbands and wives have to deal with when they are first married. There are things that are much more important in the scope of life. But the love God gives to a husband and wife covers many things and allows the couple to live in harmony.

If your spouse snores, or does something else that really bothers you, can you make a point to be thankful for them instead of complaining?

Lord, thank you that your love covers a lot of things and allows us to live peaceably with one another.

PERFECT EXAMPLE

Husbands, love your wives, just as Christ loved the church and gave himself up for her.
EPHESIANS 5:25 NIV

The Bible tells us to love our wives just as he loves the church. Wow, those are some impossible shoes to fill—but we can give it our best effort, and God never requires more than our best. So what are some of the biblical traits of a good husband? He's willing to leave his mother and father to build a home with his wife. He's patient—even when his wife scuffs the tires for the third time. There's no ego involved. He's humble and gentle. He isn't easily provoked. He teaches with love. He's trustworthy.

A godly husband works hard to mature in Christ. He loves his wife so much that he overlooks her shortcomings and mistakes, and he'd even give his life for her. Whatever he does, he does with love, and he never thinks evil about her. This is what you can become when you other as God loves you.

What can you do to love your spouse as Christ loved the church? What are two specific things you can do today?

Father, you've shown us the perfect example of love. Help us to love our spouses like that.

TRULY AMAZING

There are three things that amaze me—no, four things that I don't understand: how an eagle glides through the sky, how a snake slithers on a rock, how a ship navigates the ocean, how a man loves a woman.

PROVERBS 30:18-19 NLT

Have you ever thought about the majesty of God's creation and how that applies to marriage? Think about how the eagle glides through the sky. It's poetry in motion, a visible reminder of God's strength and power. Think about a snake. How does it slither across rough rocks without its skin being damaged or without falling? That's God and his amazing design skills.

Think about the ocean, such a vast expanse of water that stretches in such unimaginable distances. Yet a ship can navigate those waters, trusting the maps that chart its course. All of that is truly amazing, but there's one more thing that defies description—how a man loves a woman... and vice versa. If the love of a man and wife is one of God's most amazing creations, shouldn't we do everything in our power to make it thrive?

Have you ever thought about how amazing it is that you and your spouse love each other? Talk about ways you can protect your marriage.

Lord, you are an amazing God. Thank you for creating the precious gift of marriage.

THE MORE IMPORTANT ONE

Love is patient and kind. Love is not jealous, it does not brag, and it is not proud.
1 CORINTHIANS 13:4 NCV

There's something built inside us that makes us want to brag: "Look what I did!" But what if we spent more time bragging about our spouses than we did about ourselves? That's where true love comes in. When we pay attention to others—especially our spouses—that means we're taking our eyes off ourselves.

Love is patient and kind. It's about giving up our own will for someone we love more. And it's not just about being there for our spouses during hard times, but also celebrating with and for them in good times—with no jealousy involved. What if God had been selfish? What if he'd said, "My life is more important than yours?" But he didn't, and wise husbands and wives will make it a goal to follow his example to love their spouses more than themselves.

What tangible thing could you do today to love your spouse more than yourself? What do you need to change?

Lord, help us follow your example. Help us to love our sweethearts more than we love ourselves.

LESS OF ME

"I can do nothing on my own. I judge as God tells me. Therefore, my judgment is just, because I carry out the will of the one who sent me, not my own will."

JOHN 5:30 NLT

Husbands and wives often have great goals, but it usually doesn't take long for us to realize that our power to achieve those goals lies in God. We can't do anything without him. He is the source of our strength, and yet this all-powerful God is in love with us. His heart is touched when we want to do his will, when the desires of our hearts are to serve him.

When we seek to serve him our own desires are being put on the back-burner where they should be. It means less of self, and that's a good thing! In a home where a husband and wife are committed to doing God's will together and putting their spouse's needs before their own, the relationship will thrive.

How can you be more selfless in your relationship with your husband or wife? How does it impact you when you see your spouse being selfless?

Father, help there to be less of self in my life and more of you. Remind me to put my spouse's needs and desires before my own.

A RACING PARTNER

Since we are surrounded by such a huge crowd of witnesses to the life of faith, let us strip off every weight that slows us down, especially the sin that so easily trips us up. And let us run with endurance the race God has set before us.

HEBREWS 12:1 NLT

Many of us have lots of possessions. Our homes are filled with way more than our basic necessities, and often our basements, garages, and sheds are crammed full of all the extras. But sometimes "things" can weigh us down. The more possessions we have, the more things there are to care for, and what was once a blessing can become a burden as it takes time away from our spouses and families.

God advises us to get rid of the things that slow us down—especially those sins that can trip us up and cause problems in our homes. He looks at our lives as a race, and when we got married, he even gave us a racing partner. Just as runners prepare, couples need to condition their hearts by spending time in prayer and in God's Word. Be sensitive to his instructions, and run the race of life with endurance.

What things are weighing you down? How can that keep you from serving God?

Lord, help us to cast off the things that will slow us down from serving you. Help us to finish the race together.

NO CALLOUSES

"For this people's heart has become calloused; they hardly hear with their ears, and they have closed their eyes. Otherwise they might see with their eyes, hear with their ears, understand with their hearts and turn, and I would heal them."

MATTHEW 13:15 NIV

Have you ever been somewhere that was so loud you couldn't hear what your spouse was saying? Or somewhere the sun was so bright you had to close your eyes? Do you know that we sometimes do the same thing with God? He tries to communicate with us, but we've allowed our hearts to become calloused, and we close our ears or shut our eyes so we don't have to hear what he wants to tell us.

But if we want our homes and marriages to be healed, we have to be sensitive to his voice, we have to turn away from the things that he doesn't want us to do, and we have to give our hearts permission to understand. Let's determine that we will work to keep our hearts soft and sensitive to him.

How can our hearts become calloused? How does that affect our marriages?

Lord, we don't want our hearts to be calloused toward you. Give us eyes that see and ears that hear so we'll understand your instructions.

A LOVING REBUKE

Do not rebuke mockers or they will hate you;
rebuke the wise and they will love you.
PROVERBS 9:8 NIV

Rebuke is not a very modern word. But it is a strong word. There is nothing weak or pleasant about being rebuked. To be reprimanded in an angry or negative way can be devastating, especially to a sensitive person. When someone you love does something out of line, gentle, loving correction is a much better way. If you need a reminder you have overstepped boundaries, appreciate the one who loves you enough to bring you back into line.

We count on our mates for many things. Many are fun. But one of the things we need to be assured of is that our spouses will let us know when we need correction. Love will permeate the correction as we help our mates grow to become better people. Coming from one who loves us more than anyone else in the world, it makes us feel secure and helps to diminish feelings of rebellion and sensitivity.

Have you ever been rebuked by your mate? Discuss those times and why it was easier coming from him or her.

Lord, thank you for a spouse who loves me enough to help me become a better person.

PEACE THROUGH LAWS

Great peace have those who love your law;
nothing can make them stumble.

PSALM 119:165 NRSV

Peace is a wonderful thing to have in a marriage, but it's often hard to achieve. God promises that if we'll love his law, we'll have great peace. When our hearts are sensitive to him and to what he wants us to do, it will keep us from stumbling, and that will keep us from harming the ones we love.

God gave us his law for a reason—not because he wants to rule over us with an iron fist, but because there are consequences when we don't. Those commandments are guard rails for our lives. We can't choose one here and one there and make it work. We must obey all of them. Our attitudes can make a big difference. There's joy in the journey when we have willing hearts that want to obey his laws. And there will be a sweet and amazing peace in our homes when two hearts are united in pleasing God.

Why is it important for us to love God's laws? How will keeping them impact our marriages?

Lord, help us to keep your laws. Help us to have willing hearts that obey you. Keep us from stumbling.

SERVANT'S HEART

He sat down and called the twelve. And he said to them, "If anyone would be first, he must be last of all and servant of all."

MARK 9:35 ESV

Whenever they go out in public, David steps aside when they approach a doorway to allow Addyson to enter first. The same is true if they are in a cafeteria line or waiting to ride at an amusement park. David does that out of love and respect for his wife and as a way of making sure she is well cared for. Addyson knows that David loves her so much that he will put her first in every way.

Bringing a servant's heart to a marriage is something to be applauded. It is not always easy to put others first, especially in a society that screams, "Me, me, me first!" But when God gives you a mate for life, you must love with a serving kind of love.

Does your spouse put you first in every way? How could you do a better job of putting your spouse first?

Lord, thank you for a spouse to serve you with each day. Help us to serve each other in a way that shows your love.

SHARING

If you help the poor, you are lending to the LORD—
and he will repay you!
PROVERBS 19:17 NLT

Love notes are important in a relationship. One of the fun ways that Doug shows his love to Brenda is with potato chips. Potato chips? Brenda loves the extra crunch you get from a folded chip. There aren't many in each bag but when Doug finds one, he passes it to Brenda with a smile.

Is there something in your relationship that you share with your spouse that creates a special bond between you? It may not be potato chips, or even food. There may be a household chore that you know your mate prefers not to do. When you pitch in, the load becomes lighter and the job becomes fun when you do it together. As a married couple you share many things, both good and bad. The greatest thing you can share is a common love of God and the commitment to putting him first in all things.

What is your favorite thing to share with your sweetheart?

Father, thank you for the blessing of sharing everything with my wonderful mate.

EXTENDING A HAND

Is not this the kind of fasting I have chosen: Is it not to share your food with the hungry and to provide the poor wanderer with shelter—when you see the naked, to clothe them, and not to turn away from your own flesh and blood?

ISAIAH 58:6-7 NIV

Early marriage brings challenges: making ends meet, adjusting to life as a couple, combining two sets of family values into one, and so forth. One question may arise: how do we operate our family and still be able to give to others? For some couples, it seems like there is never enough extra to go around. But God directs us to help others in whatever ways we can. In the beginning it may be small. In time those ways will become bigger.

Find ways to share with others. Gifts of time, good used items, or services are additional things you can do together. If your interests are different, schedule one evening a week to serve in different places. Offer your gifts as a sacrifice to God and enjoy the rewards of serving him.

What would you like to offer to God as an act of service?

God, thank you that we can share what we have with others.

SHARING ETERNITY

"Anyone who has two shirts should share with the one who has none, and anyone who has food should do the same."
LUKE 3:11 NIV

Reality shows are popular on television. One focuses on the subject of hoarding. Most couples hoard in some way. You save things that are duplicates or that you don't really need. If you are saving things for children or grandchildren, that is not unreasonable. But we have lots of saved things we really don't need and we probably won't ever use. Assess the things that fill your closets and share things with someone who needs them. If this is really hard, set a goal of getting rid of just a few things the first time around.

As couples, one of the best things we have to share is our faith. As you pare down and share your material possessions, don't forget that God's love within you is the greatest thing you have to share, and there is plenty of it. When you help a friend by sharing an item, share a bit of eternity with them as well.

Do you consider yourself a hoarder? What do you save? Can you make time soon to go through your belongings and share with someone who needs them more?

Lord, thank you that we don't have to hoard your love. There is plenty for everyone.

CAREFUL WORDS

If anyone speaks, they should do so as one who speaks the very words of God. If anyone serves, they should do so with the strength God provides, so that in all things God may be praised through Jesus Christ. To him be the glory and the power for ever and ever.

1 PETER 4:11 NIV

Our words can get us into so much trouble—especially with our spouses. For many of us, our mouths engage before our brains do, and then it's too late. Sometimes words are spoken in innocence with no intention to harm. And, at other times, we're angry and we mean the hateful, ugly things we say in the heat of the moment. We only feel remorse when we see the pain we've caused.

We wouldn't have those problems if we chose to speak like Jesus, if we spoke in love, if the words we verbalized were said to help our spouses rather than to hurt them.

What difference would it make in our marriages if we spoke God's words instead of our own? What do we need to know about serving him?

Lord, give us spontaneous moments where we speak your words with kindness. Help us to see that our strength comes from serving you. Help us to give you the glory you deserve.

PRECIOUS PROMISE

The God of peace will soon crush Satan under your feet. The grace of our Lord Jesus be with you.

ROMANS 16:20 NIV

Stress can work havoc on a marriage. Becoming stressed is easy—getting rid of it is not. Overwhelming demands at work, health issues, trouble with kids and families, tension with spouses, lack of time with God, and exhaustion can all take a toll. And an over-stressed spouse can become snippy and impatient, further compounding the problems at home. So how do we get out of that pattern?

We can pray for our spouses, lifting their needs to the God who can fix them. We can help shoulder the burden. Two carrying a load is much better than one. We can provide tender affection and words of encouragement. And we can be spiritual helpers to our spouses, reminding them of God's sweet and precious promise of grace.

How can you help your spouse when he or she is stressed? How has God's grace helped you in the past?

Lord, help us to be true helpers to our spouses—especially when they're stressed. Thank you for your grace that gives us hope.

PART OF THE EQUATION

The human body has many parts, but the many parts make up one whole body. So it is with the body of Christ.
1 CORINTHIANS 12:12 NLT

Being single can lead to some fun adventures, but most single folks will admit that life is lonely. They miss having someone to talk to at the end of the day and a helpmate to share life's burdens. That's a good reminder to those of us who are married, to thank God for those very things.

God says it's not good for a man to be alone. That's why he created a helper. And since the marriage relationship is based on helping each other, sometimes it's good to take stock and make sure we are truly being a good helpmate. When a husband gets up early and empties the dishwasher or loads it because he knows his wife is tired, that is true romance. When a wife cares for a sick husband with tenderness, that love wraps around him like a comforting warm blanket. Marriage is a precious gift, and a wise couple will make teamwork part of the equation.

What can you do to be a better helpmate to your spouse? How does it make you feel when your spouse does something nice for you?

Lord, remind us that we're a team. Help us to work together to make our marriage the best it can be.

BETTER DAYS?

God is our refuge and strength,
an ever-present help in trouble.
PSALM 46:1 NIV

In times of trouble it is easy to look back on better times. If you could only go back to the way things were earlier in your marriage. Back before you had children or lost your job, before the house got cluttered or your mother-in-law moved in. But were those *really* better times? Living involves moving in the present and on into the future. Our yesterdays may seem better or less hectic, but God has a future for us. Without going through trials or hard times we would face the days ahead without maturity and wisdom that comes through perseverance. Each test brings with it the ability to stay the course.

Worrying about the future will not benefit anyone. Together, the two of you can use your experience and expertise to safely navigate whatever bumps in the road you encounter. Trust that the Lord has your best interests at the center of his heart, and rely on his promises. Seek his wisdom and guidance.

Can you let go of worry? How can you help each other to trust God in hard times? What strengths do you see in each other that have resulted from previous hard times?

Father God, show us the way to trust in you. Help us put worry behind us and focus on your Word. We want to walk deeper in you each day. Thank you for caring for us.

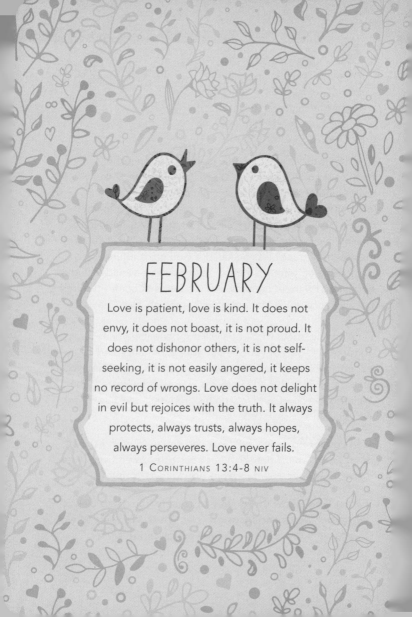

FEBRUARY

Love is patient, love is kind. It does not envy, it does not boast, it is not proud. It does not dishonor others, it is not self-seeking, it is not easily angered, it keeps no record of wrongs. Love does not delight in evil but rejoices with the truth. It always protects, always trusts, always hopes, always perseveres. Love never fails.

1 CORINTHIANS 13:4-8 NIV

RULING A KINGDOM

Lord, the God of our ancestors, are you not the God who is in heaven? You rule over all the kingdoms of the nations. Power and might are in your hand, and no one can withstand you.

2 CHRONICLES 20:6 NIV

God is our chief authority figure and our role model in marriage. Someone needs to be in charge for a relationship to work, but that authority needs to be dispensed with love and respect. God, who created the universe and rules over every kingdom, demonstrates how to provide a comforting hand and loving compassion as an authority figure.

Power can go to a ruler's head, but a wise spouse will use authority with God-pleasing intentions, led by God's guidance and his love.

Can you remember a time when you used your authority role in the wrong manner? How did that impact your marriage, and what can you do to improve in the future?

Lord, whenever I'm in an authority role in my marriage, help me to lead with wisdom and with love, remembering to come to you for guidance as the ultimate authority figure.

OPENNESS IN LOVE

Better is open rebuke than hidden love.
Wounds from a friend can be trusted,
but an enemy multiplies kisses.

PROVERBS 27:5-6 NIV

Relationships vary. Some are good, others less so; some are open and honest, and others are superficial. All relationships fall on a spectrum. The very best relationship we can have here on earth is marriage. A spouse is a lover, but also a best friend, confidant, and partner for life.

When your marriage is solid and based on God's love, you have the freedom to discuss any subject with your spouse. If you need correction or have stepped out of line, your spouse can bring it up in a kind way. If you need encouragement, your spouse is the best one to give it. What a treasure to have someone with whom you can be open in every way! When you are secure in God's love and in your partner's, honesty is expected and appreciated.

Has there been a time when you and your spouse talked openly and lovingly about a difficult subject?

Father, thank you for the open communication that marriage gives. Help us to be receptive to counsel from each other, and let that counsel be given in love.

WHO'S IN YOUR INNER CIRCLE?

Whoever walks with the wise becomes wise,
but the companion of fools suffers harm.
PROVERBS 13:20 NRSV

Every couple needs friends. These are the people who know us and love us. They are our confidants and counselors. They bring fun, companionship, and encouragement, and they serve God with us. Because friends are so influential, we need to be careful about who we bring into our inner circles.

God's Word says it best. If we want to be wise, we need to hang around wise people, and if we choose fools for our buddies, it will hurt us. Our friends impact us on many levels. If we hang out with people who are loose with their marriage vows, or are unloving and unkind to their spouses, that can rub off on us. But if we have friends who love God and base their relationships and daily lives around him, we are blessed by their example. Let us choose our friends wisely, and be godly friends for them in return.

Would God consider your friends wise or foolish? As a couple, what safeguards can you set to help you pick the friends of your inner circle?

God, we realize that we become like those closest to us. Help us choose friends who will encourage us to chase after you and keep loving each other.

BUILDING A HOUSE

One who has unreliable friends soon comes to ruin,
but there is a friend who sticks closer than a brother.
PROVERBS 18:24 NIV

When building a home, you must first pour a foundation. Soon after, the framing is done. Without a solid foundation and framing, a home will not stand the test of time. The first storm would destroy it.

In marriage, God is the most solid foundation; friendship with your partner should be the framework. Passion is like the finishing touches in a home—it changes over time. Romantic feelings come and go, but friendship remains. Support that framework by spending time with your spouse. Dating shouldn't end when you get married. When the kids leave the nest and the two of you are alone, let your sweetheart be the one who sticks closer than a brother.

What things do you love to do together? How can you nurture your friendship?

God, thank you for the gift of friendship that is vital to a successful marriage. Draw us closer to each other. Help our home to stand firm during the storms of life.

YOUR GOD-POSITIONING SYSTEM

In all your ways acknowledge Him,
and He will make your paths straight.
PROVERBS 3:6 NASB

Have you ever thought about how marriage is like a road trip? When we take our wedding vows, we start a long journey often without a clue about where we'll end up or how we'll get there. Is there a map? When we pack our families into our cars and head out for vacation, we have to trust our maps or our GPS to get us where we're going.

God's Word is life's GPS—our God-Positioning System. As we go through life, he takes us on some major twists and turns down roads that don't make sense to us. But we trust the one who's been down them before, who knows the pitfalls and dangers along the way. We need to acknowledge that he's the one in charge, trust him, and follow the path into the future that he has mapped out for us.

Why is it so hard to trust God when we don't know where he's leading us? As a couple, what have you learned about trusting God in uncertain situations?

Father, help us to trust your GPS and to follow the route that you've charted for us. Help us to remember that even when we don't understand you, we can still trust you.

A CUP OF COLD WATER

"If anyone gives even a cup of cold water to one of these little ones who is my disciple, truly I tell you, that person will certainly not lose their reward."

MATTHEW 10:42 NIV

Have you ever seen your spouse take food to a homeless person or dig into his pocket for money to help someone going through difficult times? Have you observed your sweetheart carrying a home-cooked meal to someone who's just had surgery or holding someone's hand as she prayed for them? Doesn't it make you love them even more?

God says he will reward us for our good works, but our marriage gains love from such moments of kindness too. There's something about generosity, about watching each other dispense compassion, that makes us love each other more. Why? We are watching our spouses reflect Jesus. It's even more special when we can share those moments together.

Can you recall a time that your spouse was compassionate to someone? Is there something that you can do as husband and wife to touch the lives of others?

Lord, as the source of compassion, you are so good to us. Help us touch the lives of others—to bring a cup of cold water to those who need it.

UNMERITED FAVOR

*The God of all grace, who called you to his eternal glory in Christ,
after you have suffered a little while, will himself restore you and
make you strong, firm and steadfast.*

1 PETER 5:10 NIV

Grace is showing kindness when someone doesn't deserve
it. It is unmerited favor. God gave us the perfect example
of grace when, while we were still in sin, he gave his Son to
die for us. We deserved death, but he gave us life. Christ's
sacrificial, grace-filled relationship with his church is often
compared to marriage.

Grace in marriage is essential. Overlooking when your
spouse squeezes the toothpaste in the middle is grace. Not
getting angry when your partner speaks harshly after a hard
day is grace. Since God shows us grace, we can follow his
example and give it freely to those we love.

*Where are some areas where you need your spouse to
show you grace? Thank your spouse for a specific time in
which he or she was gracious.*

**Jesus, thank you for providing us such a perfect example of
unmerited favor. When things get heated because one of
us makes a mistake, help us to show grace to each other.
May our example of a grace-filled marriage draw others to
you.**

SHINING THROUGH THE GOLDEN RULE

Stephen, full of grace and power, was performing great wonders and signs among the people.
ACTS 6:8 NASB

The world tells us to treat people the way they treat us. The Bible, on the other hand, says, "Treat others the same way you want them to treat you" (Luke 6:31). This is called the *golden rule*, but people in today's society, so focused on rigid fairness, rarely live by it. When Christians turn the other cheek, offering forgiveness, others take notice.

A marriage where both husband and wife practice the golden rule is a grace-filled relationship. That godly level of grace attracts the attention of the world and reflects Christ. God can use your golden marriage to show great wonders and signs and draw people to him. As you gracefully love your spouse, let God's love shine through.

What will others learn about Christ from watching your marriage relationship? How will they see grace in you?

God, use our marriage to draw others closer to you. Open our eyes to those who are watching us. Help us show grace by living out the golden rule and, in doing so, help us to reflect you.

CHANGING TOGETHER IN CHRIST

We all, who with unveiled faces contemplate the Lord's glory, are being transformed into his image with ever-increasing glory, which comes from the Lord, who is the Spirit.

2 CORINTHIANS 3:18 NIV

"She's not the same woman I married."

"He's changed."

These words have been uttered to many marriage counselors.

The counselor's response is almost always the same. "You are correct. Your wife isn't the same person you married, and your husband has changed."

Your experiences grow and change you. Imagine that you planted two trees on your wedding day, one to represent each of you. You would expect to see them gain height and breadth and blossom. Growth is a good thing. Don't expect your spouse to stay the same. Focus instead on how, when rooted in Christ, you can grow together.

How have you each changed since the day you married? Can you tell what caused that change? What remains the same?

Heavenly Father, help us to grow together and not apart. Help us recognize that our love is always changing.

PRUNING FROM THE MASTER GARDENER

Leaving the elementary teaching about the Christ, let us press on to maturity, not laying again a foundation of repentance from dead works and of faith toward God, of instruction about washings and laying on of hands, and the resurrection of the dead and eternal judgment.

HEBREWS 6:1-2 NASB

Any amateur gardener can tell you the value of pruning, which involves cutting away a portion of a plant to encourage more growth. God prunes Christians in the same way. "Every branch in Me that does not bear fruit, He takes away; and every branch that bears fruit, He prunes it so that it may bear more fruit" (John 15:2).

While the Lord prunes us as individuals, he also prunes us as couples to help our marriages grow. Sometimes he uses undesirable circumstances, like health problems or job losses, to strengthen relationships. When you fully rely on him and lean on each other, God prunes your union into a shape that will flourish.

How has God used circumstances to prune you as a couple? How has it made you stronger?

Almighty God, you are the master gardener. Thank you for pruning us in all kinds of circumstances. Help us to blossom and grow under your watchful care.

KID AT HEART;
MATURE IN LOVE

When I was a child, I used to speak like a child, think like a child, reason like a child; when I became a man, I did away with childish things.

1 Corinthians 13:11 NIV

When we were children, we acted like children. We were immature. We squabbled over stupid things. We said hurtful things without thinking about the consequences. Our reasoning was skewed and usually focused on ourselves. But we were children, so those issues were expected.

Unfortunately, we can carry immature traits into our marriages, causing damage and friction. Recognizing those traits in ourselves is the first step to maturity; admitting them is the next. Spiritual and emotional maturity comes from spending time in God's Word, praying and asking him for help, and having honest conversations with our spouses. As we mature, we grow closer in our marriages and in our relationship with God. While it's fun to spend life with someone who is a kid at heart, we must outgrow hurtful, childish traits when we get married. Every spouse deserves a husband or wife who is mature in faith and love.

What childish behaviors affect your marriage? How can you become more spiritually mature as a couple?

Father, none of us is perfect, and old habits die hard. Make me mature spiritually and emotionally so I can be the helpmate my sweetheart needs and deserves.

ARTIST, BUILDER, WRITER

Do not neglect the gift that is in you, which was given to you by prophecy with the laying on of the hands of the eldership. Meditate on these things; give yourself entirely to them, that your progress may be evident to all.

1 TIMOTHY 4:14-15 NKJV

Do you ever think about the fact that God gave unique gifts and talents to each of us? Wise husbands and wives look for those skills in their spouses, and they help nurture and grow those interests. Is your wife a talented artist? Set aside a place in your home for her to paint. Is your husband gifted at building things? Buy him some tools or hang out at the building supply store with him. Does your spouse want to be a writer? Save your pennies and send him or her to a writer's conference.

Encourage each other. Give sincere praise. Pray about ways to use your talents for the Lord, and be the proudest one there when others are admiring your sweetheart's handiwork. Don't waste the gifts that are inside you. Work together as a couple to help them grow and flourish.

What are the special talents that God has given to you and your spouse? How can you encourage each other to use those gifts?

God, thank you for the talents you have given us. We don't want to waste them. Help us to encourage each other to use them for your glory.

BETTER BALANCE

Grow in the grace and knowledge of our Lord and Savior Jesus Christ. To him be the glory, both now and to the day of eternity. Amen.

2 PETER 3:18 NIV

Some days it feels like we're on a merry-go-round that keeps going faster and faster. We're bogged down with heavy responsibilities at work, at home, with our families, and we scramble to get everything done, usually without success. Sound familiar? That stress can take a toll on our bodies, our marriages, and our time spent with God. Overwhelming moments are a good reminder to sit down and take stock of how we can get our lives and marriages in better balance.

Nobody can do everything and do it all well, but one thing must be a priority—spending time with God. Hours spent in his Word, in prayer, and in still moments where you listen for his voice have a big impact on your marriage and everything else in your life. Knowing God and growing in grace with your spouse will put your life into better balance.

Is your life out of whack? Pray together as a couple and ask God to be the keeper of your schedule.

Father, time with you is time well spent. Show us how we can grow in you, and help us to know you more each day.

EVERYDAY SWEETNESS

A person finds joy in giving an apt reply—
and how good is a timely word!
PROVERBS 15:23 NIV

Valentine's Day is a time for giving flowers or heart-shaped boxes of chocolates, but often it's the carefully chosen words in a card or a hand-written love note that mean the most. This day for sweethearts gives us a chance to express our love and our appreciation and to say the things that often go unsaid.

It's also a time to reflect on how God joins two lives together in marriage, giving thanks for the relationship that makes us complete as a couple. Wise couples take advantage of Valentine's Day, but they also carry that sweetness into the following days. We don't have to buy gifts on a daily basis, but we can share the gift of our words—heartfelt thoughts that will touch the soul of our God-given spouse.

What words can you use to encourage and uplift your
spouse? What words do you need to hear most?

Father, remind us that true love comes from you. Give us
words that will touch the heart, that we may always feel
secure in our love.

DON'T LOOK BACK

Let not your heart turn aside to her ways;
do not stray into her paths.
PROVERBS 7:25 ESV

Have you ever been to a theme park and seen a tour group? As they walk through the park, the group follows the leader carrying a flag. Imagine your thoughts are that flag, and your heart is one of the people on the tour. Where you allow your mind to go, your heart will follow.

When your spouse upsets you, do you dwell on it, mentally listing all the things they do to annoy you? If so, you stoked your anger by remembering past grievances. Often, your reaction becomes greater than the actual issue. The Bible tells us to "take every thought captive to obey Christ" (2 Corinthians 10:5). Next time you are upset with your sweetheart, don't look back. Deal with only the issue at hand, and you will both be happier in the end.

What are some ground rules you can establish about discussing hurt feelings or grievances?

Father, you forget our sins when you forgive us. Help us to stop negative experiences from taking root in our minds. Instead, replace any bad thoughts with memories of times we have been blessed by each other.

WISDOM GRANTED

For the Lord grants wisdom!
From his mouth come knowledge and understanding.
PROVERBS 2:6 NLT

Jim is the go-to person when folks need wise counsel. He has a gift for dispensing advice with love and compassion. His wife, Margaret, has appreciated that since their dating days and she always runs concerns or decisions by him first before she moves ahead with anything.

It's easy to get opinions on things. Everybody has one and they're usually glad to share it with you—whether you want it or not. But wise counsel is a rare and special gift. Jim would be the first to admit that his wisdom isn't his own—it comes from hours and hours of time spent in God's Word, and from many moments where he sought to hear from God. None of us want to give bad counsel—especially in our marriages—so we'd be wise to remember the source of all knowledge, understanding, and wisdom.

Where do you go when you need wise advice? Others?
Your spouse? How can the two of you seek true wisdom
together?

Lord, help us to remember that the best advice always comes from you.

KNITTED TOGETHER

Every day they continued to meet together in the temple courts.
They broke bread in their homes and ate together with glad and
sincere hearts.

ACTS 2:46 NIV

Nothing cements a marriage better than spending time with God together. It's hard to go to bed angry when you kneel or hold hands and pray before bedtime. When we pray with and for each other, it provides a shield of protection around our marriages and our homes. When we spend time talking about wisdom we've gleaned from God's Word, and how it has touched our hearts, we feed our souls. When we attend God's house together, he knits our lives together with a strength beyond all worldly ties.

If you are newlywed, decide now how you will establish habits of faith. If you've been married for a number of years and haven't done it before, it's never too late to start. Your heart and your home will benefit, and you will be glad you did it.

How can you and your spouse build habits of faith? If you
have faith habits already set, how do they affect your
relationship?

Father, we want you to be the head of our home. Let our habits include time together with you each day. Knit us closer to you and to each other.

REFRIED BEANS AND PUPPIES

With joy you will drink deeply from the fountain of salvation!
ISAIAH 12:3 NLT

Do you know the big difference between happiness and joy? Happiness is short-lived. You are happy when you have tacos for dinner. Later, when the refried beans hit, you may not feel so light-hearted. You are happy when you get a new puppy, but when it chews up the edge of the carpet, happiness is far from your mind.

Joy is long-term. It is delight deep in your heart. It starts with Jesus, and it spills over into other areas of your life—like your marriage. There may be moments when you aren't happy with your spouse. We are all human and make mistakes. But remember the deeper joy your relationship brings and focus there. A great marriage brings joy that works its way out from inside. It starts in your heart and ends up on your face.

In what ways does your spouse bring joy to your life?

Jesus, thank you for the joy and happiness in marriage. Waking up next to my best friend is a gift. On days when circumstances aren't going my way, help me to remember the deeper joy my spouse brings.

REJOICING IN SUFFERING

Rejoice inasmuch as you participate in the sufferings of Christ, so that you may be overjoyed when his glory is revealed.
1 PETER 4:13 NIV

No one likes hard times. They can be rough on a marriage. Financial difficulties impact every aspect of our lives. Health crises wear on us physically and emotionally when we can't help our partners. Sometimes, circumstances beyond our control create chaos in our marriages.

Suffering is hard on all of us, but joining together in those moments makes all the difference. We can make a conscious choice not to let bitterness ruin us. We can say, "God, I can't fix this. I need your help!" We turn our suffering over to him. Walking together, united with God and each other, provides the strength that's needed. Let us use moments of suffering—and God's provision through those times—to share the glory of what God does for us and through us.

What difficult circumstances have you gone through as a couple? How did you react to the problem, and how did it strengthen you?

Lord, you know more than we do the pain of suffering. When we struggle, help us to trust you through difficult circumstances, and show us your glory through them.

PLEASING PRESENCE

How happy your people must be! How happy your officials, who continually stand before you and hear your wisdom!
2 Chronicles 9:7 NIV

Are your friends and family happy to be around you? Some people are pleasing by nature; everyone likes to be around them. The Queen of Sheba felt that way about King Solomon. When she met him for the first time, she was amazed at his presence and assumed the people who spent daily time with him were happy.

Does the way you go through life make your spouse happy to be in your presence? Choose to do something today just to make your sweetheart smile. Tell a joke, take him a cup of coffee, or rub her feet. Challenge yourselves to make each other smile as many times as possible during the day. You have each other! That's a lot to be happy about.

What can you do to make your spouse smile? Talk about past deeds that made you smile.

Father God, happiness comes from you, as all good things do. Thank you for the gift of our marriage. Be a pleasing presence in our relationship, and help us to start and end each day with smiles.

HARMONY AT HOME

Live in harmony with one another. Do not be proud, but be willing to associate with people of low position. Do not be conceited.
ROMANS 12:16-18 NIV

Living in harmony is a great marriage goal. Conflict causes real damage, eroding our love and security. It can impact our homes in many ways. One of the best securities we give our children is a mom and dad who love each other. If they hear frequent fights, it can put fear into their hearts. No parent wants that.

How can we rid our homes of conflict? We can take our eyes off ourselves and put them on others. We can put our spouses' interests above our own, saying "I love you" louder than words. We can get rid of the "I'm always right" syndrome that affects so many of us. Only God is always right, and when we are willing to talk with our spouses and admit that we're wrong, we let them know that they are valued and loved. Harmony. It's a good thing!

What keeps you and your spouse from living in harmony? How can you put your spouse's needs above your own?

Lord, we want our home to be filled with love and peace, and we want our children to always feel secure there. Show us how to put each other's needs above our own.

MIND READING

Have unity of mind, sympathy, brotherly love, a tender heart, and a humble mind.
1 PETER 3:8 ESV

Ruth stood at the stove, stirring soup. This was her family's favorite, but today she was cooking it for her neighbor, Miriam, who was ill. Ralph walked in the door and sniffed appreciatively. "Mmmm. Smells good," he said. "Greg stopped by as I got the mail. He said Miriam just had surgery. Could we do something? Maybe take some soup?" Ruth turned around and smiled.

This was not the first time Ruth and Ralph had the same idea about something they hadn't even discussed. As they grew closer to God in their marriage, they found that they often had similar thoughts. Their desire to love and serve God manifested itself in a desire to love those around them. God's love overflowed to their family, neighbors, and friends. Let God bring you and your spouse together, and you may be surprised at the results.

Have you and your spouse ever thought simultaneously of a response to a challenge, a way to meet a need, or a change you needed to make? What drew you to that choice?

Father, thank you for the unity of mind and spirit that only comes from you. Let that unity bless our marriage and overflow into our relationships with others.

OPEN YOUR PANTRY

The crowds asked, "What should we do?"
John replied, "If you have two shirts, give one to the poor. If you have food, share it with those who are hungry."
    LUKE 3:10-11 NLT

John and his wife, Mary, talked after dinner. Mary said, "Did you know Bobby lost his job last week? His wife can't work because of her health, and they have five children to feed. I don't know what they're going to do."

"Well, I know what we're going to do," John replied. "We're going to help them. We don't have a lot, but we can share what we have."

We don't have to look far to see how abundantly God has blessed us, even if we're not wealthy and don't have big homes or fancy vehicles. With our blessings comes a responsibility to help others. Sometimes, it's just a box of groceries from our pantries. It can be a monetary gift to help with clothing or other expenses. It is our privilege and joy to help, but it also impacts our marriages. There is nothing more attractive than a spouse with a loving and generous heart.

How can you be a blessing to someone? Tell your spouse of a time you saw him or her helping someone else.

Father, let us be sensitive to the needs of others. Make us a blessing to those who need a helping hand.

PUT ON AN APRON

Pure and undefiled religion in the sight of our God and Father is this: to visit orphans and widows in their distress, and to keep oneself unstained by the world.
JAMES 1:27 NASB

One of the best activities that husband and wife can do together is serve. God calls each of us to serve others. Meeting the needs of "the least of these" is one way to weave Christ into the center of your marriage.

Make a list of ways you can serve as a team. Perhaps God is calling you to teach a Sunday school class. Maybe you can tie aprons on each other and offer your help at a soup kitchen. Are there local schools that need volunteers to help at-risk kids with homework? Consider your gifts and brainstorm how you can be the hands and feet of Jesus together.

What are some of your gifts or areas of strength? How can you use those to serve others?

Lord, open our eyes to ways we can help others together. Use us, Lord, and show us how serving weaves you into our marriage.

TITHING TIME

Suppose someone has enough to live and sees a brother or sister in need, but does not help. Then God's love is not living in that person.
1 JOHN 3:17 NCV

Need is all around you. Rarely do you drive through town and not see a homeless person needing food or clothing. Young couples struggle to balance jobs, children, and more. Elderly people find even the mundane tasks of life harder to manage. What is your response?

Most married couples have what they need but not everything they want. Look around and see who is hurting or in need. Is there something you can do? Could you take food to the homeless man? Could you keep the young couple's children for an hour or two so they could have a quiet meal together? Could you shop at the grocery store for your elderly neighbor? When we talk about tithing, we think of money. Wouldn't it bless you as a couple to tithe your time as well?

Have you ever thought about what you could do as a couple to help others? Brainstorm together and one of you take notes.

Lord, thank you for providing for our family. Open our eyes to ways we can share your blessings with others.

SUPPORTING OTHERS

We who are strong ought to bear with the failings of the weak and not to please ourselves.

ROMANS 15:1 NIV

Jimmy and Linda's friend, Al, struggled for a couple of years with an addiction to alcohol. He tried to overcome it, but failed repeatedly. He sat in Jimmy and Linda's living room, tears streaming down his cheeks as he said, "I need help."

"I've never been where you are, or fought an addiction like that," Jimmy replied, "but I can promise you one thing—Linda and I will be here for you. We're going to walk this journey with you, we're going to pray for you, and we're going to assist you in getting the help you need."

Through the following year, Linda watched her husband as he helped his friend. She saw his godly character on display time and time again. And she reaped an unexpected benefit from the situation. Watching her husband's compassion in action made her love him even more, tightening the bond of their already good marriage. A spouse who goes out of his or her way to help others will be an exceptional caretaker of a family.

Can you be strong for someone else? How has someone helped you when you've been weak?

Father, there are so many people who need someone strong to help them through difficult days. Help us to be that support for those who need us.

HONEST COMMUNICATION

Love does not delight in evil but rejoices with the truth.
1 CORINTHIANS 13:6 NIV

Nothing drives a wedge between a husband and wife faster than dishonesty. In marriage, that could be unfaithfulness, untruths, half-truths, finances, and the like. Avoiding these can be much easier if your marriage relationship is based on truth and trust.

A truthful marriage is a healthy one, and we all want healthy marriages. If your marriage is not healthy, schedule regular sessions, alone or with a therapist, to discuss what is going on openly and honestly. Agree on rules for the discussion, such as no hurt feelings, no interrupting, just discussion with no defense, etc. Communication is an excellent way to practice truth in your marriage. It takes work, but it is well worth it.

Do you need to discuss areas of your marriage with your spouse? Take time now to set aside a few moments for that discussion.

Father, thank you that we can communicate with our spouses in a way that strengthens our marriage. Thank you for communicating with us, and let our relationship with you deepen.

LITTLE WHITE LIE

If we claim to have fellowship with him and yet walk in the darkness, we lie and do not live out the truth.

1 JOHN 1:6 NIV

What's wrong with a little white lie? If a statement is not one hundred percent true, you may think it will not hurt anyone. Often the problem is not whether one lie will be hurtful, but the next one, or the next. Little white lies pile up. When you lie, you have to remember exactly what you said in order to keep the lie going. If you slip up, you may have to tell another lie to continue the first one, and suddenly there is little truth in your lie.

Honesty is always the best policy. When you tell the truth, there is no worry of tripping up later, but that is not the best reason to be truthful. God directed us to always be truthful, and that command extends to our marriages. Married couples living in an honest and truthful manner develop trusting relationships. When that bond is sure, they can also build trusting relationships with others, sharing God's love with them in truth.

Is your relationship a trusting one? Share what is on your heart. Have you shared the blessings of a Christ-centered marriage with another couple?

Lord, thank you that you are truth to us in every way. Help us live that truth in our marriage and in our relationships with others.

MARCH

"The rain and snow come down from the heavens and stay on the ground to water the earth. They cause the grain to grow, producing seed for the farmer and bread for the hungry. It is the same with my word. I send it out, and it always produces fruit. It will accomplish all I want it to, and it will prosper everywhere I send it."

ISAIAH 55:10-11 NLT

ASK FOR WISDOM

In the same way, wisdom is pleasing to you. If you find it, you have hope for the future, and your wishes will come true.
PROVERBS 24:14 NCV

Wisdom must be present in every marriage. In order to make good choices, we need to contemplate choices in a godly manner and trust in the hope of our future. From day one of our marriages, there are decisions that will affect our lives in the near future and beyond.

Asking God for wisdom should be part of every couple's daily routine. In your quiet time together, ask God to grow your love for each other, to provide for and protect you as a couple, to draw you closer to him, and to lead you to wise choices that honor him. While decision-making is not always fun, choices must be made every day. Some are very small; others are monumental. All require wisdom to assure you choose God's way for your marriage and life.

When making decisions, do you pray together about the right choice? Do you search God's Word for answers?

Lord, thank you for the wisdom of your Word and for the opportunity to ask for your direction in our lives. Let that wisdom give us confidence to follow you in our decisions.

ETERNAL FUTURES

We do not lose heart. Though outwardly we are wasting away, yet inwardly we are being renewed day by day. For our light and momentary troubles are achieving for us an eternal glory that far outweighs them all. So we fix our eyes not on what is seen, but on what is unseen, since what is seen is temporary, but what is unseen is eternal.

2 CORINTHIANS 4:16-17 NIV

When hard times come, it is devastating if we lose hope. Those moments can either tear our marriages apart or pull us closer together. To survive, we need to spend time together in God's Word, pray together, and encourage each other.

Sometimes, we get so bogged down with our current situations that we fail to look ahead to our future. We focus on things that aren't important. Christ has already won the battle for us. With eternal hope ahead, we can keep this life in perspective. Sometimes God allows us to look back and see that what we once thought was a terrible situation was a blessing in disguise, sent to us for his glory.

How can we help each other when things seem hopeless? What can we learn from those situations?

Lord, you have already saved our souls for eternity. Help us to not lose heart as we face battles, but to fight them together as a couple with our faith and our eyes fixed firmly on you.

CHRIST'S HOPE IN MARRIAGE

Blessed be the God and Father of our Lord Jesus Christ! By his great mercy he has given us a new birth into a living hope through the resurrection of Jesus Christ from the dead.
1 PETER 1:3 NRSV

Hope. Life without it is despair. With hope, discouragements become challenges, pessimism gives way to optimism, and sadness is replaced by joy.

Hope is the difference in a marriage without Christ and one with Christ. When you married and promised to love each other forever, you knew there would be difficult times. Standing at the altar before God, you knew that he would be present in your marriage. You knew you could always find hope in him. Even in the bleakest times, you can put your faith, hope, and dreams in his hands. That is what is called our blessed hope.

Are you aware of God's hope in your life? Talk to your spouse about the hopes you see for you and for your marriage.

Lord, thank you for being there on our wedding day. You are the hope in our marriage. Even when life is difficult, continue to provide us with hope—hope for our future, and hope for eternal life with you.

IT'S ALL ABOUT ME

Humility is the fear of the Lord;
its wages are riches and honor and life.
PROVERBS 22:4 NIV

Are you guilty of having an "it's all about me" mentality? We like to think that we don't, but it can creep into our lives unnoticed. One doesn't have to be married for long to recognize that there are going to be problems when a husband thinks he is more important than his wife or vice versa. We reflect that attitude in little moments, like when money is tight and one partner goes out and buys something frivolous, while the other goes without. Perhaps one knows the other is exhausted, yet chooses to sack out in the recliner without offering to help with the dishes or the kids.

When we humble ourselves and put God and our spouse first, we reap many benefits. Humility builds character, appreciation, and honor. It gives us an assurance of being valued, and a life and marriage that is rich in love.

How can you put your spouse's needs before your own?
How does it affect your home when your self-importance is out of line?

Lord, please take away my "all about me" mentality. Give me a heart of humility, and help me to honor you by putting my spouse's interests ahead of my own.

GODLY PRIDE

Pride brings a person low,
but the lowly in spirit gain honor.
PROVERBS 29:23 NIV

There are good and not so good kinds of pride. When your spouse is promoted, completes a work project, or is a good dad or mom, you have reason to take pride in that. Such pride is the result of our God-given love. If you are proud of accomplishments with gloating or haughtiness, then pride is not a good thing.

Doesn't it feel good to go out in public on the arm of your sweetheart? Do others wonder how you snagged such a great partner? You hold your head high, knowing it was part of God's plan for the two of you to be together. This is the good pride, because it comes from confidence in knowing you can trust the plan of God in all things.

When was the last time you told your spouse you were proud of him or her? If it has been a while, change that right now.

Lord, protect us from the wrong kind of pride. Instead, fill us with a pride in you that will draw others to you.

CRUSHING CONCEIT

Do not be proud, but be willing to associate with people of low position. Do not be conceited.

ROMANS 12:16 NIV

Conceit is not a nice word; it even sounds sinister. No one should think so highly of himself or herself that others feel inferior. In marriage, conceit has no place. Many vows have a phrase about each person loving the other one more. Those words kick conceit to the curb. Outside marriage, conceit can create disdain for others.

When marriage is based on godly love that puts others first, conceit is not a problem inside or outside the relationship. Let your marriage overflow with the love of God, and it will transcend financial, social, and professional barriers in other areas of your life. Work to live in harmony, both in your marriage and in the world.

If there are areas of conceit in your marriage, talk about them and ask God to remove them. If you don't have those areas, thank God together.

Lord, we know you made all your children different, yet you love them all the same. Help us to extend that same love to each other and to everyone we meet.

THE US IN FOCUS

Don't be selfish; don't try to impress others. Be humble, thinking of others as better than yourselves.

PHILIPPIANS 2:3 NLT

Selfishness is a trait that none of us want, yet we all have it. We are devoted to ourselves, to what makes us happy, and to what will benefit our interests. If that's not enough, we sometimes make ourselves out to be more than we are to impress others. If we're honest, we've all been guilty of that from time to time. Our focus is on us; even the last two letters of the word *focus* spell *us*. What if we put that much effort into putting others first, especially our spouses? Can you imagine the difference that would make in our homes and marriages?

God has given us a great example to follow. With him, it has always been about us, because we are the loves of his life. The great blessing of following his lead? When our focus is on others, there is no selfishness or guilt.

Can you think of a time when you were selfish about something, or you tried to impress somebody else? How did that impact your relationship with your spouse?

Father, take my focus off me and put it on you, my spouse, and others. Give me eyes that will see the specialness of others.

TEARS OF LAUGHTER

Then our mouth was filled with laughter,
and our tongue with shouts of joy;
then they said among the nations,
"The Lord has done great things for them."

PSALM 126:2 ESV

Mark and Ellen laughed until they were wiping away tears and their sides hurt. One of the gifts of their marriage was that they shared the same quirky sense of humor. And when Mark thought something was funny, all he had to do was to look at Ellen, and the laughter would start.

Whenever they looked at photos from their many years of marriage, the joy caught in the pages was a tangible reminder of how laughter helped them through many difficult times when they'd encountered job losses, health crises, or other hurtful or bewildering situations. God sent funny moments to brighten their days.

Today, thank God for the gift of laughter, for the joy he places in our marriages, and for the way he binds our hearts together.

When was the last time you laughed with your spouse? How can you bring joy to the heart of your sweetheart?

Father, thank you for the gift of laughter and for the joy that fills our home. You have done great things for us, and we thank you for blessing us far more than we deserve.

PEOPLE OF INTEGRITY

I know that you are pleased with me,
for my enemy does not triumph over me.
Because of my integrity you uphold me
and set me in your presence forever.
PSALM 41:11-12 NIV

You may not talk about integrity every day. However, you are aware if it is there. You know people in your relationships, your church, and your workplace who are people of integrity. You can trust them in any situation, knowing they will do the right thing.

The same should be true about your spouse. No matter what the situation, you should always be able to count on him or her to make godly choices, whether personal or for your marriage. If a question arises about what to do or say, you are confident your husband or wife will speak for you as you would want. Integrity endears you to each other.

Spend time talking about integrity today. How important is that to you and your marriage?

Lord, help us to be people who can be counted on in our marriage and in life. Bind us close to each other and to you.

YES AND NO

*Do not swear, either by heaven or by earth or by any other oath,
but let your "yes" be yes and your "no" be no, so that you may not
fall under condemnation.*

JAMES 5:12 ESV

Some folks are just wishy-washy. They have a hard time
making decisions: when to buy a new car, whether or not to
take a vacation, or what to have for dinner. Sometimes it is
hard to choose one thing over another.

Being a wishy-washy mate can cause dissention and
instability in your marriage. You have taken the marriage vow
which means you pledged to be part of a couple who heads
up a family. You and your mate will have lots of decisions to
make. Pray about them, discuss them, and weigh the pros and
cons. Then make a firm decision and stick to it—no second
thoughts. Having a unified and secure decision-making
process in your marriage will allow you to live without wasting
moments second-guessing yourself, and it will give you time
to enjoy your family.

*Are you wishy-washy? Is your mate? What can you do to
help your decision making process?*

**Lord, help us to always rely on you to help us make
decisions and then once made, help us stand firmly on the
outcome of those decisions.**

FOLLOW ME

"Come, follow me, and I will show you how to fish for people!"
MATTHEW 4:19 NLT

The call for our lives can be pretty simple. Jesus said, "Follow me!" to his disciples, and they dropped their lives to obey his call. In the same way, God calls us to work in ways we might not expect. Fortunately, God also calls partners together in marriage.

With our spouses, we can pursue a life after Jesus, together. Marriage is richer and more fulfilling when we realize our common, Christian calling to be fishers of people. We can combine individual strengths into a mighty force for God's work.

What strengths do you have that can work together to follow Jesus? Who are the people in your lives that you can reveal Jesus to together?

Jesus, thank you for leading the way and asking us to follow you. We acknowledge that you have called us, and we pray that together we would follow your calling and spread the good news to those who need it.

MANY ADVISERS

Without counsel plans fail,
but with many advisers they succeed.
PROVERBS 15:22 ESV

The planning of a wedding takes a lot of organization. Whether the occasion is grand or simple, we rely on a number of experts to get us through the day. After that special day, we don't stop needing advisors; the same holds true for our marriages.

With our spouses, we plan our lives in hopes of fulfilling our dreams for the future. Goals are great, and they are even better when we invite wise counsel into the planning process. We need to set aside pride and ask for advice from a variety of people. God, our ultimate advisor, tells us that this is the path to success.

What plans have you and your spouse discussed for your future? Who can best give you counsel for each plan?

Lord, thank you for the hopes and dreams you placed in our hearts, for our family and our future. We ask for godly counselors and advisers as we plan our steps according to your will.

HOME AMONG THE WISE

If you listen to constructive criticism,
you will be at home among the wise.
If you reject discipline, you only harm yourself;
but if you listen to correction,
you grow in understanding.

PROVERBS 15:31-32 NLT

God has given us a community of believers so that we have a wealth of knowledge to draw from when we need guidance.

At times, we need to lay aside our pride and ask for advice on our relationships. It doesn't matter how long we have been married; each stage has its challenges, and it will bless our marriages to seek out godly wisdom from those who have traveled the road before us.

Are there people in your lives that could give you solid marriage advice? Acknowledge the need to get some healthy counseling every once in a while, and make yourself at home among the wise!

Lord, we acknowledge that we cannot walk our marriage path alone. Thank you for the wise people that you have placed in our lives. Help us to seek out advice and correction so we can grow in understanding of each other and our marriage.

DISPLAYS OF AFFECTION

Love each other with genuine affection, and take delight in honoring each other.
ROMANS 12:10 NLT

Do people describe you as a hugger? Affection comes more easily to some than to others. However, it is important to remember that genuine affection is not limited to physical touch. The above verse from Romans is more about a deep care for one another, and that kind of love is visible when you put others first.

In marriage, being authentic about your affection means that you take into consideration what your spouse needs to experience your love. Each person has different affectionate needs, and you honor them by giving them that affection openly and honestly.

In what way do you most appreciate affection? Share this with each other, so that you can both share love that will reach the other where it is needed.

Father, thank you for giving us each other in marriage. Help us to communicate our affections honestly and gratefully, and lead us to discover renewed and deepened affection for each other.

MARKED BY THE MAKER

Woe to those who quarrel with their Maker, those who are nothing but potsherds among the potsherds on the ground. Does the clay say to the potter, 'What are you making?' Does your work say, "The potter has no hands."

ISAIAH 45:9 NIV

Have you ever watched a potter work? The clay starts as a lump and doesn't look like much until time and careful molding takes hold. The process is messy for a long time, and the final product looks nothing like the beginning.

The same is true in our lives. At times, you wonder how God is molding you. You may question why your lives look messy, why your marriage is a little rough, and where God is in the midst of it. Remember that you are the clay, and the master potter knows what he is doing. He makes all things beautiful in his time.

Are you questioning where God is right now or why your lives look the way they do? Talk with your spouse about what is messy in your marriage.

Master Potter, thank you for taking the time to mold us and make us into something beautiful. Let us see your handiwork in our marriage and continually trust in your plan.

CELEBRATE OFTEN

Live happily with the woman you love through all the meaningless days of life that God has given you under the sun. The wife God gives you is your reward for all your earthly toil.

ECCLESIASTES 9:9 NLT

People like parties. Seasons, holidays, birthdays, accomplishments—we celebrate them all. However, we can get so caught up in the toil of everyday life that we don't find time to celebrate. Scripture tells us that many of these earthly pursuits are pointless. The most meaningful parts of life are the people in them, and they deserve to feel like a reward.

Your spouse is an immensely meaningful part of your life, and what better reason to celebrate? Celebrations are important to your marriage. They acknowledge your commitment to each other and renew the appreciation and joy that you have for one another. Celebrate each other, and celebrate often!

Have you celebrated your marriage lately? Is there a way that you can celebrate each other this week?

God, we thank you for each other. We recognize the joy and blessing that marriage brings. Help us to find ways to celebrate our love.

ETERNAL BLESSING

May the Lord bless you and protect you.
May the Lord smile on you
and be gracious to you.
May the Lord show you his favor
and give you his peace.
NUMBERS 6:24-26 NLT

What does blessing really look like? We try to find God's blessing in our finances, in feeling comfortable, or in experiencing happiness in our relationships, but those are worldly blessings. Bank accounts can empty, and arguments are part of life. What can we do when earthly blessings fail us?

The scriptures say that God's blessing is found in his protection, in his grace, and in his peace. While his blessings can be found in our homes and jobs, it is always found in his Word. Turn to him on your own and as a couple, and he will give you true peace.

Do you see God's blessings around you each day? Share them with your spouse.

Dear Lord, you have already blessed us with eternal grace. Continue to bless us with your protection, your grace, and your peace. Open our eyes to your blessings, and give us grateful hearts.

GOOD WORK

We are His workmanship, created in Christ Jesus for good works,
which God prepared beforehand so that we would walk in them.
EPHESIANS 2:10 NASB

We spend a great deal of time dreaming about our futures and what God wants us to do with our lives. As a couple, we can often find ourselves asking the same questions over and over again. What is God's next step for us? What is his calling for our lives? How do we move forward together?

Ephesians is clear; we were created for good works. While we can work for God as individuals, we can apply this to our marriages too. God crafts spouses into one tool, each person bringing different talents to the table. Together, couples can do good works for God that they could not do alone.

What does "good works" mean to you as a couple? Are you involved in doing these things?

Jesus, we can do all things through you. We bring our hopes and dreams before you. Mold them into your calling for us to do good works together.

DO YOUR GIFT WELL

In his grace, God has given us different gifts for doing certain things well. So if God has given you the ability to prophesy, speak out with as much faith as God has given you. If your gift is serving others, serve them well. If you are a teacher, teach well.
ROMANS 12:6-7 NLT

In a marriage, we cannot pretend to be something or someone that we are not. It is often said that our spouses see our best and our worst, and there is comfort in that. We need to be ourselves with the one who loves us the most. Our spouses encourage and advise us with full knowledge of our gifts and weaknesses.

In the same way, we cannot hide ourselves from our creator. He fashioned our gifts, and he knows where we should use them. Be confident in your design. To rephrase this scripture, do your gift well!

Discuss your gifts with each other. Are you doing the things that represent who you really are? Brainstorm together on how you can use your individual talents for God.

Holy Spirit, thank you for giving us gifts to use for your glory. Help us to be true to who we really are, and guide our choices and our work.

LET HIM TAKE OVER

"My grace is all you need. My power works best in weakness." So now I am glad to boast about my weaknesses, so that the power of Christ can work through me. That's why I take pleasure in my weaknesses, and in the insults, hardships, persecutions, and troubles that I suffer for Christ. For when I am weak, then I am strong.

2 CORINTHIANS 12:9-10 NLT

We have two ways to face challenges; we can allow ourselves to become discouraged, or we can allow God to take over in our weakness. When we acknowledge our failings, we give God room to make himself known. We no longer operate in our own strength; we rely wholeheartedly on him. It is in these times where God is glorified through us.

One of the great gifts of marriage is that we never face challenges alone. Support each other, and take time to pray together. Instead of asking God to give you strength, it might be time to ask him to be present in your weakness.

Are you facing any seemingly insurmountable challenges right now? Are you discouraged about your failings? Share these with your spouse, and encourage each other.

Jesus, you are all powerful. You are everything that we cannot be. Thank you for our strengths, but thank you even more for our weaknesses, that your power might be displayed through us.

FAMILY SUPPORT

Children are a heritage from the LORD, offspring a reward from him.
Like arrows in the hands of a warrior are children born in one's youth.
Blessed is the man whose quiver is full of them.
They will not be put to shame when they contend with their opponents in court.

PSALM 127:3-5 NIV

Whether you have children or not, it is good to acknowledge them as a blessing. Sometimes, parenting is an unrewarding job. The hours are long, and no one is always appreciative. God, however, created family as a support system.

If you are devoted to your children, they are likely to return this devotion. They will be faithful because you have been faithful. In times when you most need your family, they will be there. This is a wonderful reward of parenting, and it is worth it!

Who are the children in your life? Is there a way you can show appreciation for them?

Dear Lord, thank you for the gift of family. Strengthen our family, and help us to grow in your ways so that we can support each other in all things.

CONTINUAL

They were continually devoting themselves to the apostles'
teaching and to fellowship, to the breaking of bread and to prayer.
ACTS 2:42 NASB

The early church seems like an impossible standard for
community. A continual fellowship would never work in
modern society. We rarely live as neighbors, and our lives are
increasingly busy with things outside of church.

The use of the word *continual* is there for emphasis. God
wants to confront us with the strong dedication that early
believers had toward one another, toward teaching and prayer.
These things are important to us as Christians and vital for a
healthy, holy marriage. Don't get too caught up in the world;
learning from God and speaking with him in prayer are more
important.

Do you have other Christians in your life who encourage
your faith? Do you need to get back to church or invite
some Christian friends over for a meal?

Jesus, thank you for making us part of the body of Christ.
Thank you for putting other believers in our lives. Grant
us stronger connections with these believers, and let us
encourage others around us. Help us devote ourselves to
teaching, prayer, and fellowship.

STRENGTH IN NUMBERS

If one can overpower him who is alone, two can resist him.
A cord of three strands is not quickly torn apart.
ECCLESIASTES 4:12 NASB

Unity is at the core of God's being. He exists as three in one and created us to live in community with one another. This Ecclesiastes verse reminds us of what God said from the very beginning: it is not good for humans to be alone.

When we have each other, we are not easily overpowered. Your marriage bond can overcome many challenges. When we are more than two, we are even stronger. When you invite other believers into your difficulties, you build up your resistance. Draw close to your Christian friends for advice and comfort; there is strength in numbers.

How is your spouse an ally in hard times? What can you do build each other up, and how can you join forces with other believers to strengthen your spiritual lives?

Lord, thank you for blessing us with each other. We are stronger because we are together. Help us to keep you at our center, and give us others who can help us with our battles, that we may also help them in theirs.

UP-WORDS

Worry weighs a person down;
an encouraging word cheers a person up.
PROVERBS 12:25 NLT

Family life is full of stresses. We worry about our finances; we worry about our health; we worry about whether we made the right choice in jobs, cities, or houses. When we add children to the equation, worry often increases. Our love parallels worry; the more love we have, the more we may worry.

The Bible recognizes that words are powerful. Encouraging words cheer the soul. The next time you feel that worry has taken over, use God's Word to give you words of encouragement. His Word is full of promise and hope, and it will bring peace into your stressful situations.

Are either of you feeling stressed or worried about anything today? Take time to share this with each other and then offer some words of encouragement.

Heavenly Father, thank you for caring about our needs. Your word says to cast our cares on you, and so we do that now. Grant us peace and hope to our troubled hearts, and reassure us of your presence in our lives.

WOUNDING WORDS

If you bite and devour each other, watch out or you will be destroyed by each other.
GALATIANS 5:15 NIV

Words of criticism towards our spouses are like wounds; they are painful and take time to heal. Unfortunately, it is often too easy to make unpleasant comments here and there, especially if we are retaliating from similarly harsh words.

Scripture says that such battles lead only to destruction. If you are feeling unloving toward your spouse, take your wounding attitude to the Lord. Repent of unkind words, and allow his grace to give you the right words to say.

Do you need to repent of unkind words? Take the time to apologize to each other if needed, and give new words of love.

Heavenly Father, thank you for your grace. Forgive us when we have been unkind to one another, and help us to tame our destructive tongues. Let us see one another in love and act graciously, as you have done for us.

WHAT IS BETTER?

What pleases the Lord more: burnt offerings and sacrifices or obedience to his voice? It is better to obey than to sacrifice. It is better to listen to God than to offer the fat of sheep.

1 SAMUEL 15:22 NCV

We might say that we work long hours so our family can live a comfortable life. We might say that we keep the house incredibly clean to ensure a peaceful environment. These are both true, but often we set our own ideas of what sacrifice means for our family, and we sound the trumpet when we think we have sacrificed enough!

Sacrifice looks different to each person. What might be a sacrifice for you is not for your spouse or child. We should look for God's appreciation above all else. When you are frustrated, take a moment. It may be that the Lord wants you to obey his command to love, rather than to work for it. Work is good, but love is greater.

What do you think you sacrifice for your family? Discuss this together and consider whether this is God's requirement or your own. How does the Lord want you to serve?

Lord, forgive us when we get self-righteous about what we sacrifice for our family. Help us to listen to you and obey. Give us wisdom to know when you simply require us to be loving.

OUR SAFE PLACE

A gossip betrays a confidence,
but a trustworthy person keeps a secret.
PROVERBS 11:13 NIV

Marriage should be a safe place where partners can confide in matters of the heart and openly discuss thoughts about anything: silly or serious. Each spouse must be the one person that the other can depend on.

Perhaps we are pretty good at keeping our private conversations private, but there are times when we might share intimate knowledge with those outside of our marriage. Talkative or not, any of us can slip up and reveal what we should not. God intends for marriage to be a safe place for our hearts, and many discussions don't need to be shared beyond that space. Let us actively work to keep our marriages intimate.

Are you able to open up with one another about most topics? Do you feel like you can trust each other with your words? Make sure your marriage is a safe place for each other.

Jesus, thank you for our marriage. Thank you for creating a space where our hearts can be intimate and safe. Help us respect the confidence that we have in each other, and help us keep that trust. If we fail, help us forgive each other.

KEEP THE DAM SHUT!

Starting a quarrel is like breaching a dam;
so drop the matter before a dispute breaks out.
PROVERBS 17:14 NIV

Have you ever heard the saying, "Choose your battles?" It saves a number of senseless arguments when you stop to evaluate whether the problem is worth fighting for. Unfortunately, quarrels can become frequent in a marriage. Little problems can turn into bigger ones, if you let them.

This is why Scripture cautions you to stop before you even start. This requires self-control of the tongue, and it starts by taking a moment to reflect on your anger and irritation. If it's not worth the dam of emotion that you think might follow, then drop the matter. As you practice this self-control, it will become easier to do, and you and your partner will both be happier for it.

Do you feel as though you often quarrel about nothing? What are some strategies you can adopt to drop a matter before the dam breaks?

Father, you are perfect patience. We ask for your wisdom when we grow irritated with each other. Help us to check our hearts and control our tongues, that we may prevent unnecessary quarrels. Give us an extra measure of grace for one another, today and always.

CONQUERING THE QUEST FOR POWER

Better to be patient than powerful;
better to have self-control than to conquer a city.
PROVERBS 16:32 NLT

The nation of Israel expected their Messiah to come as a king: one who would defeat their enemies and make them the reigning nation. Instead, Jesus entered the world through the humblest of means and said that if they wanted to be great in God's kingdom, they had to serve all.

In our relationships, we get involved in power struggles, though we don't often recognize them. When we war against each other, even in a silent struggle, our cities crumble, and we will learn the hard way that holding the power hurts our marriages.

When you are struggling to hold power in your marriage, how can you pursue patience and self-control over your need for power? Talk with your spouse about ways you can avoid power struggles.

Lord, we are sorry when we lose our self-control and battle for power in our marriage. Help us recognize the times when we need to surrender, and let us work together to build up our family rather than tear it down.

COLLECTED BAGGAGE

Cast your cares on the Lord and he will sustain you;
he will never let the righteous be shaken.

PSALM 55:22 NIV

A man took a long journey carrying an empty sack over his shoulder. Along the way he saw a rock on the path. He bent down to pick it up and placed it in his bag. He found another and then another. Along the way he filled that sack and staggered under its weight. He could hardly walk and his destination seemed further away than when he began. Did he need that heavy burden? No! The rocks had blocked his path and the man needed to remove them to reach his destination.

Is your marriage suffering under so much collected baggage? God wants to shoulder your burdens. He wants the two of you to be free from the hardship and pain of the trials you face and problems you encounter. Do not punish yourselves by carrying the load on your own. Allow the Lord to give you peace and happiness. He delights in blessing you with his assistance when you need help.

Do you hold onto your burdens? Can you let the Lord take care of your problems? Can you share grievances with God?

Lord, help us to see when we are trying to shoulder our own troubles. We need help. Ease our sorrows and fill us with joy. We want to depend on only you.

DEEP YEARNINGS

"For this child I prayed, and the Lord has granted me my petition which I asked of Him. Therefore I also have lent him to the Lord; as long as he lives he shall be lent to the Lord."
1 SAMUEL 1:27-28 NKJV

Hannah was barren. She yearned deeply for a child. In her culture, bearing children was paramount for a woman. Elkanah, her husband, also had another wife who gave him children year after year, but Hannah was barren. She viewed this as a great personal failure and embarrassment. Hannah approached the Lord and vowed that if he granted her request she would give the child back to him. No doubt you will remember she gave birth to Samuel and when he was weaned she took him to be raised at the Temple.

Do you ache for a child, yearn for a house of your own, or desire to go to the mission field? Hannah's vow was to give back the son she so craved to repay the Lord for his kindness. She prayed for years. God wants to answer your prayers. Let the Lord know how deeply you appreciate the blessings he has given you.

Do you share your deepest yearnings with the Lord? What prayers have gone unanswered? How do you feel about them?

God, we want to acknowledge that everything we have and everything we are is because of you. We thank you and praise you for our many blessings. Help us to learn patience to see the answers to our prayers.

APRIL

Let us know; let us press on to
know the Lord; his going out is
sure as the dawn; he will come to
us as the showers, as the spring
rains that water the earth.

ISAIAH 6:3 ESV

WAY OF FOOLS

The way of fools seems right to them,
but the wise listen to advice.
PROVERBS 12:15 NIV

Do you listen to the "talking heads?" Do you follow every self-help link on Facebook: who to vote for, what to eat, what not to eat, how to get rid of male-patterned baldness or tone up the midriff area? There is advice coming from every corner. Should you listen to the next get-rich scheme or should you get your finances in rein? Do you need to get another credit card? Should you buy into a pyramid scheme to get discounted cleaning products or buy memberships to save money?

Take care to know which way you should go. As a married team you are the head of a household. It is your duty to point the direction the house goes. Don't be swayed by every notion you read about. Test everything against the Word of God. Find wise counselors. Ask your pastor. Do your research. You know the song, "Fools rush in, where wise men fear to tread." Don't be in a hurry to make important decisions.

Are you ready to make important decisions at the drop of a hat? Can you go to someone who knows more about the subject than you? Together can you research the answers to your questions?

Jesus, we want your help in finding the answers to life's dilemmas. Help us to make wise decisions based on knowledge and facts. Help us to seek wise counselors when we have questions.

SPEAK GOOD, DO GOOD

Let us think of ways to motivate one another to acts of love and good works.
HEBREWS 10:24 NLT

One of the many joys of marriage is that your partner knows you well. You both understand what the other person needs, whether it be a cup of coffee or help in a life transition. Use your understanding of each other to give effective encouragement. Think of what motivates your spouse to carry on, stay strong, and not lose heart. It might be a long walk, a night out of the house, or a letter to remind them of God's promises. We have hope in a God who deserves all our trust, and we can communicate this hope to each other when it is most needed.

Have you or your partner been discouraged lately? In what ways can you encourage each other to trust God and continue to love and do good to those around you?

Lord, we trust in your unwavering promises. Help us encourage one another to acts of love and good works.

ASK FOR DIRECTIONS!

*Look here, you who say, "Today or tomorrow we are going to a
certain town and will stay there a year. We will do business there
and make a profit." How do you know what your life will be like
tomorrow? Your life is like the morning fog—it's here a little while,
then it's gone. What you ought to say is, "If the Lord wants us to, we
will live and do this or that."*

JAMES 4:13-17 NLT

It is easy to become dissatisfied with your current
circumstances. Life is full of "what next?" discussions. We
aspire to hold better jobs, houses, and leisure opportunities.
These desires are not wrong or to be dismissed. Scripture
simply cautions us against trying to take control of our lives
out of God's hands, planning out every step ourselves.

Before you become anxious about what's next, take some
time to pray with your spouse, and ask God for direction. He
may not show you the final destination, but he will guide you
into the next step.

*What plans have you made lately about your future? Have
you remembered to surrender them to Jesus to find out
what he wants for you?*

**Father God, thank you that you have great plans for our life
together. Thank you for blessing us as a family and taking
us further into your will. Help us to know you are leading,
and give us trust in your guidance to a blessed future.**

GRACIOUS HOMES

The Word became flesh, and dwelt among us, and we saw His glory, glory as of the only begotten from the Father, full of grace and truth.

JOHN 1:14 NASB

As part of the Trinity, Jesus existed before time, and he shared the glory of God. Instead of coming to earth as an exalted king, he clothed himself in graciousness for the sinners, the poor, and the oppressed.

When we say that Jesus is the way and the truth and the life, we recognize that his life is the one to imitate. In our marriages, we can quickly become critical and harsh with each other. Grace starts at home, and it is successful only when we let Jesus work through us. Be uplifted by the grace that is in Christ, and allow him to work in your everyday actions.

Do you need forgiveness for being ungracious to one another? Allow the truth and grace of Jesus to be present in your conversation.

Lord Jesus, thank you for showing us humility and guiding us with your grace. Forgive us for the times that we have not reflected your grace. Help us walk together, confident that we are loved and we are able to love in all fullness.

JESUS' HABITS

Jesus traveled to Nazareth, where he had grown up. On the Sabbath day he went to the synagogue, as he always did, and stood up to read.
LUKE 4:16 NCV

Jesus went to the synagogue on the Sabbath day. It was a habit in his life, but it wasn't just to follow some rules to impress God—he *was* God! Instead, he lived as an example for us.

As Jesus demonstrated, we need to decide on some godly habits in our relationships and our daily activities. Perhaps you need to set up some regular prayer times or spiritual check-ins with your spouse. Maybe you need to go to church more. You will find freedom in having some good habits. You won't need to be obsessed with trying to be better; you just will be!

What habits are important for you to put in place as spiritual leaders in your family? Ask yourselves if you are following the example of Jesus.

Jesus, thank you for living on earth and showing us the importance of walking with God daily. Help us to set life-giving habits in our relationship and family life, and give us the resolve to put them into practice.

KEEP THE PEACE

"Every kingdom divided against itself will be ruined, and every city or household divided against itself will not stand."
MATTHEW 12:25 NIV

Divisions can start off small. They might be a few different thoughts with the way a friend is doing things, or it may come out in a few disgruntled comments to your co-workers. Chances are you have made it clear to your spouse when they have irritated you.

If there are children in your household, there are more opportunities for disharmony, between siblings or your parenting styles. We need to actively look for common ground and keep God's will for our families at the forefront. Be encouraged that God didn't make us exactly the same; he made us to complement one another.

Are you letting your spouse or your kids bring out the best in you? Think of the areas that need some adjusting and bring them to the Holy Spirit in prayer.

Heavenly Father, thank you that you brought this family together to be a unit of strength in a needy world. Bring healing where there has been division, and give us guidance in bringing peace into our home.

PRACTICE LOVE

Dear children, let us not love with words or speech but with actions and in truth.
1 JOHN 3:18 NIV

We all have ways in which we naturally give and receive love. For many, words are meaningful, but they become empty if there is no action to give truth to the words. You might tell your spouse that you respect them, but if you are continually unsupportive or selfish, your words of respect will mean nothing.

Scripture tells us that love is an active quality. There are many tangible ways to give and experience love, and they need to be more than empty speeches.

Are there ways that you can show love to your spouse through meaningful actions this week? Ask each other what would best show your love.

Dear Lord, help us to love each other in actions and in truth. As we put our love for one another into practice, let this spill into our interactions with others, that they may experience your love through us.

HUMBLE ARGUMENTS

When pride comes, then comes disgrace,
but with humility comes wisdom.

PROVERBS 11:2 NIV

What is your natural response in an argument? Do you go to all lengths to prove that you are right? Do you walk away, unwilling to meet in the middle? We all expose weaknesses when it comes to disagreements, and most of us do not respond as we should.

God's Word talks about our heart attitude and the consequence of holding onto pride instead of accepting the road of humility. If we are willing to understand things from the other person's perspective, we might learn something about each other and ourselves.

Is there a recent argument that you need to apologize for? How can you make a commitment to approach the next disagreement with humility instead of pride?

Father, we are sorry for letting pride rule our disagreements. Please give us your wisdom to approach each other with humility. Allow our love for one another to shine through the rough patches.

SURVIVING THE DROUGHTS

Though the fig tree does not bud and there are no grapes on the vines, though the olive crop fails and the fields produce no food, though there are no sheep in the pen and no cattle in the stalls, yet I will rejoice in the Lord, I will be joyful in God my Savior.

HABAKKUK 3:17-18 NIV

Droughts are a real and natural part of any lasting relationship. We can find ourselves facing seasons of life that seem unproductive, discouraging, and just plain dry. In these times, your love might feel dormant.

If you are experiencing this right now, be encouraged to find the depth of character that comes with persevering through droughts. If you both agree to face dry times together, you will find that your love will come into a new season. Praise God, and find his joy in every circumstance.

Are you experiencing a dry season in your relationship? Do you feel there is no fruit in your lives? Take some time to consider what season of life you are in, and plan for future droughts.

Lord, forgive us for blaming each other in times of drought. Help us to recognize the season of life and love that we have. Give us patience in the dry times, and help us to remain joyful in one another, encouraging each other until the fruit comes.

CONSIDERED CONVERSATIONS

These commandments that I give you today are to be on your hearts. Impress them on your children. Talk about them when you sit at home and when you walk along the road, when you lie down and when you get up.

DEUTERONOMY 6:6-7 NIV

What dominates conversations between you and your spouse? Is it the next purchase, holiday, or chore? Is it your work or your children? Perhaps you spend a lot of time discussing finances or people you know. It's okay to talk about what is on your mind, but do you give much thought to the Scriptures and how God might be speaking to you throughout your day?

If you have children, chances are they are going to pick up on a lot of your dialogue. When the Word of God is on our hearts, we naturally spend time talking about Jesus at home, when we're out, and as we go to bed. Pass your love for God's ways on to your children. Discuss them with your family. When you share your heart, your children and spouse will be able to share theirs.

What have you spent a lot of time talking about recently? Can you think of ways to bring Jesus into your conversations with each other and your children?

Lord, sometimes we get caught up in daily necessities, and we spend little time reflecting on your Word. Enter our conversations, and fill us and our children with lasting impressions of you.

NEARSIGHTED

"How can you think of saying, 'Friend, let me help you get rid of that speck in your eye,' when you can't see past the log in your own eye?"
LUKE 6:42 NLT

This verse points out that spiritual nearsightedness is universal. Our farsighted vision easily sees another's defects while remaining blind to our own. Often, a defect we see in another is a mirrored reflection of ourselves.

It's easy to self-righteously point out our spouse's errors without seeing our own gargantuan faults. And how often do we rise in self-defense when our errors are pointed out? (Can you hear echoes from the Garden of Eden?) Before you critique your spouse, take a moment to examine yourself.

What is one thing I can do to become less nearsighted? Am I mature enough to ask my spouse to point out my faults?

Father, point the mirror back at me when I rise to my own defense. Grant me humble ears and lips to accept criticism from my spouse. Let me be quick to hear and slow to speak.

RECEIVED

"Anyone who receives you receives me, and anyone who receives me receives the Father who sent me."

MATTHEW 10:40 NLT

People marry with the best intentions not to make the same mistakes their parents did. Then, reality hits. The wife finds herself getting irritated when her husband doesn't pick up his clothes and leaves shaved facial hairs in the sink, and the husband gets upset because his wife is picky and hard to please. When they are calm and not in a pointing-fingers mood, loving spouses will hear each other out and humbly ask for forgiveness, promising change. What if that only works for a week?

The verse for today compels us to look beyond ourselves and our problems. Jesus says to receive our spouses as if we were receiving him. Wow! In other words, look beyond your spouse's shortcomings, and receive him or her as you do Christ.

How can we acknowledge Christ's presence each morning as we start our day and look beyond each other's faults?

Father, we invite you to be an integral part of our marriage. Make us conscious when we start pointing fingers at each other. Help us to accept each other where we are right now, just as you accept us.

USING YOUR GIFTS

Who are you, O man, to answer back to God? Will what is molded say to its molder, "Why have you made me like this?"
ROMANS 9:20 ESV

A popular belief dished out to today's young people is that they can be anything they aspire to be. The big flaw in this encouragement is ability. There is always hard work and practice, but what if your gifts don't line up with your desires? At times, we all fall prey to longing for different talents.

We are content when we accept our gifts, and we must accept our spouse's gifts as well. So your husband isn't a handyman, but perhaps he quickly spots the flaws in a theological argument. Maybe your wife doesn't feel comfortable in the kitchen, but she loves to paint and creates beautiful art. Rejoice with and encourage your spouse to excel in his or her gifts.

How can you accept the unique gifts God gave you and your spouse? Brainstorm ways you can use those gifts in the coming weeks.

Father, you wisely gave different aptitudes and talents to each of us, and your choices are always right. Give us grace to accept our gifts and each other's.

SCHEDULE SHIFTS

Make every effort to keep yourselves united in the Spirit, binding yourselves together with peace.
EPHESIANS 4:3 NLT

Jared and Abby were like two ships passing in the night. He worked the evening shift. She worked days. Both of them were involved in different service projects at church, and they each volunteered at different charities in their town. Add in family responsibilities and tasks around the house, and they barely saw one another. It was impacting their marriage as their once close relationship became distant and cold.

They were doing good things. Responsible things. Even spending time serving the Lord. But they had allowed their schedules to start the destruction process for what had once been a thriving marriage. A wise couple will remember a simple equation: put God first, your spouse and children after that, and then other people. Be a united front as you ask God to become the keeper of your schedule, and then sit down with your calendar and put first things first.

Are you drifting apart because of your schedules? Sit down together and see how you can change things.

Lord, keep unity in our home. Help us to ask you before we take on tasks that will take time from our spouses and families.

ATTENTIVENESS

Wise people can also listen and learn;
even they can find good advice in these words.

PROVERBS 1:5 NCV

The stats prove what we all suspected: in general, women talk more than men. The numbers vary from 15,000 words a day to 30,000, but the average woman speaks three times more than the average man. Have you observed couples walking—be it on a street, path, or beach—and often the woman is talking, while the man listens? The need to talk is part of a woman's DNA, and that hasn't changed since the beginning of time.

When a wife comes to her husband with a question, she isn't always looking for a solution. She just needs to talk it out, and in talking, she often finds the answer. If a husband doesn't know that, he gets out his mental tool box to suggest a fix. The wise wife will preface her talk by saying, "I'm not looking for solutions. I just need to share." The wise husband will then listen attentively, without offering three steps to solving her problems.

How can you improve your dialogue? Talk together about communicating clearly.

Dear Lord, help us come to terms with our differences. We should not try to change each other; we need patience to listen and wisdom to know when to speak. Thank you for giving your Holy Spirit to help us.

UNDERSTANDING

As you do not know the path of the wind, or how the body is formed in a mother's womb, so you cannot understand the work of God, the Maker of all things.

ECCLESIASTES 11:5 NIV

Can you predict where the wind is going to blow next? Even weather forecasters have trouble and they have equipment to help them. Or as you've awaited the birth of a child, have you ever thought about how that baby is forming in the womb? Sonograms provide a precious window into the womb, showing tiny arms and legs waving around, occasional somersaults, and even an opportunity to see your unborn child sucking his or her thumb. It's beyond amazing—and beyond our comprehension how God causes that child to grow.

Our minds aren't big enough to understand something so complex and miraculous. The same is true in how God works in our marriages. Consider the way he takes two people and turns them into one loving union. We can't understand the depth of that—but we can be grateful for all of it and stand in awe of a creator who does all things well.

Does it boggle your mind how big God is? What can you do to understand him more?

Father, we aren't able to understand all that you do, but we are in awe of you!

CAUSE AND EFFECT

A glad heart makes a cheerful face,
but by sorrow of heart the spirit is crushed.
PROVERBS 15:13 ESV

Cause and effect. A joyful heart causes a cheerful face. A sad heart produces a broken spirit. What would happen if we always chose to be joyful—even in difficult circumstances? Is that even possible? Fanny Crosby, a famous hymn writer, went blind at six weeks old. She wrote her first poem when she was eight. It begins, "O what a happy soul am I although I cannot see..." and it concludes, "To weep and sigh because I'm blind, I cannot and I won't!"

As a couple, we can help each other live joyfully, even when we don't feel joyful. It is difficult to be objective when we are suffering. That's where our spouses play a pivotal role in helping us look at the situation through a different lens, giving us new perspective on the situation. We can choose to be happy in spite of our circumstances.

Has your spouse encouraged you in a recent challenge?
Thank each other.

Heavenly Father, make us encouragers for each other, and lead us to choose joyful hearts.

PEEKING IN AT HEAVEN'S DOOR

Through the praise of children and infants
you have established a stronghold against your enemies,
to silence the foe and the avenger.

PSALM 8:2 NIV

A mother lost her way driving home with her two children after visiting a friend in a large city. Following that first wrong turn, she couldn't get her bearings. She drove uphill and down, around a lake, and past unfamiliar streets without finding anyone to ask for help. She began to feel she would never find her way home. In desperation, she cried aloud, to no one in particular, "Where am I?" A little voice from the back seat immediately replied, "God knows."

A child's perception of spiritual matters can astound adults. With their innocence and trust, they open heaven's door for us, allowing a peek inside that silences the voice of our own doubts. Two words spoken by that little voice brought peace to a troubled mother's heart, and eventually, they did find a familiar road that took them home.

In what ways have children, whether your own or someone else's, been God's voice to you?

Heavenly Father, thank you for children and the ease with which they believe. Give us a child's trusting heart, as we must become like little children in order to enter the kingdom of heaven.

SET IN STONE

Everyone should be quick to listen, slow to speak and
slow to become angry.
JAMES 1:19 NIV

"Guilty, your honor." We are all guilty of blurting out information we promised to keep secret. We rail on someone for offending us, or interrupt to tell our story while growing bored at others' tales. We are guilty of hurling angry words at our spouses and not listening to instructions, counsel, or criticism. We are guilty of half-truths, exaggerating, and outright lies.

Sadly, we cannot retract our words. Once out of our mouths, they embed into someone's heart and soul. We ask for forgiveness, yet what has been said is set in stone. How much better if we had never uttered those words! The good news is that our holy God is within us, and he is waiting for an invitation to help us.

Will you yield your tongue to him each morning? Apologize
to your spouse for any poor words, and renew your vows
of kindness and grace to one another.

Father, thank you for living in us. Help us to be attentive to the quiet voice of the Holy Spirit, which tells us when to stop talking and listen. We yield our tongues to you today, in the expectant hope that you will help us on this daily journey.

COMBAT LONELINESS

Two are better than one, because they have a good reward for their toil. For if they fall, one will lift up his fellow. But woe to him who is alone when he falls and has not another to lift him up!

ECCLESIASTES 4:9 ESV

Loneliness is toxic. Studies show that not only does it hurt our emotional and physical wellbeing, it is also detrimental to our brains, causing memory loss and shortened lives.

The antidote to loneliness is healthy relationships, and marriage is one of the best.

The psalmist David says God combats loneliness with family. God planned for husbands and wives to be not just sexual partners, but best friends. It's about sharing a good joke, enjoying a meal, going for a walk, watching a favorite TV show, reading quietly, or playing a round of golf. It's knowing someone cares for you and enjoys sharing life with you for as long as you both live.

Have you taken time to enjoy one another? What is something you could do this week to strengthen your relationship?

Thank you, Father, for giving us each other. Help us to value our relationship and protect our quality time together from the busyness of life. Show us ways to strengthen our bond and build beautiful memories together.

THE PASSION IN COMPASSION

Put on then, as God's chosen ones, holy and beloved,
compassionate hearts, kindness, humility, meekness, and patience.
COLOSSIANS 3:12 ESV

We associate passion with marriage, but compassion? Yes. Compassion literally means *with passion*. Compassion is more than a strong emotion; it compels us into action to alleviate another's sorrow or suffering.

Some people are compassionate by nature. Most of us, however, find our compassion thermometer hovering close to zero at times. In marriage, we have endless opportunities to practice compassion. When our spouse has a headache or comes down with the flu, the natural response is to get out the Tylenol and make sure he or she can rest comfortably. But if our spouse contracts a debilitating disease? Can compassion walk that long road, day after day, year after year? If that day comes, we can count on God's enabling grace to fill us with his compassion. God doesn't expect us to serve with only our strength, and that is our greatest encouragement.

Have we shown compassion when one of us has a bad day? What practical things can we do to alleviate each other's afflictions?

Father, thank you for your perfect and endless compassion. Sometimes we find ourselves lacking true and selfless compassion. We feel incapable of going the extra mile. Please fill us with your compassion and your desire to love unconditionally. Show us how.

YOKED FORCES

Do not be yoked together with unbelievers. For what do righteousness and wickedness have in common? Or what fellowship can light have with darkness? What harmony is there between Christ and Belial? Or what does a believer have in common with an unbeliever?

2 CORINTHIANS 6:14-15 NIV

Is a yoke a positive or negative thing? Some might see it as forced submission to another's will. Others may see a yoke as an enabler that unites forces to do something one could never do alone. In the old days, if one ox could not pull a cart by himself, he needed a partner yoked with him, and their doubled strength could pull the cart.

In marriage, we submit ourselves to a yoke both legal and sacred—only one partner out of billions—to form a unique nucleus. We submit ourselves to the yoke of interdependence, and we pull together as a team. It is no longer about finding solitary fulfillment, but of enabling each other to reach our dreams together.

Am I willing to submit myself to my spouse in order to enable them to be all God wants? Ask each other what you might do to help pull your cart forward.

Father, with your infinite knowledge, your plans are always right. You understand how two independent people can enable each other through a simple act of mutual submission. Help us to look at our marriage through your lens and see all the wonderful possibilities for mutual fulfillment.

CHOOSING CONTENTMENT

Not that I speak from want, for I have learned to be content in whatever circumstances I am.

PHILIPPIANS 4:11 NASB

Wouldn't it be nice if contentment were automatic? Life would be more pleasant, and we would be too! The hard truth is that contentment is a choice, but it is one we can all make. Even the apostle Paul admitted he had to learn how to be content.

Contentment is a by-product of accepting what you cannot change. It does not mean you agree with the way things are or that you like the way things are. Rather, it is a statement of faith. You acknowledge your circumstances while trusting God to change what you cannot change, and you accept what he sees fit to change. Then, you can rest, and inner conflicts cease.

Is there a circumstance in your lives that you cannot change but would like to? Can you choose to be content in this situation?

Father, give us grace to choose contentment even in situations we cannot change. You can change what we are unable to change, and we trust you to do what is right for us. Grant us patience and perseverance.

DESERVE-O-METERS

Bear with each other, and forgive each other. If someone does wrong to you, forgive that person because the Lord forgave you.
COLOSSIANS 3:13 NCV

Forgiveness is never about merit. We don't forgive our spouse because he or she deserves grace. We forgive because Christ forgave us. We all seem to possess a built-in "deserve-o-meter," and it starts blinking whenever someone wrongs us.

To help us understand the dimensions of Christ's forgiveness of our sins, and why we should then forgive others, Jesus told the parable of a man who had a massive debt forgiven. Freed from his own debt, the man turned around and refused to forgive another man who owed him a mere pittance. He did not pass on grace and forgiveness. We are the ones with the huge debt that Christ forgave. As a result, we should be just as prompt in forgiving our spouse for an angry word, selfish act, or moral failing. Anything another human being could do against us is, in God's sight, a mere pittance compared to the huge debt we owe God.

Am I unwilling to forgive my spouse for a wrong done to me? How does God view my lack of forgiveness?

Heavenly Father, you are the perfect example of forgiveness—willing, unreserved, and complete. Destroy our "deserve-o-meters," and help us, as a couple, exemplify your forgiveness to each other every day.

UNCHAIN YOUR PAST

Forget the former things;
do not dwell on the past.
Isaiah 43:18 NIV

Our capacity to remember is a great gift from God. Life would have no meaning if we were unable to recall what we did an hour ago, a week ago, or last year.

Good memories are energizing, but bad memories can drag us down. Hurtful memories form links in a heavy chain we drag around, links of resentment, grudges, and wrongs done to us or by us. God invites us to let go. Through repentance and forgiveness, the manacles on our ankles unlock, and we can walk away from those memories—free. When they come back to taunt us, God holds the key to keeping those chains away.

Are you carrying around a heavy chain of crippling memories? Can you give them to God right now?

Heavenly Father, thank you for forgiving our sins and casting them in the depths of the sea. We give you the bad memories that haunt and hurt our relationship. Give us a new life of forgiveness and freedom in Christ.

SUBLIME UNITY

My lover is mine, and I am his.
SONG OF SOLOMON 2:16 NLT

Those eight words succinctly sum up marriage. *I belong to you. You belong to me.* We belong to each other. It is the essence of married life. "No man is an island," said the poet John Donne, and he was right. God saw that it was not good for man to be alone, and he made us to live in community.

There is no closer relationship on earth than that of husband and wife. In sexual unity, we fully comprehend what belonging feels like. It is joyful abandonment to each other, a oneness of body and soul that is total acceptance of who we are. Our words and touches are tender, our consideration for each other sweet and thankful. In sublime moments, we taste eternity, but those moments don't last. Daily life dulls past moments, and we soon forget to be tender and kind. Sexual intimacy can bring us back to "I belong to you, and you belong to me."

Talk together about how you can fully appreciate the blessing of belonging to each other.

Father, in your wisdom and love, you gave us each other. You created sex to make our relationship fulfilling. Watch over us and our relationship, and help us to guard it as a treasured gift.

A COMMAND AND A PROMISE

So do not fear, for I am with you;
do not be dismayed, for I am your God.
I will strengthen you and help you;
I will uphold you with my righteous right hand.
ISAIAH 41:10 NIV

Isaiah's message to Israel was both a command and a promise. They had reason to be afraid – they lived during a stormy period when their sin was leading them on a fast track to judgment and captivity. Yet, God had not forsaken them. His judgment was coming, but so was his mercy. One day he would deliver them as he had their ancestors long before.

This command and promise is for us too. Our country and culture is being taken captive spiritually. Blatant disobedience to God's Word is leading us further from God and closer to the enemy. These are tumultuous and potentially fearful times. We don't need to fear because God is with us and he will give us the strength we need to make it through.

As you see our nation turn increasingly away from God, are you fearful? Take some time to search the Scriptures for more promises of God's protection, help, and strength.

Lord, it's hard to watch our country support the very things you detest and refuse to acknowledge your presence. Please help us each day to trust you and to know in our heart of hearts that your righteous, strong arm will hold us fast.

OVERFLOWING

"Give, and it will be given to you. A good measure, pressed down, shaken together and running over, will be poured into your lap. For with the measure you use, it will be measured to you."

LUKE 6:38 NIV

The imagery of Christ pouring blessings into our laps comes from the ancient Middle Eastern grain market. People went into the market and literally bought a lapful of grain! A part of their garment was folded up and secured by a sash, and the pocket created held the grain, filling their laps. The crowd listening to Jesus would have understood the illustration completely.

Many years ago, a young couple discovered this verse and decided to put it to the test. Having nothing to give away, they prayed that God would channel some money in their direction so they could pass it on. Within a week or so, a friend handed them $15 for reason at all, just as a gift. They quickly gave it away. Within three weeks, they received the equivalent of $630 from various sources. Amazed and grateful, they learned a life lesson that we can learn, too. God wants to pour out his blessings on us, but our own generosity is the trigger. We do not give to get, but we also cannot out-give God! He will bless us as we bless others.

Would you consider yourselves a generous couple? Are you willing to put God to the test and sacrificially give?

Lord, help us to become cheerful givers. Show us ways we can pour blessings out on others, with the knowledge that our investment will be returned many times over.

A GUARD AT THE DOOR

Set a guard, O Lord, over my mouth;
keep watch over the door of my lips!
PSALM 141:3 ESV

"Sticks and stones may break my bones, but words will never harm me," claims a familiar saying. True, words cannot cause physical harm, but they can do as much damage to the spirit as a 2 x 4 would to the body. David, our psalmist, understood it. James, the brother of Jesus, did as well. They both knew the impossibility of controlling the tongue. "No human being can tame the tongue," said James. David beseeched God to put a guard over his mouth so that, even when provoked by his enemies, he would not utter a cruel word.

Think of the mouth as a one-way exit door. If there were a guard on duty, his post would be on the inside, preventing any unauthorized escapes. David pleads that God be a guard for him, to prevent him from saying anything that would displease God and harm others. Should we not do the same?

Think about your conversations. Are the words you use uplifting or damaging? Be honest with each other, and be ready to make some speech adjustments!

Post a guard at our mouths, Lord. Set a watch at the door of our lips, that we may not sin against you and hurt each other.

FULL ACCEPTANCE

Accept one another, then, just as Christ accepted you, in order to bring praise to God.
ROMANS 15:7 NIV

There is a deep need in the human heart for acceptance. The longing to belong is a powerful, significant factor in our choices. Outside of Christ, it can lead us down the wrong path. In Christ, the need for acceptance is satisfied—not by our own striving, but through the relationship we have with the one who fully accepts us.

In Romans 15, Paul spoke to Jews and Gentiles, two groups of people who were polarized by culture and background. The Jews, God's chosen people, believed that Christ came exclusively for them, and they had difficulty accepting Gentile Christians into their fellowship. Paul urged them to accept one another just as Christ had accepted them. The message to us is the same! As believers, can we love and accept those in the Body of Christ who are radically different than we are? Jesus said our love for each other would cause people to be drawn to him.

Is it difficult for you to accept others who look different, have different backgrounds, or express different tastes? Do you have difficulty accepting each other just as God created you, or are you intent on changing one another?

First of all, Lord, help us to accept each other fully. Forgive us for any judgments we have made toward others, and give us the grace to love and accept them that your name may be glorified.

MAY

For behold, the winter is past; the
rain is over and gone. The flowers
appear on the earth, the time of
singing has come, and the voice of
the turtledove is heard in our land.

SONG OF SOLOMON 2:11-12 ESV

WALKING WITH INTEGRITY

The one whose walk is blameless is kept safe,
but the one whose ways are perverse will fall into the pit.
PROVERBS 28:18 NIV

Walking hand-in-hand with your spouse brings heartwarming security; walking hand-in-hand with God brings spiritual confidence. Ideally, couples join hands with each other and place their joined hands firmly in God's hand. Faith brings integrity and will keep your marriage focused on God and filled with his love.

Walking the straight and narrow path is not easy, and having a spouse to hold you accountable is a blessing. Spouses make a covenant with each other that as they walk through life they will keep each other accountable and help each other walk closely with God.

Can you remember a time when your partner held you accountable for an action? Thank him or her.

God, thank you that we have each other. Help us to hold each other accountable to live the life you have planned for us.

BE A BUILDER

Let us therefore make every effort to do what leads to peace and to mutual edification.

ROMANS 14:19 NIV

In Paul's day, there were disagreements among the Christians about things that were, in the grand scheme of things, rather petty. Some felt that being a vegetarian was best and certain days should be celebrated as holy days. Others felt differently. Paul knew there was nothing inherently evil about meat that was not kosher and that certain days were not holier than others. Conflict over such things was discouraging, especially to the new believer. Paul exhorted them to stop insisting on their own ways and to encourage one another in the faith.

Sometimes we become petty and nitpicky with each other over unimportant things. We need to remember that God has not called us to transform one another, but to encourage and build each other up.

Are you easily irritated by each other's quirks and habits? Be honest! Make a covenant to be cheerleaders for each other.

Lord, we want to work on building each other up. We want to live with peace ruling our lives and home. Give us grace to overlook any faults, and make us builders instead of discouragers.

BE STRONG AND COURAGEOUS

"Have I not commanded you? Be strong and courageous. Do not be afraid; do not be discouraged, for the Lord your God will be with you wherever you go."

JOSHUA 1:9 NIV

It must have been a terrifying time. Moses, the Israelite leader, was dead, and Israel was headed into major warfare. The Promised Land was there for the taking, and they had to prepare under new leadership. "Get ready to cross the Jordan River, into the land I am about to give to you," God said to Joshua. "As I was with Moses, so I will be with you. I will never leave you nor forsake you! Be careful to obey all the law. Keep this Book of the Law always on your lips; meditate on it day and night" (verses 2, 5, 8).

Be strong! Be courageous! Was this really possible? Yes, because God would be there. As long as the people meditated on the law and were careful to obey it, God's presence would be a constant. From that place of security, strength and courage could rise. Take strength and courage from Joshua; God can do the same for your marriage in the 21st century.

Are you and your spouse experiencing the presence of God daily? Are you consistently in the Word, letting it permeate your very being, making obedience second nature?

Lord, thank you for the magnificent promise of your presence. Thank you that we don't need to be afraid or discouraged, because you will never leave us or forsake us. Reassure us of that promise, and keep us safe in you.

BECOME LIKE JESUS

In your relationships with one another, have the same mindset as Christ Jesus: Who, being in very nature God, did not consider equality with God something to be used to his own advantage; rather, he made himself nothing by taking the very nature of a servant, being made in human likeness…he humbled himself by becoming obedient to death.

PHILIPPIANS 2:5-8 NIV

A very rich king was unhappy. He longed to share his life with someone. One day, he saw the most beautiful woman he had ever seen. He lost his heart, but she was a peasant. How could he win her over? He could write an edict, but she would marry him only out of obedience. He could court her, but she might marry him just for his money and position. He decided to approach her as a peasant, and in doing so, give up his royal palace and all his wealth and become just like her in order to win her heart.

This is what Christ did for us. He had equal status with God, yet he set that aside and became human. He lived a selfless, obedient life, sacrificing himself on a cross to save us. Christ led by example, selfless and sacrificing. His love inspires us to love in the same way.

Do you serve one another gladly, giving up your wants in deference to the other's needs? Talk about ways you can best help one another.

Lord, thank you for your sacrifices. Help us to follow your loving, selfless example.

HEAR AND OBEY

"Blessed rather are those who hear the word of God and obey it."
LUKE 11:28 NIV

Jesus spoke these words when he introduced the template for prayer—the Lord's Prayer. He urged his listeners to keep on asking, seeking and knocking; God, as a good Father, would answer with good gifts.

Jesus demonstrated the authority of his Word and power over Satan by casting out a demon. In the crowd, a woman, perhaps overcome with admiration and joy, cried out, "God bless your mother who bore you!" Jesus quickly shifted her perspective from temporal to spiritual by responding, "Blessed are those who hear and obey the Word of God."

Hear and obey. Sometimes, there is a gap between what we hear and know to be true, and how we live. As Christians, we need to be hearing God's Word on a regular basis, but hearing and obeying are poles apart. Obeying is the path to blessing.

Are you reading the Word of God together? Are you obeying what it says? Find a time for the Word, and discuss how to hold each other accountable.

Lord, thank you for your Word; it is the truth that sets us free! Give us discipline to read it, and grant us obedient hearts.

BOAST IN THE LORD

Those who wish to boast should boast in this alone: that they truly know me and understand that I am the Lord who demonstrates unfailing love and who brings justice and righteousness to the earth, and that I delight in these things. I, the Lord, have spoken!

JEREMIAH 9:24 NLT

Boasting about one's accomplishments is generally distasteful to others. We are told many times in Scripture that we should be humble, defer to others, and value others more than ourselves. God gives us permission to blow only one horn, and that is God's! Our successes pale in comparison to his justice, unfailing love, and righteousness.

Paul must have had this passage in mind when he wrote to the Corinthians, "If anyone wants to be proud, he should be proud of what the Lord has done. It is not what a man thinks and says of himself that is important. It is what God thinks of him" (2 Corinthians 10:17-18 NLT). Be confident in God's greatness and in his love for you.

Talk with your spouse about all God has done in you and through you. Thank God, and take a moment to brag about him!

Thank you, Lord, for being our God. Thank you for the many blessings you pour out on our lives. How great you are!

COME BOLDLY

Let us come boldly to the throne of our gracious God. There we will receive his mercy, and we will find grace to help us when we need it most.

HEBREWS 4:16 NLT

Our heavenly Father invites us into his presence. "Come to me. Come confidently, without reservation or fear. I have what you need!"

As a child, you probably struggled with your shoelaces or zipping up your jacket and, frustrated, ran to your mom or dad for help. As a teenager, perhaps you had troubles with friends or classes and turned to your parents for comfort. As an adult, you've made big decisions. There have been times of sorrow and discouragement. Your needs are endless, but so is God's grace. So come.

As a couple, what are your needs today? Can you run to the throne of grace right now and receive the help you need?

Thank you, Lord, for inviting us into your presence at this moment to receive mercy and grace. We humbly ask for your help, and we look forward to what you will do in our lives.

ETERNAL CONTENTMENT

Make sure that your character is free from the love of money, being content with what you have; for He Himself has said, "I will never desert you, nor will I ever forsake you."

HEBREWS 13:5 NASB

The promise to never leave nor forsake was first given to the nation of Israel in Deuteronomy. Moses would soon hand his leadership to Joshua, and the battle to possess the Promised Land was about to begin. Disobedience and discontent had cost them forty long years in the desert. Paul quoted the same promise to the Jewish converts who needed a different reminder—to keep their eyes on the big picture and not to be ensnared by materialism. The true Promised Land, an eternity with Jesus, lies ahead.

Don't be covetous, be content. The presence of God dwells in a contented spirit because when we have Jesus, we have everything we need.

Are you and your spouse content with what you have? Do you spend too much time aiming for more while not being grateful for what God has given you?

Lord, forgive us for our lack of contentment; we know that what we have is really what we need. Thank you for your gracious abundance. Give us an eternal perspective and the peace and contentment that come with it.

GETTING ADVICE

Get all the advice and instruction you can,
so you will be wise the rest of your life.
PROVERBS 19:20 NLT

Proverbs is the Christian's go-to book for practical, common sense directives to navigate life. According to the above verse, listening to and receiving counsel leads us to wisdom. Looking for it in the right place is, of course, imperative. The story of two kings in 1 Kings 12 is a case in point.

Rehoboam and Jeroboam reigned simultaneously in Israel's divided kingdom. Jeroboam and the entire community appealed to Rehoboam to lighten the harsh labor demands and heavy taxes his father, Solomon, had laid on them, promising to be his loyal subjects if he did so. Rejecting the wise advice from his father's counselors, he echoed his foolish, young friends' wishes and threatened the people with an even heavier burden. His foolishness cost him most of the kingdom.

Good counsel and instruction received will lead us to wisdom. First, we intake the Word daily, and then we listen to others who can explain, expound, and challenge us to live according to it.

Are you willing to ask for advice when you need it? Can you humbly receive the wise counsel of a godly man or woman, be it your spouse or someone else?

Lord, you are the wisdom, righteousness, and redemption. Help us to receive your wisdom, whether it comes directly from your Word or from the mouth of a wise spouse or friend.

GIVE GENEROUSLY

They share freely and give generously to those in need.
Their good deeds will be remembered forever.
They will have influence and honor.

PSALM 112:9 NLT

Psalm 112 is a beautiful poem that lists the characteristics of those who joyfully fear the Lord and delight in obeying his commands. Their children will be successful; an entire generation of godly people will be blessed. Their good deeds will last forever; their light shines in darkness. They are generous and compassionate; good comes to them. Evil will not overtake them; they do not fear bad news. They confidently trust in the Lord; they can face their enemies boldly. Last but not least, they are generous and share freely with those in need. Because of their generosity, their good deeds will be remembered, and honor and influence will be theirs.

These are the beautiful characteristics of a Christian. In loving God, we are given these blessings, not only to bring praise and honor to God, but also to bless others. God is indeed generous.

Are you by nature a generous couple, or does it take some effort? Talk about ways you can bless others in need.

Lord, you are more than generous with your people. Your blessings know no bounds. Help us to freely give and joyfully share with others out of that abundance.

GOD IS FOR YOU

What shall we say about such wonderful things as these? If God is for us, who can ever be against us? Since he did not spare even his own Son but gave him up for us all, won't he also give us everything else?

ROMANS 8:31-32 NLT

God is for you. He's on your side. How can you be sure? According to Romans 6, the cross is proof. God did not spare his own Son but gave him up for you, so that you could be fully forgiven and adopted into his family. He helps you in your weaknesses. The Holy Spirit prays for you according to God's own will. God causes everything to work out for good and he has chosen you! Nothing can separate you from his love.

In light of that, does it really matter if others oppose you, or if you make a terrible choice? Consequences will come, but God is still on your side. He's waiting to mend the rips and forgive your sin. If you have Jesus, you have everything!

Do you need to be reminded today that God is on your side? Are you on each other's sides, supporting and cheering each other on?

Lord, it is amazing to know that the God of the Universe is actually on our side! Help us to live in that reality and extend the same loving affirmation to each other.

GROWING UP

Anyone who lives on milk, being still an infant, is not acquainted with the teaching about righteousness. But solid food is for the mature, who by constant use have trained themselves to distinguish good from evil.

HEBREWS 5:14 NIV

There's nothing wrong with being a babe in Christ. Everyone begins at the beginning. However, when one remains in the infant stage, or digresses back to it because of malnourishment, there is a problem. Paul was frustrated by the lack of understanding as he taught on the meatier subjects of faith. He said they were dull of hearing. Their spiritual immaturity was apparent. For the amount of time they had followed Jesus, they should have been teachers rather than elementary school kids.

It's good to evaluate our spiritual growth, remembering that it is our responsibility. We grow in spiritual maturity by dining on the solid food of the Word and trusting God to teach us through it. We can't wait around for someone else to make sure we grow up in God.

As a couple, are you complacent or disinterested in going deeper with God? Are you more enamored with things in this world than you are with seeking things above?

Lord, we really do want to go on to maturity in our walk with you. Life often gets in our way. Give us what it takes to devote ourselves to you and to seek you with our whole hearts.

HUMBLE HARMONY

Be of the same mind toward one another; do not be haughty in mind, but associate with the lowly. Do not be wise in your own estimation.

ROMANS 12:16 NASB

Paul hammers home the importance of harmony and humility in many letters. He repeats it again to the Romans, the Philippians, and to the Corinthians, and the message resounds to Christians everywhere in all stations of life.

In essence, he says, "Do not court the rich and the powerful while neglecting the lowly and in so doing exalt yourself to a higher place." He calls for peace, unity, like-mindedness—a harmony of love and acceptance that understands our oneness in Christ.

Is it difficult for you to associate with those who are perhaps less blessed than you are? Why not invite another couple over who could use some encouragement and friendship?

Lord, help us to remember any measure of success we have is not because of our own wisdom; it is from you. Help us to see those around us who could use a friend, and show us how to extend our love and acceptance to them.

IRON BARS

A brother who has been insulted is harder to win back than a walled city,
and arguments separate people like the barred gates of a palace.
PROVERBS 18:19 NCV

Our verse today paints a vivid picture of what can happen when a disagreement between family members becomes an offense. Iron bars of resentment are almost impossible to remove. Small matters mushroom into deep, irreparable rifts between those we once loved and trusted. For all our love, there is often less mercy for those we are closest to than to mere acquaintances or strangers.

Consider offences between brothers in Scripture. Cain killed Abel out of jealousy. Esau sought to kill Jacob for stealing away his blessing. Joseph's envious brothers sold him into slavery. Even Paul and Barnabas had a sharp disagreement about taking Mark with them on a missionary journey. Mending these kinds of broken relationships is as difficult as conquering a fortified city. Here is the lesson: Guard your marriage carefully. Avoid conflict and contention, and when it happens, reconcile quickly. Don't let resentments brew.

Are you stewing over some disagreement that you have not brought to light? If so, talk about it, and make things right.

Lord, help us to walk in the light with each other. Help us keep small issues from growing into bitter walls that separate us.

RAPHAH

Be still, and know that I am God.
I will be exalted among the nations,
I will be exalted in the earth!

PSALM 46:10 ESV

Picture a tiny child in her father's arms, while he is strolling along the seashore. The waves break on the sand, and water splashes while the undertow steadily tugs at them. It could be a frightening experience, but this child is perfectly at peace, safe in the arms of her protector. She is relaxed, because she knows who holds her.

Be still. The Hebrew term is *raphah,* and it means to let go, to relax, to cease striving. Moses knew how to do that. Remember how Pharaoh trapped the Israelites between his army and the Red Sea? To God's terrified people, Moses said, "Don't be afraid. Just stand still and watch the Lord rescue you today" (Exodus 14:13). He was still and calm because he knew his God. He knew the one holding him.

Talk about times God has intervened for you in the past. How do you both typically respond to difficulties? Can you be still, or are you striving?

Thank you, Lord, for offering us peace and tranquility in times of trouble. You have been faithful since the beginning of time, and we choose to be still and trust you.

UNQUENCHABLE LOVE

Many waters cannot quench love;
rivers cannot sweep it away.
If one were to give all the wealth of one's house for love,
it would be utterly scorned.
    Song of Solomon 8:7 NIV

There are things money cannot buy. Genuine love is one of them. It is a priceless gift, and when it is pure, no adversity can quench it.

The kind of love demonstrated in 1 Corinthians 13 is a love that waters cannot quench or floods drown out. Wealth does not hold a candle to the value of genuine love. Practice that love in your marriage, and you can overcome all adversity.

Spend some time talking about the priceless gift you have in each other. Your love is rare and to be treasured above all things.

Thank you, Jesus, for the gift of love, from you and from each other. Guard that love, and grant us continual joy in one another.

LOVE THAT WILL LAST

Always be humble and gentle. Be patient with each other, making allowance for each other's faults because of your love. Make every effort to keep yourselves united in the Spirit, binding yourselves together with peace.

EPHESIANS 4:2-3 NCV

A wedding is a beautiful event, both to experience and to observe. The bride and groom are captivated by their love for each other, and emotions run high. They exchange rings as a symbol of their lifelong vows of love and faithfulness. The rings have no beginning and no end, and at that moment everyone is convinced this marriage will be eternal too. However, after the wedding real life comes, and there will be challenges in living out the love they pledged.

The Greek word for love in this passage is *agape*, which is less about emotion and more about doing things for the benefit of the other person. What does this look like? Paul tells us it is humility, gentleness, patience, and forbearance, all wrapped up in a bow of peace. This is the substance of love.

Is your love going to endure? What are you doing to make sure it does? Talk about ways you can build peace and unity in your relationship.

Lord, we ask that you would help us preserve our love with humility, gentleness, and patience. Help us to overlook each other's faults and love wholeheartedly.

LOVING THE WORLD

Do not love the world or the things in the world. If anyone loves the world, the love of the Father is not in him. For all that is in the world—the desires of the flesh and the desires of the eyes and pride of life are not from the Father but are from the world.

1 John 2:15-16 ESV

The temptation to love the world is not a new phenomenon; such has been the human condition since the creation of man. Today's verses bring to mind the story of Eve and her temptation to satisfy her desires in the wrong way. The forbidden fruit looked delicious and good to eat, and she thought it would make her wise. The craving to satisfy herself superseded her love for God and she, along with Adam, succumbed to temptation.

The world in which we live is not essentially evil, but its inhabitants are. Wanting our own way, wanting things for ourselves, wanting to appear important—none of these wants are from God. The world and all its passions will one day pass away, but whoever follows God will live forever.

What does John 15:19 mean when it says to be "in the world, but not of the world?" Do you long for the world more than you long for God? Talk about your temptations with your spouse.

Lord, increase our desire to know you. Forgive us for spending too much energy on the temporal things and not enough on the eternal.

NEEDING HELP

Where there is no guidance the people fall,
but in abundance of counselors there is victory.
PROVERBS 11:14 NASB

Solomon, the wisest man who ever lived, still needed help, and he didn't allow his pride to stand in the way. When Solomon built the temple, he needed more talent and supplies than Israel could provide, including skilled carpenters, stonecutters, and a great amount of cedar wood. He enlisted the help of King Hiram, and after seven and a half years, the completed project was one of the wonders of the world.

It takes humility to ask for help. Many marriages do not endure because the couple is simply not willing to admit to anyone that they need advice. Pride can stand in the way of tapping into the resources of wisdom that God has placed in others.

Do you need help with your marriage, your finances, or your parenting? Assess your needs and talk about who you can get support and godly advice from. Don't let pride stand in your way.

Lord, we admit that we don't always have all the answers. Please lead us to people you have gifted with the counsel we need.

NO PAIN, NO GAIN

No discipline seems pleasant at the time, but painful. Later on, however, it produces a harvest of righteousness and peace for those who have been trained by it.

HEBREWS 12:11 NIV

Disciplining children is probably the least favorite part of a parent's job but because we know the wonderful benefits, we soldier on. Discipline is actually proof of parental love; parents love their children too much let them flounder in selfish and willful ways.

As God's children, we need discipline too. When God allows consequences to fall following a foolish decision, he is being a good Father to us. His desire is to transform us into the image of Christ. Left to our own wisdom and natural inclinations, we would fall short of that goal. At times, we need to feel his heavy hand pushing us back on track. In the end, the beautiful, peaceful fruits of righteousness will abound, worthy of all the pain they cost.

Talk about a time when you have felt the Lord's discipline in your life. Perhaps you are in that season currently. Where do you see God's love in his discipline?

Lord, thank you for loving us too much to leave us in our sin. We need your loving discipline in our lives. Help us to cooperate with you and heed your correction.

OUR SAFE PLACE

The LORD is a refuge for the oppressed,
a stronghold in times of trouble.
PSALM 9:9 NIV

In our dangerous world, people need safe places. If you live where natural disasters are common, you need strong shelter. In times of war, persecution, oppression, and tyranny, sanctuary is a necessity. Even when there is outward peace, trouble and turmoil may rage internally with financial difficulties, death, sickness, or disappointment.

God is a refuge for us. He is the strongest fortress—our best defense. When we are weak, he is our citadel of strength and our sure protection from the evil one. The door is open. Go on in; God will keep you safe.

We live in turbulent times, politically and socially. Are you afraid of what the future may hold for you and future generations?

Thank you, Lord, for being our refuge. Help us run to you in times of trouble. When we are tempted by fear and worry, remind us that you are with us, ready to shelter us from danger.

OUT OF THE MOUTHS OF BABES

He called a child, whom he put among them, and said, "Truly I tell you, unless you change and become like children, you will never enter the kingdom of heaven."

MATTHEW 18:2-3 NRSV

"Out of the mouths of babes," we say when a child surprises us with unusual wisdom or adult-sized understanding. Mr. and Mrs. Pederson were quietly arguing in the kitchen when their 7-year-old came on the scene. "You guys should get counseling!" she said. Though small and inexperienced, she implored her parents to stop fighting and be friends. A child has qualities that we lose in adulthood, and we must recapture them.

What childlike qualities should we emulate? Well, children are forthright, trusting, uncomplicated, loving, persistent, joyful worshipers of God. They trust instinctively. They are not spoiled by life's disappointments and skepticism. Unless we change our cynical thinking to simply and humbly trusting God, we will not enter the kingdom of heaven. He doesn't want us to become childish, but childlike!

Have you noticed and appreciated a child's naturally trusting nature? Talk about areas in your life where you have become cynical, and humbly repent.

Lord, thank you for the wonder of children. Help us be more like them, trusting in your Word and unspoiled by unbelief.

ROOTS

Look after each other so that none of you fails to receive the grace of God. Watch out that no poisonous root of bitterness grows up to trouble you, corrupting many.

HEBREWS 12:15 NLT

What we see is often determined by the unseen. While we see only a plant's stem and leaves, hidden underground is a complex, life-giving root system. The roots are anchors for the plant; they take up water and nutrients from the soil and propel them to the stems and leaves. Healthy roots make a healthy plant and produce good fruit.

In the Hebrew culture, a poisonous plant was called a bitter plant. The writer of Hebrews uses this metaphor to warn the church against the poison of bitterness in the heart. Hatred, hostility, cynicism, resentment, and anger can become flourishing root systems in the heart that feed the spirit with bitterness and poison others. We must watch carefully for poisonous roots. Bitter roots produce bitter fruit.

Have you allowed bitterness to take root in your heart? Is there anyone you need to forgive or an offense that you need to release to God? Are you upset with one another? Talk about all of these bitter roots.

Oh God, help us to be intolerant of sinful attitudes of the heart that can grow into bitterness. Make us sensitive, forgiving people who let go of wrongs and keep a pure heart for you and others.

SEASONED WITH SALT

Do not let any unwholesome talk come out of your mouths, but only what is helpful for building others up according to their needs, that it may benefit those who listen.
EPHESIANS 4:29 NIV

As a child, perhaps a parent put soap in your mouth for allowing certain words to pass your lips. Even though soap couldn't scrub the heart clean, it was a great reminder that the tongue needed to be controlled. In today's verse, Paul speaks of corrupt communication, or speech that is profane, worthless, vulgar, and insipid without the salt of grace. Such speech defiles the speaker's own soul, offends our pure God, and sins against others by pulling them down instead of building them up.

Words are powerful! They can be refreshing or destructive. Think of the transformation that could happen in your relationship if your words to one another were always seasoned with grace. Your marriage would be stronger, your children happier, and your home a place of peace.

How would you rate your daily conversations? Needing improvement? Needing a radical renovation? Challenge each other to add grace to your dialogues.

Lord, today we pray Colossians 4:6: "Let our conversations be always full of grace, seasoned with salt, so that we may know how to answer everyone."

SHINE LIKE STARS

Do all things without murmuring and arguing, so that you may be blameless and innocent, children of God without blemish in the midst of a crooked and perverse generation, in which you shine like stars in the world.

PHILIPPIANS 2:14-15 NRSV

Do you want to be blameless and innocent, a beacon for Jesus in our dark world? Then learn a lesson from the Israelites. Three days out from God's mighty, miraculous deliverance from Pharaoh, they began the persistent, besetting sin of complaining. There was no fresh water; there was no food; there was no meat. God met their needs faithfully, but they were never satisfied for long. It was a bad testimony to the nations around them.

Complaining and arguing about our circumstances, about each other, or about our lot in life is insulting to our Savior. It says to him that what he has provided isn't good enough. For the sake of honoring Christ and providing a good example to others, let us do everything without murmuring!

Are you a complainer? Do you naturally default to the negative and voice your displeasure? Talk about how you can share positivity and hold each other accountable.

Lord, we confess our complaints. Please forgive us. We want to influence those around us with our Christ-like attitudes; grant us the peace and courage to do so.

SIX SHORT VERBS

*You shall follow the Lord your God and fear Him; and you
shall keep His commandments, listen to His voice, serve Him,
and cling to Him.*

DEUTERONOMY 13:4 NASB

God has a way of speaking succinctly, with no wasted
words and no ambivalence. Using just six verbs, God teaches
the Israelites how to avoid deception. False prophets have
convincing rhetoric and miraculous signs saying, "Go after
other gods and serve them." Don't fall for it, Israel. Instead,
follow, fear, listen, obey, and serve the true God, and hold on
to him for dear life.

Anyone can be duped, even the wisest among us. That's
why God's message to Israel so long ago is the same to us.
The enemy is as active today as he was then. God's antidote
is the same. Fear God, listen and obey him, follow him, serve
him, and hold on to him for dear life. Six actions can save our
lives!

*Talk about some of the lies that are now being embraced in
our culture. What are some things you as a couple can do
to safeguard yourselves against deception?*

Lord, thank you for giving us clear and certain directions
to keep us safe from the enemy's plots. Increase our
perception and wisdom so we don't fall prey to lies.

SPIRITUAL FOOD

Like newborn babies, crave pure spiritual milk, so that by it you may grow up in your salvation.
2 PETER 3:18 NIV

If you're a parent, you know the demands of a newborn, especially in the eating department. Meals every two to three hours make for exhausting days and sleepless nights. It's not difficult to know when it's time for a feeding; the insistent cry is clear. While it's hard work, consistent feedings make for a healthy, strong, growing child. Similarly, if you are new in Christ, you need daily nourishment to grow.

Spiritual food for spiritual growth is found in the Bible. Its well-rounded diet of truth will provide the wisdom, strength, and direction necessary to live a life that glorifies God.

How is your spiritual diet these days? Do you need milk or meat? Are you scheduling in time for the Word each day?

God, give us a hunger and thirst for your Word, and use it to transform our lives. Help us to be disciplined students of the Word of God.

THE FREEDOM OF FORGIVENESS

"Lord, how often shall my brother sin against me and I forgive him? Up to seven times?"
Jesus said to him, "I do not say to you, up to seven times, but up to seventy times seven."

MATTHEW 18:21-22 NASB

According to Jewish law, a person could ask for forgiveness three times from the person he offended. If forgiveness was not extended, then God himself would offer it. With this in mind, it seems very generous of Peter to extend that offer to seven times. Jesus' reply went even further; it implies that there is no limit to the number of times we should forgive.

Perhaps you've experienced the wonder of being forgiven, and the freedom of granting forgiveness. Resentment chains the heart to bitterness which inevitably destroys. Forgiveness frees. If forgiveness is genuine, the relationship is as strong as before the offense, and kindness forgets the sin ever happened. We must forgive to be forgiven.

Are you withholding forgiveness toward anyone? Talk about the lasting results of nurturing an unforgiving heart.

Thank you, Lord, for forgiving our sins. Grant us the grace to extend forgiveness to others when they sin against us.

THE GREAT EXCHANGE

You know the generous grace of our Lord Jesus Christ. Though he was rich, yet for your sakes he became poor, so that by his poverty he could make you rich.

2 CORINTHIANS 8:9 NLT

History books are full of accounts of great men and women who sacrificed for the sake of others. However, there has never been a story that comes close to what Christ did for us. Yes, people have died cruel, undeserving deaths, but only Christ took the world's weight of sin on himself and carried it to the grave for us.

How can one follow Christ in this? Is it possible to make the greatest of all exchanges, one for another? At the cost of his life, Christ lavished his kindness, gracious generosity, and undeserved favor on us. How can we possibly emulate him? Perhaps we can in small, everyday ways. We can put our own desires on the shelf to prefer another's. We can consider others' needs above our own. We can drop our agenda and pick up someone else's. In all these ways, we put others first and love them sacrificially.

Take a few moments to apply these general statements to your relationship as husband and wife. Do you set aside your own desires and serve each other?

Lord, you have made us rich by your sacrifice. We have eternal life because you laid down yours. Help us to lay down our lives for each other every day.

THE HABIT OF PRAYER

Very early in the morning, while it was still dark, Jesus got up, left the house and went off to a solitary place, where he prayed.
MARK 1:35 NIV

It was the launch of Jesus' ministry. After being baptized by John in Galilee and recognized by his Father, he was led into the wilderness to do battle with the enemy for forty days. Upon returning, he was ready to be about his Father's business. "The time has come," he proclaimed. "Repent, and believe the good news!" He quickly called his first four disciples and traveled to Capernaum to preach, cast out demons, and heal the sick. He kept long hours for the crowds that came for his touch. Yet after a long, exhausting day and late night, he rose early the next morning, while it was still dark, and prayed to his Father.

It's incredible to realize that Jesus, fully God and fully man, needed to steal away to be refreshed by fellowship with his Father. If Jesus needed guidance, strength, and peace from God each day to accomplish all God had sent him to do, how much more do we?

Do you have a habit of spending time daily talking to your heavenly Father? Discuss ways you can carve out time every day to meet with him.

Jesus, thank you for showing us the importance of daily prayer and fellowship with our heavenly Father. Help us develop the habit of spending time with you.

THE LISTENING EAR

You must all be quick to listen, slow to speak, and slow to get angry.
JAMES 1:19 NLT

There is nothing more frustrating than trying to communicate something important to an inattentive listener. Checking a phone, over-the-shoulder glances, and restless hands are sure signs that your words are ricocheting around in space and not making a connection. Good listeners are not waiting for a slight lull to begin their own monologue. They keep eye contact, act interested, and respond appropriately.

James speaks extensively in his book about the power and destructiveness of the tongue. Here, his first command for the tongue is to silence it! Instead of talking, listen. Slow down, and listen without jumping to conclusions.

Do you listen to one another? Do you give each other your full attention in order to understand? Do you easily jump to conclusions or rush to judgment? Talk with your spouse about where listening is good and where it can improve.

Father in heaven, grant us the grace to slow down, both in speech and reaction. Help us to respect each other and patiently listen, with open minds and hearts.

JUNE

That is why a man leaves
his father and mother and is
united to his wife, and they
become one flesh.

GENESIS 2:24 NIV

THE PERUSAL

The LORD has looked down from heaven upon the sons of men
to see if there are any who understand,
who seek after God.

PSALM 14:2 NASB

Picture the king of the universe on his throne, leaning forward slightly, perusing the scene below. He sees his beloved creation, his children, running to and fro, busy with their lives. He zeroes in on those who don't have a friendship with him; they deny any deity and say, "No god for me!" Some are working industriously, devising wicked schemes. In another corner, people are in denial and pursue selfish desires. "Are there any down there who seek after me?" he asks himself. "Are there any who understand?" He comes to this conclusion: "There is no one who does good, not even one." What a sad moment for a father.

When God observes you, does he see a couple that is committed to loving and serving him? Does he see a marriage that glorifies him, showing a lost world how loving a relationship can be? Christ has made us good in God's eyes; we can give back to him with joy.

What does God see when he looks at you two? Is he a proud Father? Discuss how you can better model a Christian marriage to your neighbors.

Jesus, we want to make you proud. Thanks for being a good, loving Father. Help us show your love to the world!

THE SCHOOL OF HARD KNOCKS

I know what it is to be in need, and I know what it is to have plenty. I have learned the secret of being content in any and every situation, whether well fed or hungry, whether living in plenty or in want. I can do all this through him who gives me strength.

PHILIPPIANS 4:12-13 NIV

Contentment is a learned skill. So is flexibility. There are those who live with plenty, stability, and blessings who haven't acquired these skills. Others have very little and endure hardship and change, yet they exemplify these qualities. Paul experienced both, and he was able to move between the two with contentment.

You've heard the idiom "The School of Hard Knocks." It refers to the sometimes painful education we get from life's negative experiences. Paul attended that school his entire ministry, but rather than flunking out, his trust in God grew. His secret was his relationship with God, which gave him the strength to roll with the punches.

Would you describe yourselves as a content couple? Are you flexible or stuck in your ways? Are you truly settled in what God has provided for you at each given moment?

Lord, teach us how to be content. We want to learn what Paul did—how to be at peace with whatever comes each day.

TIME TO SEEK THE LORD

Sow righteousness for yourselves, reap the fruit of unfailing love,
and break up your unplowed ground; for it is time to seek the Lord,
until he comes and showers his righteousness on you.

HOSEA 10:12 NIV

In the early pioneer days, preparing the land for planting was backbreaking work. Tools were primitive, the ground hard, and rocks, brush, and trees needed to be cleared away. Without the preparation of the soil, there would be no yield, so farmers put in the work. Hosea compared the state of the people's hearts to unplowed ground, dry and resistant to the Lord. Verse 13 says they "cultivated wickedness and harvested a thriving crop of sins." It was time for them to plow the hard ground of their hearts and begin seeking the Lord. It was time to sow righteousness and reap mercy and love.

The same is true for us. If our hearts have grown cold, hard, and barren, it's time to dig out the rocks of sin and prepare for God's gentle rain of righteousness. Your marriage can be lasting, loving, and fruitful when your hearts are tender toward each other and God.

What kind of fruit does a hard heart produce? Is there
any cultivating that needs to be done in your lives and
marriage?

Lord, help us to break up any unplowed ground in our lives
so we can receive your showers of blessing. It is time to
seek you more.

TWO MASTERS

"No one can serve two masters. Either you will hate the one and love the other, or you will be devoted to the one and despise the other. You cannot serve both God and money."

LUKE 16:13 NIV

Jesus' words conclude the parable of the dishonest steward: the manager who mismanaged his master's assets. Under the threat of dismissal, he made friends with his boss's debtors, reducing their debts in the hope that they would have his back one day. Had he been a loyal servant, he would have carried out his job with integrity. Instead, he committed to his own selfish ambitions and served them instead. He found he could not do both.

Many Christians would say that they love and serve God, but their passion for material things says otherwise.

Do you think it's possible to be a slave to money even without riches? Where do you put your time and energy? For whom or what are you willing to make sacrifices?

Lord, we want to be fully devoted to you. Thank you for providing our needs. Help us to remember that material things are temporal. We want to keep our eyes on the eternal.

DAILY SAVORING

Every time I think of you, I give thanks to my God.
PHILIPPIANS 1:3 NLT

Appreciation is simply savoring the true value of something or someone. When the apostle Paul thought of his dear friends in the church in Philippi, he was overcome with appreciation. He recognized their great worth to God and the integral role their partnership played in the spreading of the good news of Jesus Christ. He didn't stop with appreciation; Paul regularly gave thanks for them.

In marriage, intentional appreciation defuses fault-finding, and it short circuits nit-picking our spouses. It helps us value their contribution. Thanking God for them reinforces our need for one another and ultimately strengthens our bond together.

When you think of each other, do you dwell on your value as beloved children of the Most High, partners in the shared gospel adventure of marriage? Are you regularly giving thanks for your spouse? What can you do today to thank the Lord for each other?

Lord, we thank you for each other. Thank you for the strengths that you have uniquely given us for this journey. Thank you for joining us as partners in this mission of marriage as we share God's grace together.

HEAVEN'S WEDDING

You make known to me the path of life;
in your presence there is fullness of joy;
at your right hand are pleasures forevermore.
PSALM 16:11 ESV

This psalm reveals intimacy our Lord desires with us, his bride. He could just tell us which path to take, and it would be good. However, we might be tempted to focus on the *direction* and forget the *director*. Instead, he invites us into the court of the king, into his very presence. A person can't forget an encounter like that, but we are more than visitors. We are invited to join him at his *right hand*: a place of honor, a place of dignity, of union—the place of the bride on that great wedding day.

Don't be content just to know which way you should walk; seek to be near him. Enjoy the presence of his majesty, and long for more. Dance down that aisle, united in purpose and passion with your heavenly bridegroom!

How did you celebrate your wedding? Who did you invite to celebrate with you? How can you and your spouse invite others into the joy of your relationship with Jesus?

Thank you, Lord, for your incredible invitation to enjoy life to the fullest at your right hand. Whatever our circumstances on this path of life, draw us near to you, strengthen our hearts, and encourage us to invite others into this great relationship with you.

AUTHENTIC MODELS

The Lord said to Samuel, "Do not look on his appearance or on the height of his stature, because I have rejected him. For the Lord sees not as man sees: man looks on the outward appearance, but the Lord looks on the heart."
1 SAMUEL 16:7 ESV

This verse is both fearsome and comforting. How delightful that we do not have to measure up to the world's standards to be selected of God for his purposes. And yet, how sobering to know that our true selves are completely laid bare to the King of the universe.

This is the relationship that he has called us to—to know him even as we are known. The marriage covenant is the closest earthly representation of that heavenly reality. This is the authenticity that we are called to model in our marriages. In no other interaction can we know and be known by another human being so intimately.

Are you completely transparent with your spouse, or do you find yourself trying to cover up? When you open up to each other, are you gentle when handling your hearts? Talk about ways you can practice becoming more authentic with each other.

God, give us your grace to nurture an authentic relationship. May we be brave enough to disclose our thoughts, dreams, struggles, and failures, and delicate enough to deal gently with each other.

OPEN EARS AND TUNED HEARTS

Carry each other's burdens, and in this way you will fulfill the law of Christ.

GALATIANS 6:2 NIV

There is sometimes heaviness in walking through life. We can be weighed down by situations, whether outside our control or the result of our own choices. If we walk alone, burdens become unbearable. Paul instructs us to fulfill the law of Christ and assist those who are pressed. Having defined this law a few verses earlier as "love your neighbor as yourself" (Galatians 5:14), he shows us how to care for one another.

Caring doesn't mean having the solution. Caring doesn't insist that burdens could have been avoided, "If only you would have…" Caring only requires awareness, a heart attuned to the needs of others, and ears to hear concerns.

Husband, is your heart in tune with what weighs on your wife? Wife, are your ears open to hear the stress of your husband's day? What does carrying your spouse's burden look like today?

Lord, draw our attention away from our own to-do lists, and help us to see the needs of others. May we be the support our spouse needs to help carry the burdens they shoulder today. Give us your Spirit's strength to truly care for one another.

ABANDONING SELF

"Respect the Lord and serve him fully and sincerely. Throw away the gods that your ancestors worshiped on the other side of the Euphrates River and in Egypt. Serve the Lord."

JOSHUA 24:14 NCV

Sincere commitment requires abandonment. We intentionally set aside everything that distracts our attention and consciously leave behind behaviors that dominated our former way of life.

Marriage requires the same decisiveness. We must abandon "looking out for number one." Spouses unite in one flesh, in one purpose. The routines that dominated single life must give way to the needs of another. While we press forward to achieve, our commitment is also demonstrated by what we leave behind.

How did your life's priorities change when you first came into relationship with Jesus? How did your life's priorities change when you made your commitment to your spouse?

Dear God, it is our desire to put you first in our marriage. Help us to abandon every distraction and pattern of life that pulls us away from you. Draw us together to be of one mind as husband and wife to serve you and each other fully and sincerely.

PERSONAL JESUS

We proclaim to you what we ourselves have actually seen and heard so that you may have fellowship with us. And our fellowship is with the Father and with his Son, Jesus Christ.
1 John 1:3 NLT

Our lives preach most powerfully what we have encountered personally. John was arguably the closest earthly companion of Jesus during his three and a half years of ministry. He was among the first chosen of the twelve. With Peter and James, he was part of Jesus' intimate circle of three, and he was Jesus' confidant.

John doesn't teach others about Jesus Christ like some kind of history lesson. He introduces God the Father and the Son, whom he knows personally. This is the companionship John invites us all to encounter: the real, living God and his real, loving family.

Is your close companionship with your spouse evident to others? How so? In what ways does your married life encourage others to a personal relationship with Jesus?

Dear Jesus, our desire is for our relationship with you to be so evident in us, both individually and as a couple, that people we encounter would be drawn into your family. We want to be an invitation to companionship with God.

LITTLE AND GREAT

"Whoever can be trusted with very little can also be trusted with much, and whoever is dishonest with very little will also be dishonest with much."

LUKE 16:10 NIV

It is easy to lose sight of what is truly important in our hectic lives. In our culture, pushing hard to accomplish great things, regardless of the casualties, is rewarded with comfortable retirement. In God's kingdom, faithfulness in the small things, regardless of the cost, is rewarded with greater responsibility.

We have great aspirations for our marriages and families, and so we should! God desires to accomplish great things in and through us. His test for our ability to steward great things for his kingdom is our dependability in the simple things. He notices our time and care with small tasks.

What "little things" have you shortcut in your family life to accomplish "greater things?"

In what ways could you reprioritize what really matters in this season of your marriage?

Dear God, we want to be dependable with the little things you have given us. Grant us wisdom to know what to put our hands to, what we should release, and peace in knowing that you bring all things to your children at the perfect time.

UNITED IN PURPOSE

There is neither Jew nor Greek, there is neither slave nor free, there is no male and female, for you are all one in Christ Jesus.
GALATIANS 3:28 ESV

The family of God is the only institution in humanity where we all stand on the same footing regardless of our nationality, our ethnicity, our social status, our income, our gender, or our age. We are all hopelessly lost without Jesus.

In God, we are all brothers and sisters, no longer lost—united in purpose. There is no hierarchy and no favorites, only family. While we are a vast variety, we are united in Jesus Christ. Our differences serve to more fully reflect the nature of God.

How can the differences within your marriage reflect God's nature more fully than either one of you could on your own?

Thank you, Jesus, that in you we equally share your eternal inheritance of everlasting life. Thank you for your great love of all people, which you showed us by laying down your life, that we might live in harmony with you and unity with each other.

FAITH AND FAILURE

Let us hold unswervingly to the hope we profess, for he who promised is faithful.

HEBREWS 10:23 NIV

What gives us the right to expect anything from God? The unshakable confidence we hold as Christians is not based on any accomplishment of ourselves or any sacrifice that we have made. The foundation of our great hope is the person and promise of Jesus Christ himself. Because of his sacrifice on the cross, once and for all, we can boldly go to God with all of our concerns and our celebrations.

How do you disarm Satan, society, and even yourself, when you hear whispers telling you that you can't go God? Are you too messed up? Are you a failure? Just agree. "Yes, I am a failure, but Jesus is not!" Because he is faithful, you can be sure that he accepts you, forgives you, and sets you free to follow him in unshackled joy.

Are there personal failures in your life you have allowed to extinguish your hope? How can you encourage each other today to hold tightly to the promise of God in Christ Jesus?

Dear God, we confess we are sinners. We ask you to clean us completely. Forgive us, Lord, for allowing our own failures to disrupt the freedom of forgiveness found in you. Thank you, Jesus, for your unending faithfulness and your promise of eternal life.

KEVLAR VESTS

Above all else, guard your heart,
for everything you do flows from it.
PROVERBS 4:23 NIV

There is a reason police and front line troops wear Kevlar vests. Our hearts supply lifeblood to every extremity. Literally, everything we do flows from our hearts. Wisdom says to protect our spiritual heart, the center of our being that connects us with others and with God.

By saturating ourselves with God's Word, we shield our hearts from the attack of the enemy. That doesn't mean we won't be attacked, but we will be prepared. In our present world, Christian marriage is often under attack. You are a target, and your hearts need bulletproofing.

Are you intentionally protecting your marriage? Is God's Word on your heart, in your mind, and on your lips? Where can you carve out ten minutes in the day to read Scripture together?

Dear Jesus, we recognize that our hearts are constantly under attack, and we are vulnerable without you. Help us to prioritize your Word in our home and in our marriage, that your life may flow through everything we do.

ALWAYS HOPE

"For I know the plans I have for you," declares the Lord,
"plans to prosper you and not to harm you,
plans to give you hope and a future."
JEREMIAH 29:11 NIV

There are times in our lives when we cannot see the hand of God at work. We cannot hear his voice. We cannot discern his purposes. We can neither comprehend the greater story God is crafting, nor can we grasp our role in it. We feel abandoned and forgotten, at the mercy of chance and catastrophe.

Such was the case for Israel when addressed by Jeremiah. God had carried them away into exile as a result of their sin, but even in discipline, God had mercy. He did not abandon his people. His plans were intact. Though they could not see it, his purpose was still at work. From Jeremiah God declared hope for Israel.

What circumstances have clouded your vision of God's purposes in your marriage or family? What does this passage speak to your heart about God's greater purposes in troubling times?

Dear God, we ask that hope be lit in our hearts. Help us to see your greater plans and purposes at work in our marriage and family. When our vision is clouded, help us to trust that you have the future of your people in your hands.

JOYFUL MEDICINE

A joyful heart is good medicine,
but a crushed spirit dries up the bones.
PROVERBS 17:22 ESV

There is no doubt that God has the greatest sense of humor. Just look at his creation. Have you ever seen a platypus? Watched a giraffe pick up something from the ground? Witnessed a baby goat frolicking? Creating must have been an act of holy hilarity!

Medical journals and research studies are full of the benefits of laughter. From heart health and lowered blood pressure to short term memory benefits, everything indicates the adage is true: *Laughter is good medicine*.

God's word goes deeper than the adage. True joy is a profound assurance in the character of God and his goodness toward his children. Joy frees us to rise above our circumstances and delight in our Creator. Life can be seriously tough, but a joyful heart recognizes happiness does not lie in our situation. Good humor lifts our souls.

Do you and your spouse take—and make—time to laugh? What are some activities you can share together to bring humor back into your routine?

Dear Jesus, as you sanctify our hearts in this marriage, please save our humor too! Help us to delight in you, enjoy one another, and walk this journey together with holy hilarity.

CLIMATES OF CHAOS

I heard a loud shout from the throne, saying, "Look, God's home is now among his people! He will live with them, and they will be his people. God himself will be with them. He will wipe every tear from their eyes, and there will be no more death or sorrow or crying or pain. All these things are gone forever."

REVELATION 21:3-4 NLT

Our world may be a broken and hopeless place, but we can always look forward to eternity. There is hope for better weather ahead even in a climate of chaos. Can you imagine it? Perfected creatures in a perfect creation in perfect communion with our Creator: the restoration is complete.

This is the future we look to! This is the reason our hearts can rise above our cloudy circumstances to glimpse the final outcome of all things. God's plan will be accomplished in his people and in this place. Genuine optimism is rooted in the character and promise of God.

How can you encourage your spouse today to press toward the goodness of God and recognize the future is bright in Jesus?

Dear God, thank you for your great promises to your children. Today, help us to see beyond our circumstances and keep our eyes fixed on you.

PEACE DURING WAR

"Peace I leave with you; my peace I give you. I do not give to you as the world gives. Do not let your hearts be troubled and do not be afraid."

JOHN 14:27 NIV

Peace in our time seems as fleeting today as it was for British Prime Minister Neville Chamberlin in 1938 at the onset of WWII. Unlike that war, true peace will never come through our battles, treaties, and agreements. True peace comes directly from the hand of the Creator to the heart of his children, regardless of the circumstances.

Whether we are stressing about global hostilities, financial burdens, relational conflicts, or daily deadlines, Jesus says our hearts can be at peace. Our internal climate reflects the confidence we hold in the perfect character of our Lord Jesus Christ. He is in control. He cares for us. He is our source, our life, our peace during war.

What words of encouragement can you offer each other today to draw attention from current stresses and toward your capable Savior?

Thank you Jesus, for being our Prince of Peace! We confess that we often allow stress to block our vision of who you truly are: savior, healer, redeemer, and friend. We ask that you open our eyes to see you clearly and enable our hearts to trust you fully. You promised us your peace; let that peace be our portion this day.

TEAMWORK

Yes, there are many parts, but only one body. The eye can never say to the hand, "I don't need you." The head can't say to the feet, "I don't need you." In fact, some parts of the body that seem weakest and least important are actually the most necessary. So God has put the body together such that extra honor and care are given to those parts that have less dignity. This makes for harmony among the members, so that all the members care for each other.

1 CORINTHIANS 12:20-21, 24-25 NLT

God never intended for us to walk this life of faith alone. We believe the enemy's lies when we try to fly solo.

God created us to function as essential parts of a whole. He designed us to work together. Nowhere is this more evident than in marriage. Despite our rugged, modern individualism, the truth is that we need each other, and we were made to need each other. Ultimately, the team outperforms the individual.

How does teamwork in marriage reflect God's intentions for his children? What complementary strengths do you value in your spouse? How can you celebrate your differences as God's intentional design for a successful marriage?

Dear God, help us to see our differences as a diversity of strengths, not as a competition. Give us insight to honor each other's abilities and bring harmony to our home.

REAL SUCCESS

Keep this Book of the Law always on your lips; meditate on it day and night, so that you may be careful to do everything written in it. Then you will be prosperous and successful.

JOSHUA 1:8 NIV

The great and fearful truth about the human mind is that what we dwell on determines our perspectives and informs our decisions. This is why we must internalize God's Word. We don't aim for religiously piety; we want a heavenly perspective. We want to know God's thoughts, understand his ways, and hear his heart for his people.

God wants his beloved children to know him. What an awesome privilege to crack the cover and know God personally. This is real prosperity. This is success.

How do you measure success in your marriage? Is it by the quantity (or quality) of stuff you've accumulated, the size of your house, or other achievements? Or is it by the depth of your relationship? What will it take to deepen your relationship with one another? What will it take to deepen your relationship with God?

Dear God, help us to delight in your Word, and give us insight as we read. Apply to our hearts your eternal truth and confirm to our spirits your lessons for us.

PRICE OF WISDOM

The beginning of wisdom is this: Get wisdom.
Though it cost all you have, get understanding.
PROVERBS 4:7 NIV

Ralph went to college and earned three degrees. He spent hours, days, and months studying his textbooks. He listened with great attention in class because he wanted to learn. He did Internet searches for extra information, taking notes, and memorizing important facts. Aaron also went to college—but he zoned out during classes and basically just used his books as decorative items on his desk. Which of these two men do you think gained the most wisdom?

Even though it would be nice, we don't wake up one morning and discover that we've become wise overnight. That's why God says that if we want wisdom we need to go search for it. If we want wisdom as a couple, we need to go get it, digging through God's Word for the treasures he's hidden there, and studying the important truths and principles that he's placed there for us to learn.

Are you searching for wisdom? How can the two of you learn together?

Lord, help us to seek fervently for your wisdom. We don't want to make decisions without it.

TURN TO THE LORD

Only fear the Lord and serve Him in truth with all your heart; for consider what great things He has done for you.
1 SAMUEL 12:24 NASB

This verse sits right in the middle of a story of Israel's stubbornness and rebellion. They didn't want to be led in God's way anymore; they wanted a king like all the other nations around them. They demanded it. But when the prophet Samuel showed them the calamity that would befall them for rejecting God as their king, the people were afraid. They recognized they had failed. They could see the devastation their decision would bring.

Like Israel, we can get caught up in the misery of our failures. But Samuel's words don't leave us there. Turn to God. It doesn't matter how we've failed; our rebellion is remembered no more. Serve him wholeheartedly. He has rescued us in the past, provided for us, established us, and given us a future of hope. He does this not because we are good, but because he is great! His promise of forgiveness in Christ Jesus is still true today.

Take time to recount with your spouse the great things God has done for you and your family in the past. How has he provided for you? How has he received you when you turn to him?

Thank you, Jesus, for your forgiveness and restoration. Help us to live in thoughtful admiration of your work in our lives.

A GOOD REPUTATION

Encourage the young men to be self-controlled. In everything set them an example by doing what is good. In your teaching show integrity, seriousness and soundness of speech that cannot be condemned, so that those who oppose you may be ashamed because they have nothing bad to say about us.
TITUS 2:6-8 NIV

A good reputation should be a desired trait for every couple. When our reputation is pure, it provides a level of trust which is one of the most important components of a marriage. God says that self-control should be encouraged. That means not flying into a rage when our spouses do something that ticks us off.

When we add integrity, a mature seriousness, and wise words to the mix, we provide our sweethearts with mates who are worthy of their love. And when we live like that, we don't give our enemies any ammunition. We won't have any big skeletons that will come out of the closet, and we won't have situations that will wreck our relationships or cause us shame. Being trustworthy is a good goal for all of us.

Would your spouse consider that you're trustworthy? Talk together about how you can live with integrity.

Lord, help me to always be trustworthy for you and for my spouse. Help me be a person of honor and integrity.

CULTIVATING PATIENCE

Whoever is patient has great understanding,
but one who is quick-tempered displays folly.
PROVERBS 14:29 NIV

We're not the first generation to struggle with quick tempers. Moses wrestled with this sinful pattern throughout his life. God knows our frailty, and he provides tools for us in his Word that address this issue.

Some people warn that we should never pray for patience; they fear that God will inevitably bring situations into our lives to test their resolve. However, if we don't cultivate this fruit of the Spirit, we reap disastrous consequences. Our goal should be understanding. As we seek to understand the situation that is presented to us, we short-circuit the fuse on temper; reason and rage cannot coexist.

What methods have you found to be effective in dealing
with your temper? How can you be an encouragement to
your spouse this week in this area? Are there ways you can
team up together to tackle this in your family?

Lord, our heart's desire is to display the light of your character through our lives and our marriage. We know that our tempers get in the way. Strengthen us as we seek to understand one another more clearly, and bless our family with grace and truth.

CREATED WITH PURPOSE

Your eyes saw my unformed body;
all the days ordained for me were written in your book
before one of them came to be.

PSALM 139:16 NIV

Every person is intricately and uniquely created by God for his purposes. How amazing to consider that God knew us before we took form, and our days were laid out before we took a single breath!

Like Esther in the Old Testament, you were created "for such a time as this;" God has a unique purpose for you and your marriage, here and now.

Have you considered your life and family from an eternal perspective, one where God sees the end from the beginning? Does this excite you or intimidate you? How can you and your spouse explore God's design for your marriage?

Lord Jesus, our desire is to serve you wholeheartedly and walk out the days ordained for us together in faith, hope, and love. Help us to explore your purposes for us in this season of life.

GOD DELIGHTS IN YOU

*"Before I formed you in the womb I knew you,
before you were born I set you apart;
I appointed you as a prophet to the nations."*

JEREMIAH 1:4-5 NIV

Is there anything more precious than a newborn baby? They aren't delightful because they accomplished some great feat for mankind. They are precious just because they exist. As parents, godparents, and mentors, we have great aspirations for our children, and we delight to see them take those steps.

God knew us even before we were born. He delighted in us before we ever had the chance to do one good thing. He has great plans to bring him glory with our lives. How incredible to know the delight of our heavenly Father and his unique design for his children!

Have you considered the thought that God delights in you just because he created you? How does this affect your affections toward him and your motivation to serve him?

Lord Jesus, thank you for inviting us to live in your delight and design for our lives. We ask for insight to understand—and conviction to own—the calling that you have uniquely given to us, that we may impact our world for your Kingdom's sake.

GOD'S ORCHESTRA

*Now may the God who gives perseverance and encouragement
grant you to be of the same mind with one another according to
Christ Jesus, so that with one accord you may with one voice glorify
the God and Father of our Lord Jesus Christ.*

ROMANS 15:5-6 NASB

There is nothing quite as moving as listening to a world-
class symphony orchestra; every member is uniquely gifted,
diligently prepared, and keenly focused on the piece set
before them. With one voice, the song rises, and people walk
out of the hall changed. It takes personal perseverance and
mutual encouragement.

How much more has the God of the universe
uniquely equipped his children to play crucial roles in his
grand orchestra of the ages? This is the apostle Paul's
encouragement to the church in Rome. You have a role to play.
You are called to unite, bringing glory to God and changing
the world.

*What role does your marriage play in this great symphony?
How can a diversity of gifts within your marriage
complement and not compete with one another? How can
you encourage your spouse today to persevere in their role
in this Kingdom orchestra?*

Thank you, Lord, for our parts in your orchestra. We ask
that you would unite us in our marriage to bring glory to
your name. We long to walk together in step with your
Spirit and encourage others to join in the song.

TUNED TOGETHER

"If a house is divided against itself, that house cannot stand."
MARK 3:25 NIV

A standard guitar has six strings. Each string has a different dimension, tension, position, and tone. Though they are different, each string must tune to a common standard in order to properly resonate together and produce beautiful music. Nothing beautiful is produced if each string tunes to a different standard.

Likewise, Jesus says that no organization, kingdom, or household can be effective if members are not in sync with each other. We must each tune our hearts to the single heavenly standard—the life of Jesus Christ.

What steps can you and your spouse take today to improve harmony within your home? What common values or goals guide the unity of your relationship? How can you encourage each other in your roles today?

Dear Jesus, we know that you desire to produce beautiful music through our marriage and family. Help us to set you as the ultimate standard in our home, and unite our hearts with your eternal purposes.

VALUE ABOVE WORRY

"Do not worry about your life, what you will eat or drink; or about your body, what you will wear. Is not life more than food, and the body more than clothes? Look at the birds of the air; they do not sow or reap or store away in barns, and yet your heavenly Father feeds them. Are you not much more valuable than they?"

MATTHEW 6:25-26 NIV

In this text, Jesus relates two concepts that we rarely see coupled: worry and value. He says, "Don't worry… you are valuable." When we worry, we subtly strive to find our life's worth in what we do, what we have, who we are, or what we can provide.

Jesus tells us to find our value in *whose* we are—we are children of the King. Jesus invites us out of our endless worries and into the security of the Father's great love.

How do you measure your worth? How would life be different if you had full confidence in your value as a child of our heavenly Father?

Dear Father, we see that the value you place on your children far exceeds the rest of your creation, but sometimes we struggle to believe it, and our lack of faith leads to worry. Please forgive us for underestimating your great power to provide for your people. Strengthen our faith as we fix our eyes on you and find ourselves as members of your royal family.

FIERCE PEACE

Do not be anxious about anything, but in every situation, by prayer and petition, with thanksgiving, present your requests to God. And the peace of God, which transcends all understanding, will guard your hearts and your minds in Christ Jesus.

PHILIPPIANS 4:6-7 NIV

The apostle Paul tells the church in Philippi how to deal with anxious worry. First, go to God (pray). Then, don't just tell him how miserable you are; ask for what you need (petition). Lastly, praise him for who he is and rejoice in his promise to provide for you (thanksgiving).

In this way, we displace anxious worry with a fierce peace. Paul says that the peace of God will *guard* your hearts and minds—like a military guard preventing a hostile invasion. Now, that's fierce! That's peace.

What in your marriage or family do you need to present to the Lord? Ask your spouse for an area of anxiety or worry that you can pray about for them.

Dear Lord, thank you for flooding our hearts with your fierce peace when we bring our prayers to you. Give us strength against this hostile invasion of anxiety and worry. Help us to trust in you alone.

JULY

"These commandments that I give you today are to be on your hearts. Impress them on your children. Talk about them when you sit at home and when you walk along the road, when you lie down and when you get up. Tie them as symbols on your hands and bind them on your foreheads. Write them on the doorframes of your houses and on your gates."

DEUTERONOMY 6:6-9 NIV

GROWING IN LOVE

Yet the Lord longs to be gracious to you;
therefore he will rise up to show you compassion.
For the Lord is a God of justice.
Blessed are all who wait for him!
ISAIAH 30:18 NIV

Oh, how the Lord longs to show his great love to us. With compassion and mercy he gently exhorts us to do what is right. God is not a harsh taskmaster. Using his example, learn to delight in each other, showing gentleness, grace, and tenderness especially in times of pressure. Strive to treat your spouse with warmth and affection. Be sure not to keep score or hold grudges.

God does not judge you for your faults; shouldn't you do the same for the one you love? A sure way to improve the bond of love you share is to treat your spouse better than you are treated. There can only be improvement. Celebrate the blessings you share, compliment each other, treat one another with tenderness and forgiveness. Your marriage will be better for it!

Are you quick to forgive or do you hold on to grudges?
Can you think of one specific compliment for your spouse?
Can you purpose to be more kind?

Dear Lord, thank you for forgiving us time and again when we repeat the same poor choices. Help us to follow your example and treat each other only with compassion and tenderness. We want to grow in our love for you and each other.

WINNING TEAMS

May the God of endurance and encouragement grant you to live in such harmony with one another, in accord with Christ Jesus, that together you may with one voice glorify the God and Father of our Lord Jesus Christ.

ROMANS 15:5-6 ESV

Every year we hear stories about a mediocre high school football team winning game after game, triumphing over superior squads, and being crowned champions. These are great, heartwarming stories! What is the secret to their success? Teamwork. Winning teams labor together, putting their individual desires aside and celebrating the combined skill of the whole. Together they are a stronger unit than just a collection of individuals.

It's like that in marriage. Working together, appreciating the abilities you each possess, and encouraging each other in times of distress will bring the two of you closer. Harmonious marriages are made up of two people working in tandem and listening to the Lord. A unified home where a couple is of one accord is a place of friendship, cooperation, and understanding.

Do we work together well? What different strengths and skills do each of us have? How can our talents complement each other?

Father God, help us to see ourselves as a team. We want to work together and not against each other. Please help us learn to live in unity and friendship.

KEEP ROMANCE ALIVE

Your love delights me, my treasure, my bride.
Your love is better than wine,
your perfume more fragrant than spices.
SONG OF SOLOMON 4:10 NLT

God certainly knows all about love and romance! Passion and tenderness are to be part of your marriage. Intimacy in your relationship is something the two of you share only with each other. In the early days of a marriage it can be an all-consuming passion. It deepens as the years go by.

Husbands should find out what makes their wives feel special and wives should learn what pleases their husbands. It may mean flowers, for no reason, a special home-cooked meal, a nighttime stroll, or new sheets. Learn your sweetheart's desires and surprise them. Keep romance alive and treat your spouse like a treasure: a true gift from God!

Is romance alive and well at our house, or is it stale and routine? Ask one another for suggestions on how to enhance intimacy in your relationship.

Father, thank you for the love you have set between us. Help us to see each other every day with loving eyes and hearts filled with tenderness and passion. Keep our love fresh and new.

BETTER THAN FIREWORKS

Trust in the LORD and do good.
Then you will live safely in the land and prosper.
Take delight in the LORD,
and he will give you your heart's desires.

PSALM 37:3-4 NLT

The Fourth of July is a time to celebrate America with cookouts and fireworks. It's also a good time for us to think about our blessings as a country. Sometimes we forget to thank God for his blessings of freedom—the opportunity to serve him without fear, to live safely in our country, for the opportunity to prosper, and countless other freedoms that we take for granted.

On this holiday, we can express our delight in God and thank him for his blessings—especially our freedom to worship him freely. We have a responsibility to protect that freedom for future generations, and we protect it by living in a manner where our faith impacts our culture and our homes. We can entrust our future to God, but let us work together, as husbands and wives, to keep freedom ringing throughout our land.

What freedoms are most important to you? How can you impact this culture?

Father, thank you for our freedoms and the happiness that comes as a result. Help us to be good stewards of our country and our freedoms.

PEACE IN HUMILITY

So humble yourselves under the mighty power of God, and at the right time he will lift you up in honor. Give all your worries and cares to God, for he cares about you.
1 PETER 5:6-7 NLT

We often try to rise above our worries under our own steam. Our culture may see this as a virtuous endeavor, but it is contrary to Scripture. We amplify anxieties in this life when we attempt to subdue them with our own strength.

The apostle Peter makes it clear that only by bringing ourselves under the power of God, bowing our will to his strength, will we find the right position to deal with our worry. On our knees we find the Father's heart for his children.

Can you and your spouse identify an anxiety that you need to release to "the mighty power of God"? Why can it be a frightening thing to let go? Why is it helpful to know that he cares?

Lord Jesus, make us humble. Help us to acknowledge that you are in control, and give us patience to wait for your perfect timing in every situation. We cannot thank you enough for your great care for us.

HEAVENLY SONGS

And they sang a new song, saying, "Worthy are you to take the book and to break its seals; for you were slain, and purchased for God with your blood men from every tribe and tongue and people and nation."

REVELATION 5:9 NASB

Worship is the process of ascribing worth or priority to someone. We all worship in some form. In heaven the constant rhythm is the chorus of creation, praising God and his incredible power that set all of existence into motion. In God's revelation to the apostle John, we catch a glimpse of the first new song in heaven. What event could change the direction of heavenly worship? The sacrifice of Jesus Christ for sinful mankind.

What a privilege to love, serve, and worship such a God! He loved us so much that he gave his life for his creation, restoring the relationship that our rebellion severed.

What is the song of your household? What gets priority? How do you and your spouse worship the Lord together? Do you prioritize time to do this? What patterns of worship can you establish in your home?

Lord Jesus, help us to put first things first. Help us establish strong patterns of godly worship in our family.

NOT WHERE, BUT HOW

"Yet a time is coming and has now come when the true worshipers will worship the Father in the Spirit and in truth, for they are the kind of worshipers the Father seeks. God is spirit, and his worshipers must worship in the Spirit and in truth."
JOHN 4:23-24 NIV

There was great dispute regarding worship in Jesus' day. The Jews said the only true worship was from the Temple Mount in Jerusalem. The Samaritans said people should worship God from their mountain in Samaria. In a conversation with a Samaritan woman, Jesus says it's not *where* you worship, but *how* you worship that is important to God.

By *how*, he didn't mean outward style; he meant inward attitude. True worship rises from a sincere and grateful heart praising the God who revealed himself to humanity. God is seeking people who will trade the trappings of human religion for the truth of heavenly relationship.

What is the climate of worship in your marriage? Is there a way in which your family worships God together? How do you and your spouse express worship differently? What can you learn from each other?

Thank you, Lord, that we have the privilege to worship you anywhere, at any time. There are no external barriers that inhibit our hearts' cries to you. We long to worship you in spirit and in truth, to know you deeper each day, and to establish patterns of worship in our home.

GRACE AGENTS

In his kindness God called you to share in his eternal glory by means of Christ Jesus.
1 PETER 5:10 NLT

We should be always thankful for God's grace toward us, but many times we don't even recognize that grace. When others extend grace to us, we are delighted. We start taking grace for granted, yet often fail to offer it ourselves.

We often have expectations of others without communicating those expectations. When the other person doesn't do what we expect, we judge, or fail to offer grace. We are to be grace agents, not in our own strength, but in the strength of the one who continually gives us grace.

Are you a grace giver, or is offering grace difficult for you? Do you take grace for granted? Are you thankful for the grace you receive? Talk together about grace you have noticed, and brainstorm ways to see and give more grace.

Lord, enable us recognize your amazing grace daily. Stir our hearts to become grace agents to each other and to those around us. We are grateful for your saving grace in our lives, and we want others to see your grace in us, for your name's sake.

LOVE IN GOD'S STRENGTH

Love is not rude, is not selfish, does not get upset with others.
Love does not count up wrongs that have been done.
1 Corinthians 13:5 NCV

Love yourself. You come first. The world's perception of love is very different from the Bible's teachings. As Christians, we must hold on to God's Word. Read the above verse again. We do not always express or experience this kind of love in our relationships. When life happens, we fall into selfish habits. We cannot love like God does in our own strength.

Isn't the Lord creative to ask of us what only he can do? We must depend on Jesus to love our spouse through us. God's unconditional love only comes through him. When we love him with all our hearts, his love naturally overflows into our relationships. We cannot produce it by trying harder; we must allow him to love through us.

Is the love you express and experience God's kind of love? Have you been discouraged because human nature interferes? Commit to loving each other with God's love flowing through you.

Lord, we admit that we do not love the way your Word commands. We want to be good spouses, and we cannot do it on our own. Let your love flow through us. Make us sensitive to the times we fail, and allow us the grace to seek forgiveness.

SPROUTING SEEDS

Do not be children in your thinking. Be infants in evil, but in your thinking be mature.

1 Corinthians 14:20 ESV

There is something very rewarding in watching what we plant grow. Just as parents raise children to become responsible adults, God intends for his children to grow spiritually. Many Christians are content with only the seed of God's Word; this verse challenges us to grow. As we grow in knowing and loving him, he invites us to be a part of what he is doing. He equips us for tasks he knew we would undertake.

God intends for your marriage to be a growing relationship, full of joy and satisfaction. Knowing him means understanding that he has a purpose for your life and marriage. The more you grow in him, the greater the blessings life brings.

Is your marriage growing? What are you doing to make sure that growth continues? Are you discovering God's purpose for your marriage? Are you seeking to know him more intimately?

Lord, we don't want to settle in our relationship with each other or with you. We want to grow more and more in love. Continue to teach us and reveal yourself to us, that others may see you in our marriage.

QUIET ANTICIPATION

Yes, my soul, find rest in God;
my hope comes from him.

PSALM 62:5 NIV

In our culture, we are bombarded with busyness and noise. TVs, phones, and computers are running all the time. We struggle to find time for each other. Sunday church can become a menu item; if there is nothing better to do, we might go. We may find ourselves substituting service for quiet time with the Lord, hoping that will find his favor, yet we don't know how to be quiet and wait on him. We want instant answers, instant solutions, even instant spirituality.

When we truly know God, trust him, and put our hope in him, waiting becomes a training ground, and we eagerly anticipate how he will work in our lives. When we slow down and quiet ourselves, we discover the rest that we need. When we make plans for future purchases or trips, anticipation grows as the trip grows closer. In the same way, the Lord uses our time of waiting on him to stir our hearts with anticipation.

Do you have times of quiet and waiting scheduled? Have you experienced rest in your relationship with each other and with the Lord?

Lord, teach us how to wait quietly. We want to experience your rest; please show us what needs to change in our schedule. We will continue to put our hope in you as we wait for you to teach us.

SHOOTING FROM THE LIP

Be filled with the Spirit, speaking to one another with psalms, hymns, and songs from the Spirit. Sing and make music from your heart to the Lord.

EPHESIANS 5:18-19 NIV

Words are a powerful tool from God. They can be an instrument of encouragement and healing. They can also be a weapon of destruction and wounds. Too often, we "shoot from the lip," not considering how those shots affect our spouse or others. In the heat of the moment, we say deeply painful words. When that happens, we must seek forgiveness, but we must also understand that there may be lingering pain.

Psalm 19:14 says, "Let the words of my mouth and the meditation of my heart be acceptable to you." We must choose our words carefully and use them to encourage one another in faith and good works.

Are you using words for encouragement? Are you brave enough to ask your spouse if there are any wounds from words you have spoken? Have you given forgiveness to those who have hurt you?

Father, we want our words to be a source of encouragement and healing. Forgive us for the hurt caused by careless words, and help us to forgive each other. By your Holy Spirit, let our words be blessings to each other, and may they bring you honor.

DATA WAVES AND CAPTIVE THOUGHTS

Don't copy the behavior and customs of this world, but let God transform you into a new person by changing the way you think. Then you will learn to know God's will for you, which is good and pleasing and perfect.

ROMANS 12:2 NLT

Living in the information age is both exciting and dangerous. Waves of data wash over us daily, and if they aren't processed correctly, they can hurt our Christian walk and relationships. If we do not take every thought captive, we may compromise our core values and our marriages.

We guard our hearts by thinking on things that are true, noble, right, pure, lovely, admirable, excellent, and praiseworthy. As spouses, we need to help each other process the information and images crafted to influence us, keeping out data that can compromise our hearts and splinter our relationships.

Are you able to discuss what is challenging your values? Can you recognize the difference between a secular worldview and a Christian worldview? How are you guarding your heart?

Lord, we want to keep our hearts and our minds fixed on you. Put a warning sign in our spirit when we let our guard down among data waves. Remind us to take every thought captive, so our lives may bring glory to you.

THE FRUIT OF KINDNESS

Praise the LORD, for he has shown me the wonders of his unfailing love.

PSALM 31:21 NLT

We often take the gifts and nature of God for granted, and they are everywhere in Scripture. Kindness is mentioned here in Romans, in the gifts of the Spirit in Galatians, and in the qualities of the Love Chapter, 1 Corinthians 13. Real freedom comes when we recognize that we draw kindness, patience, tolerance, and all other good qualities from God. We understand that we must be completely dependent on the Lord to do what he wants done in us.

Each day gives us new opportunities to submit our lives, that he may work in and through us. Think on how the Lord expressed kindness to you when he brought you into a relationship with him. It was his kindness and mercy that found you. Ask him to let his kindness flow through you to your spouse, family, and friends.

Have you ever considered that God wants to express his kindness through you? What would that look like? How can you express kindness in your marriage?

Lord, we know that we respond in the flesh. Forgive us for that. We want to be identified with you: your love, your kindness, your very life. Remind us that you have made available everything we need for life and godliness.

HEAVENLY COMFORT

I truly believe I will live to see the LORD's goodness.
Wait for the LORD's help. Be strong and brave,
and wait for the LORD's help.

PSALM 27:13-14 NCV

As children, we sought out our mother or father for comfort when we were hurt. A hug, soft words, a bandage, and a kiss on our boo-boo brought comfort and contentment. The pain might have still been there but we felt secure and loved. What a wonderful feeling that was.

Where do we go when we are hurt, afraid, or stressed now? What do we do when we feel unsure, mentally beat down, or anxious. Sharing your worries with your spouse is a good first step. It really is true that "a burden shared is a burden halved." Even better is sharing your hurts with the Lord. God has promised to help us shoulder our problems. Have faith that he will help. Praying with your spouse on a regular basis can help establish a dependence on the Lord for help when life gets tough. The love-bond between the two of you will be strengthened as you seek God's comfort through prayer.

Do the two of you make time to pray together? How do you share your worries and concerns with your spouse? Are you comfortable praying together, or would you rather pray alone?

Lord, we thank you for your goodness to us. We want to seek your help more often. Help us to depend on you. Let us see your great love for us.

SPEAK IN LOVE

Let no corrupting talk come out of your mouths, but only such as is good for building up, as fits the occasion, that it may give grace to those who hear.

 EPHESIANS 4:29 ESV

We all know how difficult it is to watch others argue. Nasty words are hurled with the intent to hurt. Accusations and bickering can lead to unhappiness and depression. How sorry and uncomfortable we feel for those involved. Look at your own relationship and the disagreements you and your partner have. Do they escalate into verbal wars? Do you say things you will later regret?

The wisdom of God reminds us to be careful with what we say. Try to think first and be slow to anger. Then try to speak in love and not hate. Choose your words carefully and without malice. Vulgar and disagreeable jabs are ungodly and can damage our relationships. Remind yourself that noxious words tear down, but love builds up and encourages.

Do you argue unnecessarily? Can you try to discuss your differences without belittling each other?

Lord God, we need help when we are upset with each other. Remind us to be slow to speak and to treat each other with love and grace. Thank you for loving us even when we don't deserve it.

DISTINCTLY UNIQUE

"I will make him a helper fit for him."
GENESIS 2:18 ESV

Marriages are all different. Why? Because each marriage is made up of two distinctly unique people. Some couples spend most of their time together and some are only able to catch up a little bit each day or on the weekends. Depending on what stage of life you are in, togetherness will greatly vary.

Know that while your marriage may not look like other marriages, God has put you together. Your relationship is a good thing. You complement each other. Find ways to spend more time together. Develop the common interests you share. If you can't think of anything you both like, try new activities. Be creative. Make time for enjoying each other's company.

Are you comfortable with each other? What do you do together that you both find fun? Are you willing to carve out time to spend with just the two of you?

Jesus, thank you for bringing us together. Help us to find common interests so we can enjoy each other's company better. Draw us closer each day.

BUMPS IN THE ROAD

Blessed is the man who walks not in the counsel of the wicked,
nor stands in the way of sinners, nor sits in the seat of scoffers;
but his delight is in the law of the LORD,
and on his law he meditates day and night.
PSALM 1:1-2 ESV

No marriage is without a few bumps. These bumps can turn into total derailment if there is no preparation. The Word of God is filled with over 5000 promises and 600 laws! Regular studying of the Bible will help us to understand how to listen to God instead of a self-help book or TV infomercial. When you need to make a decision, run to the wise counsel of God. Call your pastor. Don't let disagreements fester.

The best way to avoid big problems in your marriage is to never let them get big. Forge a friendship with a couple in your church that has been married longer than you. Ask them to share with you what they do to keep love fresh and communication good. What makes their relationship work? Don't let embarrassment or pride keep you from dealing with problems.

Do you have Christians in your life who can help you with your marriage relationship? Talk about where in the Bible you can search for help when you have trouble.

Lord, we want your wisdom and counsel when we disagree. Help us work together to heal our hurts. Help us to be aware when our spouse is hurting. We want our marriage to be strong and vibrant.

TOGETHER IN GRIEF

*"Blessed are the poor in spirit, for theirs is the kingdom of heaven.
Blessed are those who mourn, for they will be comforted."*

MATTHEW 5:3-4 NIV

When someone close to you passes away it is normal to be sad. Our grief may overcome us for a time and our heart feels broken. We fear that it may never feel full again. We mourn the loss. Heartache is difficult to describe but can lead to despondency and depression. This is one of the many reasons it is good to have a spouse. Our husband or wife is there to share that grief. They can offer understanding and comfort. What a blessing that love and care can be in the bleakness of those grief-filled days.

One is never prepared for death, even if the end was expected. One of the ways you and your spouse can comfort each other is in talking about the good times you spent with your loved ones. Remembering them and the time spent together can bring peace. God does bring blessing with comfort.

Have you suffered loss? What are the ways you can offer comfort to your grieving spouse?

Dear God, thank you that you have promised to bring comfort to those who mourn. Help me to depend on you in times of grief. Allow me to comfort those around me who suffer loss.

BE AN ENCOURAGER

Therefore encourage one another and build one another up,
just as you are doing.

1 THESSALONIANS 5:11 NASB

We all love an encourager. They walk into a room of gloomy people, and soon everyone's outlook is brighter: happiness exudes. God has called us all to be encouragers! You can start with a simple compliment. A public tribute can change hearts. How much better we feel when we are appreciated. Just as quickly, one snide remark can take all the wind out of our sails and deflate our souls.

"Sticks and stones, can break my bones. But words can never hurt me." Don't you believe it for a minute! Unkind taunts received as a child can still be hurtful long into adulthood. Try to use kindness and care when speaking to others, especially your spouse. Use encouraging words to build them up, don't tear them down.

Do you speak encouragingly to each other? Are you kind?
Do you speak with tenderness? Can you share something
your spouse said that encouraged you this past week?

Father in heaven, help us to speak with love. We want to build each other up and not tear each other down. Show us how to be encouraging.

LOVE ALWAYS

Love patiently accepts all things.
1 CORINTHIANS 13:7 NCV

The marriage relationship is a bond of love. While most of us know what love is, we are hard-pressed to define it adequately. We go on about making love, feeling special, perhaps raising a family, but we are not quite sure how to explain love with words. In 1 Corinthians 13, the Bible defines love as patiently accepting, always trusting, hoping, and enduring. Love is the greatest of all things.

That's pretty profound. Can you say you patiently accept everything? You always trust each other, always find hope, and your relationship will always endure? This is your goal! You can rest in the promise of the Lord that he wants to help you do just that. If one of you falls short, God says to keep it up; keep loving, accepting, trusting, hoping, and enduring. This is a lesson for every day of your lives together. You may be newlyweds, in the middle of raising a family, recent empty nesters, or enjoying your fiftieth wedding anniversary—the principles from 1 Corinthians 13 will still be appropriate.

Are you patient with one another? How can you look for the good in your partner and encourage them?

Dear Lord, we thank you for bringing us together in marriage. Teach us each day about love. Help us to love each other with a pure love—a love from you. Thank you for loving us.

COUPLE FRIENDS

"Do to others as you would have them do to you."
LUKE 6:31 NIV

Most couples come into marriage with their own friends. Sometimes these friends and their partners will become "couples" friends, and sometimes not. While it is good for each of you to have your own buddies, it is important to cultivate other couples as friends too. Relationships with Christian couples can provide fun, companionship, child-rearing advice, and counsel. If you seem to be without these relationships, look around your church. Join a small fellowship group, or ask around if anyone is interested in seeing a ball game, going on a picnic, or grabbing their kids and going for a hike with your family. Don't wait to be asked.

Doing things together with other couples can strengthen the bond you share and help make joint memories you can look back on together.

Are you spending most of your free time with others and not your partner? When was the last time the two of you spent time with another couple? What can you plan to do with friends together in the near future?

Lord, we want to be good friends. Give us ideas to have fun with other couples. Teach us how to show your love to those around us. Thank you for our church family.

GOD DECISION

I will instruct you and teach you in the way you should go;
I will counsel you with my loving eye on you.
PSALM 32:8 NIV

Josh and Rachel were stressed. She'd been offered an amazing job that would allow her to help children get forever homes, but Josh would have to give up his job and they'd have to move far away from their family and friends. Josh was willing to support Rachel for this huge opportunity, but they wanted to make sure it was the God decision for them instead of just a good one.

We don't have to be married long to realize our lives will be full of decisions. Sometimes they're easy, and at times, they take us so far out of our comfort zones that it feels like we've ended up in a zone in another country. When we're stressing over what to do, we tend to forget God's promise that he will instruct us and teach us in the way we should go. Just as a loving mama keeps her eyes on her little ones while they walk to the neighbor's house down the street, God's loving eyes are always on us.

Do you have a difficult decision to make? How can you understand what God wants you to do?

Lord, teach us to follow you. Help us to ask you for understanding, and cause us to dig deeper into your Word to listen to your whispers of instruction.

SERVING TOGETHER

I have been a constant example of how you can help those in need by working hard. You should remember the words of the Lord Jesus: "It is more blessed to give than to receive."

ACTS 20:35 NLT

We have been charged by God to be generous. We can support our church endeavors, missionaries, various service charities and the like. We can help our neighbors in time of need, providing meals or transportation. We can be generous with our time, assisting others with the talents the Lord has given to each of us. We can act as mentors, coaches, leaders, Sunday school teachers, community garden helpers, or small group leaders. Why not find something that the two of you can do together. The time you spend in a common activity can enhance your marriage.

If you donate money to causes, be sure to involve your spouse. Discuss and decide monetary gifts before they are given. If one of you is volunteering a large time commitment, be sure to talk it over together. Your first commitment is to your spouse, but the two of you will find blessing in your kind generosity.

Are you generous with what God has blessed you with? Do you have talents you aren't sharing? What plan for charity or service can you try?

Lord Jesus, thank you for the many blessings you have bestowed upon us. We desire to use those blessings for good. Help us to have generous and giving hearts.

GRATITUDE ALWAYS

Giving thanks always for all things unto God and the Father in the name of our Lord Jesus Christ.
EPHESIANS 5:20 KJV

When everything is going well it is easy to be grateful to God. We can appreciate the goodness of the Father when our hopes and dreams seem to have come true. We praise the name of Jesus and rarely take the time to ponder the ramifications of trials and tribulations. The Word of God tells us to give thanks *always* in *all* things. What does this mean? When you lose your job, give thanks. When the house of your dreams is beyond your budget, be grateful to God for the home you have.

Make thankfulness and gratitude to God a habit each day. When the hard times come, you will be able to praise the Lord even though you may not feel like doing so. This act of obedience will fill you with love you never expected. Trust God to touch your heart with expanding love. His mercy and grace will sustain you through your trials.

What trials have you experienced during your marriage? Were you able to give thanks? How might praising God help you through a troubling time?

Dear Lord, we thank you and praise you for the many blessings you have shown us. Help us to find the strength to be grateful in hard times. We appreciate your wisdom in joining us together so we can support each other in times of stress and difficulty.

A GOOD HABIT

LORD, every morning you hear my voice.
Every morning, I tell you what I need,
and I wait for your answer.

PSALM 5:3 NCV

Do you pray together regularly? Spend time studying God's Word? It doesn't matter if you are newlyweds or have been married for thirty years, your relationship will benefit with regular time spent seeking God's will and wisdom together. You may make a habit of prayer and praise with dinner or before you turn out the lights at night. Read a book, taking turns reading passages and talk about it. Count your blessings together and thank the Lord for each one. Share your worries and problems and pray for each other.

Even if you can only find time to study together once a week, make it a habit. Studies tell us that if you continue an activity for six weeks, it will become a routine. Intimacy in marriage can be physical *and* emotional. The more you share innermost thoughts, fears, and hopes with each other, the closer you become, and the more satisfying your relationship will be.

What could the two of you do to make a habit of praying and studying together? Are you willing to try to make time for it?

Dear Lord Jesus, we hope to continue to grow closer to you and closer to each other. Thank you for loving us. Help us learn how to praise you together.

HAPPY DAYS

There is a time to cry and a time to laugh.
There is a time to be sad and a time to dance.
ECCLESIASTES 3:4 NCV

Do the two of you have fun together? As we grow and mature it is easy to put playtime and levity behind us. Jobs, children, house payments, daily responsibilities all take up precious time. All work and no play really *does* make Jack a dull boy! Bring some fresh humor to your marriage. It doesn't take much to make the day fun.

Start the day by telling a joke, take a walk together, go to the zoo, pull out a board game. Find things to laugh about, watch some old comedies, go people-watching. Life is serious enough and responsibilities will always be there, but your outlook will change when you fill your life with happiness.

What do the two of you do for fun? Are you playful with your spouse? Can you think of new ways to add amusement into your marriage?

God, sometimes in the daily grind we forget the healing laughter that play can bring to our hearts. Help us to find joy and fun in each day. Bind us together with good humor.

REJOICE ALWAYS

Rejoice in the Lord always. I will say it again: Rejoice!
PHILIPPIANS 4:4 NIV

Is your life joyful? God desires to give you joy. He wants you to be happy and to celebrate each day with delight. The Lord made you for glory and triumph. Rejoice in the Lord—always! It is so important his Word says it twice. Happiness and contentment sometimes feel elusive. Choosing to rejoice and deciding to be content can make a huge difference in how we respond to our problems. Listening to praise music as you go about your day can help lift your spirit and fill your heart. Counting your blessings helps focus on what is good.

You and your spouse could begin each day celebrating the goodness of the Lord. Find joy in the little things and you will see it in new areas of your lives. Mealtime is a great time to share the blessings of the day and thank God for them. The more you speak of gladness, the more it takes root in your heart. A joyful heart is a cheerful, grateful, and rejoicing heart.

Can you share a special blessing you experienced today? Is it hard to be joyful when problems surround you? What makes it hard for you to rejoice? Can your spouse help you in difficult times?

Lord, thank you for all you've done for us. Help us to rejoice in you each day. Help us to see the good in our lives and be grateful for it.

LIES ARE LIES

Do not let kindness and truth leave you.
Bind them around your neck.
Write them on the tablet of your heart.
PROVERBS 3:3 NASB

Little white lies: benign untruths we tell ourselves are okay because we use them to spare our spouse unhappiness or uneasiness. But white lies are just as bad as big fat black lies. Husbands and wives are united in a bond of love that requires kindness, truth, fidelity, honesty, and devotion for a lifetime. Fudging the truth for whatever the reason does not show honesty or kindness. Own your actions and decisions. Trust your sweetheart to forgive you for actions that previously you felt a need to stretch the truth about.

God's lovingkindness is unending. He will always forgive us and help us become more like him. Ask him to help remind you each time you are tempted to lie. A pure tongue is greatly desired among all your dealings and relationships, but especially in your marriage.

Do we strive to be truthful to each other always? Why would we be tempted to lie? How can we help each other?

Jesus, we want to be truthful in all we do. Help us become trustworthy. Teach us the many facets of loving behavior toward each other.

LETTING GO OF THE PAST

Those who do right will continue to do right,
and those whose hands are not dirty with sin will grow stronger.
JOB 17:9 NCV

The past can haunt a marriage, forgiveness can bring freedom and delight. When you confess your transgressions to the Lord there is mercy, grace, and forgiveness. Sins are forgotten and you have a clean slate. Justification in the eyes of the Lord is a gift. Learn from your misdeeds and strive to do right. What freedom and independence comes from confession and forgiveness!

Bringing up the past can bring destruction to the joy in your marriage. God has declared confessed sin to be banished "as far as the east is to the west." Move forward with each other, start every day new and fresh. If your husband or wife has disappointed you in the past, give them the benefit of your love and God's trust in them. Help them to continue to do the right thing by building them up and not tearing them down. Treat each other with respect and love.

Can you be encouraging to your spouse? Do you bring up the past when you have arguments? How can you let go and move forward?

God, we know we aren't perfect. Please accept our confessions. Thank you for the forgiveness you give freely. Help us to forgive each other and let the past be past. We want to look forward to our future.

DEVOTED TO PRAYER

Devote yourselves to prayer, keeping alert in it with an attitude of thanksgiving.

COLOSSIANS 4:2 NASB

How do you pray? On your knees, in your car, running after your toddler, on a picnic, while you fix the fence? Do you sing praise songs along with the radio, ask God's forgiveness with tears streaming down your face? All of these encompass what it is to pray. The Lord desires a relationship with us that is deep and personal. It is by sharing our thoughts, our thanks, and our innermost desires with him that true relationship forms. Petition or requesting from God is certainly one form of prayer but so is praising the Lord for his grace and mercy.

Together you can seek wisdom and solutions. Prayer can take practice. Make it a habit. When the two of you met it took time to get to know one another. You shared your past, your hopes and dreams, and your future plans. God loves you and wants to hear these things too. Approach prayer as a conversation, an expression of thanks, and acknowledgement of all God has done for you.

Are you comfortable in prayer? What have you heard from God recently? Do you pray together?

Lord, we desire to know you more. Help us to learn to pray more effectively. Show us how to listen to you.

AUGUST

"A new command I give you:
Love one another. As I have
loved you, so you must love one
another. By this everyone will
know that you are my disciples, if
you love one another."

John 13:34 NIV

COMBINED TALENTS

God arms me with strength, and he makes my way perfect.
He makes me as surefooted as a deer,
enabling me to stand on mountain heights.
He trains my hands for battle;
he strengthens my arm to draw a bronze bow.

PSALM 18:32-34 NLT

You and your spouse are a team. Together you have a collection of skills, talents, and passions that make your team unique. You can't compare your relationship to others in all respects because there is no other couple exactly like you. As soon as you said, "I do," the two of you began to form habits, rituals, and routines. You took on certain jobs.

As time goes by and the dynamics of married life change, you need to find ways to be flexible. All days are not the same; all seasons in your lives will not go exactly as you plan. God has prepared you with tools and savvy to use the intelligence and competence you both possess to aid you in all circumstances. When you encounter bumps in the road, seek guidance and help from the Lord. All you are and all you have comes from him. Trust him to continue to supply your needs as you walk forward.

Do you have a hard time accepting change, or are you flexible? What talent or skill do you possess that will help your relationship in the future? Why do you think change elicits a certain response in you?

Father God, thank you for making us the way we are. Help us to be prepared for change. Help us to keep our relationship on an even keel in times of adjustment.

ASK THE TEACHER

If any of you lacks wisdom, you should ask God, who gives generously to all without finding fault, and it will be given to you.
JAMES 1:5 NIV

Teachers often say there is no such thing as a stupid question, yet children can still be afraid to raise their hands to find the answer the teacher wants to give. Let's consider a young boy, Sam. He is embarrassed, shy, or too prideful to ask the teacher to help him. The kind teacher pursues little Sam and asks him some revealing questions. Sam realizes the teacher is compassionate and won't judge him, and he decides it's safe to ask his question.

If the fear of God is the beginning of wisdom, we should humbly ask God to bless us with wisdom. He is the source of all compassion, and we can always trust his answers.

Do you believe that sometimes we don't get something simply because we don't ask for it? What can you and your spouse ask for today?

Oh Jesus, help us to believe in you as our trusted teacher and giving father. May we not be afraid, ashamed, or too prideful to call out to you for wisdom and help.

BILLIONS OF CELLS

You created my inmost being; you knit me together in my mother's womb. I praise you because I am fearfully and wonderfully made; your works are wonderful, I know that full well.

PSALM 139:13-14 NIV

There are times we are guilty of putting ourselves down. We can be bitter toward God for not making our noses smaller, our arms stronger, or our reading skills better. The list gets long. When we think of the flawless creation of our body, the findings are astronomical! Think of the billions of cells formulating us into who we are today.

The rapid division of cells that continued to multiply with our parents' DNA made us unique human beings. The fact that we are created in God's image is astounding when we take a moment to contemplate it. Just think; we were part of God's eternal plan before he laid the foundation of the world!

Do you question God about who he made you to be, or the fact that he wanted you to be born in the first place? Do you take joy in knowing he designed you with a plan?

Father, we are awed and honored at being part of your creation. Help us to agree with you and accept ourselves as your children.

STRESSFUL MARATHONS

We have this treasure in jars of clay to show that this all-surpassing power is from God and not from us. We are hard pressed on every side, but not crushed; perplexed, but not in despair; persecuted, but not abandoned; struck down, but not destroyed.

2 CORINTHIANS 4:7-9

Paul was speaking to the believers in Corinth, who were being persecuted by the Roman government because they had chosen to follow Jesus. Talk about stress! We know what even little stresses can do to us mentally and physically. Sometimes, we feel we have an unfair dose of stress.

We run the marathon of a busy schedule: appointments, church obligations, school, lessons, games, and so forth. We have to get the money to get the gas to get to work, where that big project needs to be done by its deadline. We have many first-world problems that we regularly need to put into perspective. We must remember that we have God's all-surpassing power. We don't go through life alone.

Do we recognize the difference between God-assignments and our own assignments? What should you and your spouse prioritize this week? This month?

Jesus, save us from ourselves when we take on things you never intended. Help us with the everyday assignments you have given us. We trust and rest in your all-surpassing power. Show off your glory in us.

MORNING CONVERSATIONS

In the morning, Lord, you hear my voice;
in the morning I lay my requests before you
and wait expectantly.
PSALM 5:3 NIV

Ah, morning. Some people love it; others are night owls. God's Word directs us to start our day with him, whatever time that may be. This is when we share our requests with him and wait eagerly for his responses.

If something concerns us, it concerns God. It is his grand design that we give to him the first part of our day. To say we lay our "requests before him and wait expectantly" means we believe he is powerful enough to answer our requests. When we start our morning as a faith walk of expectancy, we align our will and desires to his. It strengthens and reaffirms our faith. We are ready for the day.

When life happens, do you say, "Ok God, then you better do something about it!" Do you instead say, "Yes God, I can't wait to see what you are going to do with this one!" Talk about how God has worked in your life in the past.

Father please help us start our day with you. Help us to wake each day by listening for your voice and waiting in great expectation of your plan.

JUST STAY CALM

The Lord himself will fight for you. Just stay calm.
EXODUS 14:14 NLT

There are times in our lives when we are distressed, apprehensive, and fearful. Worry seems to plague us. It's as if the entire world is against us. God loves you and he is prepared to fight your battles. His shoulders are broad and he has the strength to carry your burdens. Don't panic, don't despair, just stay calm in your spirit and listen.

Agitation and panic will do nothing but cause more worry; trust in God's mercy and sit in the quiet and stillness. In the middle of the night when the darkness seems to close in and magnify each and every trial, allow God to comfort and assist you. You can hear him better when you are calm and listening. He will not desert you in your time of need.

Do you panic in troubled times? Do you know how to find help in God's Word? What are your biggest worries right now? Can you allow God to comfort you?

God, in our times of need please help us to remain calm and composed and let you work out our troubles. We want to rest in you. Thank you for supporting and loving us.

SAFE AND SECURE

God, hear my cry; listen to my prayer.
I call to you from the ends of the earth when I am afraid.
Carry me away to a high mountain.
You have been my protection,
like a strong tower against my enemies.
PSALM 61:1 NCV

Have you ever visited a Medieval Castle? These fortresses were built in such a way that they could protect entire villages against an enemy's attack. There were food storage rooms and a water supply in case the siege lasted a long time. There were towers and high walls for protection and battle. The Lord is your castle. He can protect you from fear and worry. He will supply all your needs. Just as the villagers could run to the castle and be safe within its walls, God will draw you near to him and wrap his arms around you.

No matter the circumstances, whatever you face, God can and will protect and defend you in times of difficulty. Relax, rest in him, feel secure in his ability to help. Remember he is your shield and your protector in times of need. Let him fight your battles.

What is your response to fear and anxiety? When you face worrisome problems do you ask for God's help? Can you remember a time when you felt safely supported by him?

Father God, help us to rely on your protection. We want to rest in you, safe and secure in your arms. Thank you for providing us with safety and security.

STEPPING AWAY

Then Achish called David and said to him, "Surely, as the Lord lives, you have been upright, and your going out and your coming in with me in the army is good in my sight. For to this day I have not found evil in you since the day of your coming to me."

1 Samuel 29:6 NKJV

King Achish thought very highly of David, who was an excellent leader and soldier. One day, the Philistines in the king's army complained that David's men would turn against them while they were fighting. They had heard that David had slain tens of thousands, even more than King Saul. If he had slain so many Philistines, what would stop him from coming after them? Because of this discord, Achish told David he would need to leave the army. David complained; it was not his fault that the Philistines were worried. Still, David obeyed and left the king's side, even though he had served him well for over a year.

Sometimes, God leads us away from opportunities, jobs, and futures that look perfect. Like David, we must obey him and walk away, remembering that he has our best future in mind.

Do you find yourself like David, completely blameless yet being asked to step away from helping somewhere even though you were a perfect complement?

Father, help us trust you when you release us from a vocation, position, or decision. In our marriage, help us to support each other faithfully. You are a good and just God; keep that in our hearts.

CLOTHED IN RIGHTEOUSNESS

Let us behave decently, as in the daytime, not in carousing and drunkenness, not in sexual immorality and debauchery, not in dissension and jealousy.

ROMANS 13 NIV

Paul encouraged early believers to live righteously because the day of the Lord was drawing near. Considering this was probably penned shortly after the Lord's death, those words were written close to 2,000 years ago. Now, the Lord's return is closer than ever. Paul's counsel is just as relevant today as it was millennia ago.

Mankind often appears to have a longing for God, or at least an acknowledgement of his existence. Nevertheless, many humans choose to live for pleasure without much consideration for God's commandments. How can we combat our earthly desires when they become too strong? Your marriage partner is the best support you have. Lean on and encourage each other, and spend time together in God's presence. Clothed in his righteousness, you will find strength.

Does the fact that we have accepted Jesus as our Savior give us license to do whatever we want? How can you grow in God together?

Father, as we stand fast in our liberties, help us not to compromise with the pleasures of this world. Clothe us in your righteousness.

FIRST-WORLD BLESSINGS

Now there is great gain in godliness with contentment, for we brought nothing into the world, and we cannot take anything out of the world. But if we have food and clothing, with these we will be content.

1 TIMOTHY 6:6-8 ESV

Think of the last time you were perfectly content. Perhaps you were on a vacation. Maybe you finished a large project, or you were finally free from the tyranny of a constricted budget. Often in the early years of marriage, money is tight, but love flows free. After many married years, some may wish for the carefree days of apartment living and surviving on noodles and butter. Minimal responsibilities were a luxury.

Some may have an abundance, only to complain about insignificant irritations. Bought items never really satisfy. They only bring temporary pleasure and, sometimes, destruction. Whether you have much or little, contentment comes from peace in Christ.

Do you want to be that couple whose aged wrinkles reflect contentment? Can you stop today and count your first-world blessings? Make a list together.

Jesus, fill us with your Spirit. Forgive us when we aren't content with the blessings you shower on us. Help us be an example to those around us, and give us your strength.

TRIUMPHANT WISDOM

A wise man will hear and increase learning,
and a man of understanding will attain wise counsel.
PROVERBS 1:5 NKJV

God created us as life-long learners; he wants us to gain wisdom. Wisdom comes liberally to those who ask for it. Sometimes, it comes from the School of Hard Knocks. Godly wisdom comes not only from the Bible, but also from those who study, teach, and preach it.

We are wise to watch and learn from the follies and successes of others. Positioning yourself among experienced people is not an act of weakness; it's a triumph of wisdom. It's common for a child to watch an older sibling's tactics, for good or bad. Did they get away with it, or was there trouble? Did they keep practicing and win the trophy?

Are you willing to find people who are smarter, kinder, gentler, or wiser than yourself and learn from them? Are you able to ask for advice? Talk together about the people who are good influences on your lives and marriage.

Heavenly Father, we want to position ourselves near you and those who represent you well. Help us to mature and glorify your name, that we may extend the favor to others. Thank you for the freedom to live our salvation.

FIRST INSTINCTS

A gentle answer will calm a person's anger,
but an unkind answer will cause more anger.

PROVERBS 15:1 NCV

Picture a child helping set the table only to drop a vintage dish on the floor. The mother has a moment to decide how to react. Does she lambast the child right into the floor, next to the broken dish? Or does she stop and recognize the difference between childish and willful behavior? The child was truly trying to help, and the mother realizes this. She tries not to giggle, but soon she is in a duet of belly laughs with her child.

This scenario could have turned poor quickly, resulting in resentment and anger between mother and child. The mother could have justifiably, or at least self-righteously, yelled, "Be careful!" or something worse in her anger. But by controlling her first instinct, she has saved the relationship from much heartache.

In the moment of decision, how can you call on the Lord to take control? Talk about strategies for diffusing tension.

Jesus, we ask that you keep kindness always on our tongues. Help us to see others as you do, and remind us that you watch everything unfold. Your kindness brought to repentance; let us extend that grace to others.

STANDARDS OF LOVE

"Do not judge, or you too will be judged."
MATTHEW 7:1 NIV

A trip to an expensive shop in Italy turned into a sad moment for a senior on her high school trip when she was treated like a shoplifter rather than a customer. The shopkeeper had mislabeled her and treated her differently.

Are we aware of our evil thoughts toward people when we judge them to be less important than others? Do you jump to conclusions or judge people for not measuring up to your standards? None of us measure up to Christ's standards, and yet we are all equally important to him. We can extend that love to others, even in the smallest gestures.

Do you generally prefer or honor certain people? If you catch yourself acting inhospitably toward another, what can you do instead? As a couple, how can you reach out to others?

Jesus, prompt us to be like you in our thoughts and actions. Help us not to judge others, but to love them as you so graciously love us.

A GOOD, CLEAN ARGUMENT

Remind everyone about these things, and command them in God's presence to stop fighting over words. Such arguments are useless, and they can ruin those who hear them.

2 Timothy 2:14 NLT

A bad apple can spoil the whole bushel. A bad word spoils a conversation. We know a soft answer turns away anger, but sometimes bruising words tumble out. We may just want to be heard, to know that what we say has worth. Sometimes we act out of conviction, wanting the other person to know that our way is the correct way of doing something.

It is a privilege to listen to each other and affirm your right to each think as you please. It is a hard right to submit to, especially when we know the person has set a destructive course. Sometimes, a person just enjoys a good argument. A spouse might want to complain to the other without hearing a solution. Keep each other's preferences in mind when tensions rise.

Do you enjoy a good argument? Do you try to fix a complaint when your hurting spouse just wants a sounding board? Discuss what each of you needs.

Lord, help us to be in the moment, to listen and really hear. We want to win the war together, not the battles between us. Help us to communicate what we need to each other.

TESTING GOD'S PATIENCE

God is not man, that he should lie, or a son of man, that he should change his mind. Has he said, and will he not do it? Or has he spoken, and will he not fulfill it?

NUMBERS 23:19 ESV

Balak of Moab wanted God's prophet, Balaam, to go with him to curse the children of Israel. God told Balaam not to go or curse the people, yet Balaam went ahead, riding his faithful donkey. The donkey stopped three times in front of an invisible angel. Balaam struck the donkey until God opened its mouth and it spoke to him. The donkey had saved Balak from God's wrath those three times.

God was angry with Balaam. Balaam wanted the earthly honor that Balak promised him. Even in the middle of his crazy desire to be esteemed by the enemy, Balaam still knew he couldn't say anything except what God told him to say. We often test God's patience in the same way, knowing what we are doing is wrong. Let's make it a point to listen to God the first time!

Have you ever tried to justify something wrong, asking God to bless it, and God, in his mercy, stopped you? Like Balaam, are you looking for God to bless something he has clearly said no to? Today, set those wishes aside.

Lord, help us not to test your patience. Forgive us. Help us trust in your Word and promises.

TWO PATHS

"One who is faithful in a very little is also faithful in much, and one who is dishonest in a very little is also dishonest in much."
LUKE 16:10 ESV

This can be a scary or encouraging verse. Which path do you follow? If we know that much is required of those with much, are we scared of commitment? On the other end of the spectrum, do we think a half-truth is not a big deal?

Our actions sear paths in our minds. Each time we get away with sin, we make the path just a little larger for more sin to follow. Each time we are faithful, we widen the path for our faith and confidence in Christ to grow. God will entrust us with more, and he will give us the strength to use his gifts well.

Which path are you on? Are you willing to ask God to help you combat even the smallest of dishonesties in you?

Lord, you know the deepest places of our hearts, and nothing is hidden from you. Please transform our hearts and minds to long for full devotion to Christ, and keep us on the path to you. We want to be honest and faithful.

WHAT IS JUDGMENT?

"Do not judge others, and you will not be judged. Do not condemn others, or it will all come back against you. Forgive others, and you will be forgiven."

LUKE 6:37 NLT

Judgment in itself is not bad. We make judgments every day. Is the stove hot? Is it safe to cross the street? Biblical Abigail said that her husband, Nabal, was a foolish man, and the Bible tells us she had "good judgment." God does not require us to lie and say something is what it is not. What is this verse really talking about?

To cast judgment on someone is to revile them, and no good comes from it. Think of a ball thrown against a wall. The velocity of its return will be greater than when it was initially thrown. So too are the consequences of judging. To forgive someone does not mean they are not responsible for their actions or that you condone their behavior. Forgiveness brings freedom to both parties.

Are you bound by a grudge? Have you been casting judgment on someone you need to free? What can you do right now to begin the process of forgiveness?

Lord, help us see judgment and forgiveness through your eyes and receive your freedom. Give us wisdom in all of our difficult situations.

UNVEILED

So all of us who have had that veil removed can see and reflect the glory of the Lord.

2 CORINTHIANS 3:18 NIV

Moses was illuminated temporarily with the glory of God on Mt. Sinai, when God gave him the Ten Commandments. When Moses appeared again to the people, he had to wear a veil, as his face was radiant from God's presence.

To unveil means no secrets can be hidden. We don't have to wait to be transformed into God's image. We are constantly changing into the image of Jesus Christ. Moses' glory came during the time of the law, and the Spirit's glory now comes from the death and resurrection of Jesus. Even now, it lives in you!

Have you ever envisioned the glory of God? Even better, have you envisioned the glory of God alive in you?

Father, show off your glory, and help us grow in you. When we don't feel worthy, help us to remember that your mercy has saved us, not our works or righteousness. Let that glory help us want to please you with lives that honor your name.

REWARDS

"I the LORD search the heart and examine the mind, to reward each person according to their conduct, according to what their deeds deserve."

JEREMIAH 17:10 NIV

Reward is a benefit received to reinforce a behavior. Sometimes, a reward is expected; other times, it is a surprise bonus. God's Word gives us encouragement in our everyday life by telling us that nothing we do for the Lord will be forgotten. Imagine what heaven will be like! It's not just a perfect place without sin, where God will live with us, but a place that we indeed can send our treasures on ahead.

We know God will reward, but we don't have to perform to receive his loving redemption. Our works won't make him love us any more, and our sins will not diminish his love for us either.

Ask yourself if your works are unto the Lord or unto man. How can you serve the Lord through your life today?

Lord, help us in our humanness to serve you. Let your promises lead us to holiness and righteousness.

OUR FATHER'S HOUSE

Let us consider how to stimulate one another to love and good deeds, not forsaking our own assembling together, as is the habit of some, but encouraging one another; and all the more as you see the day drawing near.

HEBREWS 10:24-25 NASB

Living in a way that pleases God includes gathering together with fellow believers. We are iron sharpening iron. Choosing to follow Christ, and yet not attending church, is reckless. We forfeit the many studies, groups, and activities that go along with it, and this causes us to shrink spiritually.

It also stops us from fulfilling of great commission, robbing fellow believers and unbelievers of what non-attenders have to offer. To be honest, it is selfish. Live streaming, and rebroadcasts of services are fine for those who are away from home, sick, or shut-in, but the local church is invaluable to our communities and to kingdom of heaven.

Do you find yourself making excuses to sleep in or skip church? Do you spend time with a body of believers? How can you encourage each other to get out the door?

Father, forgive us when we view church as a final option. Jesus, show us how to follow your habit of going regularly to God's house. Help us connect with fellow believers and be a fruitful part of your kingdom on earth.

ETERNAL OR TEMPORARY HAPPINESS?

To the degree that you share the sufferings of Christ, keep on rejoicing, so that also at the revelation of His glory you may rejoice with exultation.
1 PETER 4:13 NASB

It may be difficult to wrap our brains around "the sufferings of Christ." What does that mean? For some it means terrible persecution. In life, we all have trouble. It rains on one just as it does another. As Christians, we choose to honor God even in trouble.

Scripture implores us to arm ourselves with Christ's attitude in suffering. We should not live recklessly for human desires; we should seek the will of God. As we choose a life with Christ, some of our friends or relatives may judge us, according to their standards. We may be insulted, intentionally overlooked, uninvited, or even excommunicated. Still, we are called to rejoice when we are insulted for the name of Christ. Scripture says we are blessed, and the spirit of God rests on us. Eternal happiness looks completely contrary to temporary happiness. Rejoice that eternity is won for you!

Do you question God when trials and sufferings come upon you? Will you ask the Lord to help you through pain, and trust he has his best waiting for you? Share your current trials with your spouse, and celebrate your eternal happiness.

Jesus, please comfort us in our sufferings. We give them to you as a sacrifice of praise.

A VOW TO GOD

Sacrifice thank offerings to God, fulfill your vows to the Most High, and call on me in the day of trouble; I will deliver you, and you will honor me.

PSALM 50:14-15 NIV

When Kent and Jennifer got married, they vowed to love each other, but they also made a vow to serve God. Neither of them realized that their surrender would lead to Kent becoming a pastor a few years down the road. They loved sharing their lives in ministry, but with it came challenges, just as in any other profession. They dealt with moments when they faced decisions and didn't know what to do, times when they felt helpless to comfort those who were going through hard times, and days when there were financial situations to conquer.

But you know what they discovered? God doesn't call us to a task without equipping us for it. Moments of God's provision give us opportunities to share about God's faithfulness, bond our hearts together, and remind us where we need to go when trouble arises.

Have you and your spouse made a vow to God about something? What have you learned through the process?

Lord, we know you'll honor our vows to you. Remind us to come to you whenever trouble arises.

MENTORING COUPLE

Then the Lord God said, "It is not good that the man should be alone."
GENESIS 2:18 ESV

What a great idea God had in building humans for companionship! Man and woman fit together physically, spiritually, and emotionally. It is no small thing to be able to have a partner in Christ, united on the same front. Where one is weak, the other can lift and support. A married man and women are one in the sight of God.

Think about a married couple that you admire. It may be their respect, honor, or compatibility that attracts your desire to be like them. Watching older couples laugh and commiserate looks satisfying, like they have achieved something together. Isn't that something we should all wish for?

What couples do you admire in your life, and why? Share them with your spouse. How could you ask an older, admirable couple to mentor you?

God thank you for making us life partners. Help us to be kind to one another, and position us alongside a godly mentoring couple.

WISDOM

The one who gets wisdom loves life.
The one who cherishes understanding will soon prosper.

PROVERBS 19:8 NIV

Ken has a "get rich quick" type of personality, and as a result, he's tried all sorts of harebrained schemes to become prosperous. His wife, Donna, is just the opposite. She reasons through her decisions, researches, asks for wise counsel, and most importantly, she prays about it. But sometimes she can over-rationalize.

That's where the beauty of being a couple comes in. They bring balance to each other. When Ken comes home all excited about an idea to increase their income, Donna provides the background work to see if it's viable or not. As they've prayed together and sought to understand what God wants them to do, they've learned that when wisdom from God is part of the process, they love life more and don't have to deal with the fall-out. And you know what? God has honored them for seeking him and prospered them beyond what they ever expected.

How does seeking wisdom affect our lives as a couple?
What is required for God to prosper us?

Father, give us wisdom as we make decisions. Bless us and help us to then pour those blessings into the lives of others.

JUST PASSING THROUGH

We fix our eyes not on what is seen, but on what is unseen, since what is seen is temporary, but what is unseen is eternal.
2 Corinthians 4:18 NIV

Could it be possible that what we see here on earth may actually be an imitation of the reality of heaven? We may picture heaven as ethereal, with harp-strumming cherubs floating on clouds. Yet the world used to be perfect: heaven on earth. When God creates a new heaven and a new earth, what will they be like?

It's evident that a gravitational field is pulling at our bodies, and our limbs and organs don't treat us with the same respect they did when we were first born. When we keep our thoughts on the reality and glory of what is to come (such as glorified bodies that never grow old or die), we can live in this speck of time, knowing what eternity will be.

Have you ever thought about what it might be like to live in a perfect land? Have some fun describing possible heavens to each other.

Father we can be impatient, knowing that one day we will live in a faultless paradise with you. Help us live everyday as visitors passing through.

EFFECTIVE COUNSEL

Brothers and sisters, I do not consider myself yet to have taken hold of it. But one thing I do: Forgetting what is behind and straining toward what is ahead, I press on toward the goal to win the prize for which God has called me heavenward in Christ Jesus.

PHILIPPIANS 3:13-14 NIV

Many people think that going to a counselor means digging up the past and wallowing in it. Some think that transparency on such a deep level will leave them vulnerable. Seeking counsel should lead us to a safe place that shows us the root of what hurts, so we can ultimately be free from judgment, guilt, and worry.

A root of bitterness can taint the souls of all around it. Sharing the pains of our past with a trusted Christian friend can free us from the chains that weigh us down. We can then press on toward the goal God has called us to and win the prize he has for us.

Is there a repeated pattern in your life? Do you have outbursts, habits, or fears that you just can't seem to shake? Share what you see in yourself.

Father, we lay our pain at your feet. Transform us with your grace and love. Send us the right counselors so we can press on.

BRINGING CALM

Fools give full vent to their rage,
but the wise bring calm in the end.
PROVERBS 29:11 NIV

Have you ever gotten mad at your spouse, said ugly things, and then later wished you could take your words back? I suspect most of us have been guilty of that on multiple occasions. What's even worse, we seem to have an uncanny ability to hurl words that hurt our spouses most because we know the spots where they're sensitive or vulnerable.

Rage can cause so much damage in a marriage. Words spoken in anger can seep into our souls, wounding us deeply. The next time we're in those situations, we'd be wise to practice quietness until we get ourselves under control. Stop and pray and ask God to make your attitude right before you say angry words that could be remembered forever.

Do you have a problem with anger? How does that impact your relationship?

Lord, please seal our lips before we hurl angry words at our spouses. Keep us quiet until wisdom kicks in.

UNBIDDEN WORDS

"By your words you will be justified, and by your words you will be condemned."
MATTHEW 12:37 ESV

At first glance, these words sound like they rolled off the lips of a stern judge. Actually, they were spoken by Jesus to the Pharisees in response to a severe criticism they made concerning the source of Jesus' healing power.

Our words do matter. More than that, words reveal our motives and our heart. Not the carefully crafted responses we give, but rather the words that tumble out of our mouths, unbidden. Like a pop quiz in school, caught off-guard, we hear ourselves saying things we never planned on saying or even thought we were capable of saying. These circumstances reveal our true heart. The Holy Spirit allows it, not to embarrass us, but to change us. We only seek change if we acknowledge we need it.

Do you have the courage to ask God to reveal your heart to you? Have you or your spouse ever said anything that surprised both of you?

Heavenly Father, your deep love for us is the reason you sometimes allow embarrassing situations. Stripped of our polished words and vanity, we see ourselves as we really are. We desire to be true through and through, like sterling silver. Give us your grace to accomplish this.

YOU HAVE A GIFT!

If your gift is serving others, serve them well. If you are a teacher, teach well. If your gift is to encourage others, be encouraging. If it is giving, give generously. If God has given you leadership ability, take the responsibility seriously. And if you have a gift for showing kindness to others, do it gladly.

ROMANS 12:7-8 NLT

A blessing of marriage is that between the two of you there are a variety of gifts to share with your family, the church, and your wider community. At times, it can be a burden to teach, to give, to encourage, or to lead. If your spouse is feeling this way, encourage them to recognize the gift they have received, and remind them God gave us these gifts for a purpose.

Today's scripture then moves on to the hardest command; use your gifts cheerfully. God wants our heart's attitude to be one of joy. Isn't it frustrating when your spouse does something nice for you and then complains about it? Be a cheerful giver of yourself and all your gifts!

What are your God-given gifts? Is your heart cheerful about using them? Talk with your spouse about times you have seen each other's gifts in action.

Father, thank you for the gifts that you have given us. Between the two of us, we can accomplish much for your glory, so help us to give generously with cheerful hearts.

GOOD STEPS

So follow the steps of the good,
and stay on the paths of the righteous.
For only the godly will live in the land,
and those with integrity will remain in it.
PROVERBS 2:20-21 NLT

God wants us to follow him, and he wants us to be men and women of integrity. As Christians, we want to follow him, but we need safeguards to keep us on the right path. Honesty, honor, and good character positively impact our homes and marriages, but it can be hard to achieve those traits if we spend the majority of our time with friends who don't share our values and love for God.

Picking friends wisely is important because we often become like the people we give our time. We must choose godly companions who encourage us to live for God—those friends will also value the sanctity of marriage. As husbands and wives, we need to be godly friends for each other, encouraging one another by pointing to God and living our lives with integrity.

How can you encourage your spouse spiritually? Do your friends encourage you by their godly example, or are they leading you astray?

Father, help us to walk our paths with integrity and honor. Remove any influences that harm our marriage or keep us from serving you.

A BALL OF YARN

He will yet fill your mouth with laughter
and your lips with shouts of joy.
JOB 8:21 NIV

Tim dropped to the floor while Kristin slumped to the side of her chair. They were watching the family cat discover the best way to play with a ball of yarn. The ball had rolled under the sofa, and she got stuck trying to retrieve it. Her back paws waved in the air. Instead of getting up immediately to get her out, Tim and Kristin couldn't help but laugh at her antics.

There's nothing more exhilarating than a good belly laugh. It is cleansing, therapeutic, and heartening. The Bible tells us a merry heart is like medicine. When you laugh with your partner, you experience an unspoken closeness—a deep, unified enjoyment that puts other concerns aside. Laugh often together.

When was the last time you and your spouse enjoyed a good belly laugh together? If it's been a while, plan an activity that will make you both laugh.

Lord, thank you for the ability to laugh. In a world full of turmoil, we need some lighter moments.

SEPTEMBER

There are three things that are too
amazing for me, four that I do not
understand: the way of an eagle in the
sky, the way of a snake on a rock, the
way of a ship on the high seas, and
the way of a man with a young woman.

PROVERBS 30:18-19 NIV

JOB'S HEART

"Have you considered my servant Job? There is no one on earth like him; he is blameless and upright, a man who fears God and shuns evil. And he still maintains his integrity, though you incited me against him to ruin him without any reason."
JOB 2:3 NIV

Notice how God characterized Job in this verse—honest, righteous, respectful, a man who shunned evil. Job was a man of integrity. He was so faithful that even God sang his praises. Could there be a higher honor? And yet God challenged Satan to attack Job, confident that he would stand through the trial. Job's great love for God and his commitment to righteousness would see him through. His deep-seated desire to please his heavenly Father would cause his faith to hold fast.

As a couple, can you make a similar commitment to God and each other? Could it be said of you both, that you are honest, you do what is right, you respect God and shun evil? If so, your marriage will last and will be a shining example to the world.

As a couple, do you desire to please God? Are you standing strong when trials come? Can God trust you with difficulties?

Father, give us the heart and testimony of Job. Help us to encourage each other to live faithfully for you.

THE LITTLE THINGS

The Lord has done it this very day;
let us rejoice today and be glad.
PSALM 118:24 NIV

Sometimes we forget to thank God for the little things—things that in reality perhaps aren't so little! Consider the simple gift of a single day—twenty-four hours to spend with our sweethearts and one more opportunity to serve God. Often we get so bogged down with responsibilities that we pass right by those blessings, missing the joy that God has for us each day. Missed moments with our loved ones are irreplaceable. We simply cannot retrieve time.

Wouldn't it be wise to sit down together as a couple and figure out how to make time with God and each other a priority? Ask him to become the keeper of your schedule. It would be a shame for you and your spouse to miss the fresh joy that's waiting for you with each new sunrise. This is the day that the Lord has made. Rejoice and be glad in it!

Have other things gotten in the way that keep you from experiencing the joy God has for you each day? How can you and your spouse remedy that problem?

Lord, please be the keeper of our schedules. Show us how to use our time wisely, putting you first always while never overlooking the small, daily joys you set before us.

INEXPLICABLE JOY

You believe in him and are filled with an inexpressible and glorious joy.

1 PETER 1:8 NIV

Living a life of joy is a great goal for all of us. That doesn't mean that we'll be happy every day of our lives and that everything will be rosy, or that we won't have any problems. Joy is more than momentary happiness when something exciting happens. True joy is being contented in our circumstances. It's a commitment to trust in the one who loved us so much that he gave his life for us. Joy brings a special and inexplicable peace. It's a deep sense of contentment that comes from spending time in God's presence, studying his Word, and talking with him.

As we spend time with God and follow the path he has laid out for us, we discover the true joy that can only be found in him.

Have you ever been in the midst of hard times, and yet experienced real joy? Do you and your spouse spend time each day in God's presence?

Father, give us joy in the journey, and contentment and peace when tough circumstances come along.

WHEN LOVING IS DIFFICULT

"Love your enemies! Do good to them. Lend to them without expecting to be repaid. Then your reward from heaven will be very great, and you will truly be acting as children of the Most High, for he is kind to those who are unthankful and wicked."

LUKE 6:35 NLT

Ouch! It's hard to be good to our enemies—especially difficult if someone has hurt our sweetheart. If we're not careful, bitterness, anger, and even plans for revenge can emerge. Bitterness is always destructive, hurting us as much as the offender. Revenge causes even more damage.

When Albert's pastor preached about loving our enemies, it hit hard. At first, it made Albert angry. But after some thought, he told God, "Okay, I'll try." He and his wife, Sue, decided to pray about it together. The next day, Albert set a basket of tomatoes and cucumbers from their garden on the porch of his enemy's house with a note that read, "From Albert and Sue." The next week, Albert mowed their lawn. Over the next several months, their good deeds continued. It wasn't easy, but as they followed God's command together, their marriage was strengthened. They discovered the rewards of truly acting as children of the Most High, being kind to those who were unthankful.

Discuss this verse from Proverbs 25:21-22 NLT: "If your enemies are hungry, give them food to eat. If they are thirsty, give them water to drink. You will heap burning coals of shame on their heads, and the Lord will reward you."

Father, help us to see our enemies through your eyes. Help us to love like you love.

THE FRUIT BASKET

The fruit of the Spirit is love, joy, peace, forbearance, kindness, goodness, faithfulness, gentleness and self-control. Against such things there is no law.

GALATIANS 5:22-23 NIV

Holiday gift baskets are typically filled with beautiful fruit and other tantalizing goodies. They are a joy to both give and receive. Have you ever thought about creating a spiritual gift basket that would be filled with the fruit of the Spirit? What if you carried peace and joy home with you after a busy day? What if you shared forbearance and patience even in an aggravating situation? What if you daily expressed kindness, goodness, faithfulness, and gentleness in your relationship with your spouse? What if you practiced self-control instead of losing your temper, or doled out generous helpings from your spiritual fruit basket to your mate every single day? What if?

Perhaps you need to dip into your basket more often and become consistent users of the fruit of the Spirit. What a perfect gift to give to your spouse.

Are you lacking in any of the spiritual gifts? If so, ask God to help you cultivate those that are needed so each of you can bear much fruit together.

Lord, help us dip into our spiritual baskets and generously distribute the fruit of the Spirit to one another.

INCOMPREHENSIBLE GOODNESS

Do you think lightly of the riches of His kindness and tolerance and patience, not knowing that the kindness of God leads you to repentance?

ROMANS 2:4 NASB

The goodness of God is beyond our comprehension. As the vastness of the universe baffles the human mind, so does God's universal benevolence. Who but a loving, kind, patient and wholly good God, would tolerate our rebellion and patiently lead us to a place of repentance? He could employ fear, intimidation or coercion to force us to a place of repentance. But instead, he woos and gently guides us to the light.

You have been the recipients of God's amazing kindness, and because of it you have been transformed. Have you been showing kindness in your marriage relationship? God's patience, tolerance and kindness have been granted to you in full measure. Are you allowing it to overflow to your spouse?

Are you by nature impatient people? Talk about ways you can show more kindness and be more patient with each other.

Father, thank you for my spouse. Take us through our years with hearts full of love for you, hearts that are filled with kindness, tolerance, and patience for each other.

GENUINE LOVE

Love is patient and kind. Love is not jealous or boastful or proud.
1 CORINTHIANS 13:4 NLT

Love is patient. It is a simple statement, yet so difficult to put into practice especially in the context of marriage. Consider this scenario: The husband gets home later than expected. The wife responds impatiently, "Where have you been? We're going to be late!" without thinking that perhaps he had been unavoidably detained. Or perhaps the wife is taking too long trying on clothes at the mall. A big game is on in thirty minutes, so instead of letting her enjoy herself after a long day with the kids, he grumbles and hurries her along.

Impatience can easily take root and become a habit in marriage. Wise couples work hard on developing patience and kindness. They put aside the jealousy, the selfishness, and the insistence on their own way because genuine love puts other needs before its own. The surprising and wonderful truth is the more these qualities are demonstrated, the more they are returned!

Are you patient and kind to your spouse? Discuss some practical ways you can show real love to each other.

Lord, teach us to be patient and kind. Help us to put our spouses before ourselves.

A RECORD OF RIGHTS

Love is not rude, is not selfish, and does not get upset with others.
Love does not count up wrongs that have been done.
1 CORINTHIANS 13:5 NCV

In our early dating days, we looked at that gorgeous person across the table from us and imagined a lifetime of romantic days filled with sweetness and love. We innocently did not dwell on the fact that marriage is between two imperfect people—people who are at times rude and selfish, and can become upset at the slightest provocation. As flawed individuals, we may even start keeping tabs of our spouse's wrongdoings. "I remember the time you told me I could spend the money and then you fussed about it for a week!" "Remember how you introduced me at the company dinner? I was so mortified. I still can't believe you said that about me!" Negative memories have a tendency to accumulate and resurface if they have not been washed away through forgiveness and forgetfulness.

What if you put more effort into keeping a record of the good things your spouse does instead of counting the wrongs? Can you imagine how that would change the dynamics of your relationship?

Do you ever keep tabs of your spouse's wrongdoings? Is there a list that needs to be eradicated by forgiveness?

Lord, quicken our memories to retain the good things and forgive and forget the wrongs.

REKINDLE THE FLAME

If I had the gift of prophecy, and if I understood all of God's secret plans and possessed all knowledge, and if I had such faith that I could move mountains, but didn't love others, I would be nothing. If I gave everything I have to the poor and even sacrificed my body, I could boast about it; but if I didn't love others, I would have gained nothing.

1 CORINTHIANS 13:2-4 NLT

Love trumps all! Every spiritual gift could be ours and we could possess the wisdom of Solomon and sacrifice all we have, but without love, it is meaningless. The building blocks of a good marriage are varied—among them trust, compatibility, common interests, attraction, and passion. However, if there is no love, the relationship cannot exist.

Love covers; love is selfless; love seeks the other's good, and puts the other first. Love allows discussions and decisions to happen in peace because there is an innate desire to please the other. Self-sacrifice comes easily and joyfully.

If you feel like the love factor has diminished in your marriage, can you figure out why? Sit down with your mate and discuss how you can reclaim your first love.

Lord, help us to fan the dimming flame of our love. Make our marriage so strong that nothing can shake it.

THE SONG OF ENCOURAGEMENT

Be filled with the Holy Spirit, singing psalms and hymns and spiritual songs among yourselves, and making music to the Lord in your hearts.

EPHESIANS 5:18-19 NIV

Has discouragement ever brought your spouse to the point of despair? No matter what you did to help, or how you tried to bring some cheer, you couldn't find a way. Betsy experienced a time like that with her husband, Charles. His job situation was bad and they were hurting financially. His ego had taken a hit and he doubted his ability to care for his family. It was a tough time. They prayed together. Betsy texted him verses of encouragement each day, but he still struggled with the discouraging circumstances. Betsy prayed, "God, I don't know how to help him. What can I do?"

And God said, "Sing." *Really?* So that night when Charles arrived home from work, Betsy sat him down at the dining room table, pulled up some praise music on YouTube, and the two of them began to sing—comforting words of God's provision and hymns about a faithful God. Both of them wiped away tears as the words of praise brought healing to their hearts.

Are you discouraged today? Sing praises with your sweetheart. The gloom will begin to lift through the healing presence of Jesus. There is power in praise!

Lord, give us a song in the night. Help us to praise you through good times and through bad.

IS YOUR CUP HALF EMPTY?

Now the Berean Jews were of more noble character than those in Thessalonica, for they received the message with great eagerness and examined the Scriptures every day to see if what Paul said was true.

ACTS 17:11 NIV

It is often said that opposites attract. In a marriage, the husband and the wife each bring strengths and weaknesses to the relationship. One spouse might have the propensity to see things in a negative light, while the other has a more optimistic outlook. Different people have different temperaments. The optimist can encourage the pessimist to lighten up and see the fun in life. The pessimist needs to grow in trust and gratitude to begin to see life through a new lens—one focused on God's goodness and blessings.

What is your outlook? Are you the eternal optimist, always seeing the good? Or are you a pessimist, desperately needing someone to help you see that there is light at the end of the tunnel? A great marriage is one where there is mutual encouragement and willingness to grow and change.

Is your cup half full or half empty? Do you look at the bright side of everything, or do you need your mate to help you lighten up? Talk about your differences.

Lord, thank you for making us unique and for being the balance in our lives we so desperately need.

THE CHALLENGE OF DISCIPLINE

*Discipline your children, and they will give you rest;
they will give delight to your heart.*
PROVERBS 29:17 NRSV

Children are a gift from the Lord—made in the image of God and entrusted to us to raise in the fear of God. There are days when our patience is tested to the limit and days when our hearts melt with love and gratitude. A young mom with three small children had one of those days. She put a sign in the window for her husband's benefit upon his return home from work. "Children for Sale." Three words said it all.

A vital component of child rearing is discipline. It's never an easy task especially if mom and dad have differing styles. Rather than allowing a discrepancy to be problematic, why not use this opportunity to search the Scriptures to see what God says? You will find that our mandate is to raise children who love and obey God by teaching them obedience. So, parents, keep a united front! Do whatever is necessary to stay on the same page, and in the end your children will bring delight to your hearts!

How do your parenting styles differ? How can you complement one other and provide a united front?

Lord, help us to teach our children to obey you. Give us the wisdom to administer discipline with love.

PLANTING SEEDS

Start children off on the way they should go
and even when they are old they will not turn from it.
PROVERBS 22:6 NIV

At the conclusion of an exhausting day, a young mom lamented to her husband, "I don't think these kids have learned a thing we've taught them. Even our discipline is not working." The wise dad responded, "We're in this for the long haul. We just keep on keeping on." The following day was different. The kids were obedient and kind—a much-needed affirmation that indeed God's methods are best. What the parents had faithfully taught and modeled was lodged deeply in their children's hearts and minds after all.

Think of the analogy of planting seeds in a garden. The gardener faithfully waters, fertilizes, and weeds the garden to provide the best environment possible for the seeds to take root. Nothing appears to be happening for a long period of time, but eventually the seed sprouts and fruit appears, beautiful and delectable. In the same way, we plant seeds of faith in our children's hearts by teaching them the Word, taking them to church, praying together, and modeling Jesus before them each day. We provide the best environment we can for spiritual growth. We may not see results right away, but the seeds are there and God will cause them grow and flourish whenever the soil of their hearts is ready.

What can you do to plant seeds of faith in your children?
Are you faithfully instilling in them the truth of God's
Word? Are you modeling Jesus' love each day?

Lord, help us to be faithful in planting seeds of faith in our
children. Help them to flourish.

ALWAYS A CHILD

Children, obey your parents because you belong to the Lord, for this is the right thing to do. "Honor your father and mother." This is the first commandment with a promise: If you honor your father and mother, "things will go well for you, and you will have a long life on the earth."

EPHESIANS 6:1-3 NLT

Just because you are now married does not mean you stopped being children. You are still your parents' kids. Although there are changes in your relationship because you are now peers, you are actually stepping into a new place of blessing. Your parents are now a greater source of wisdom and have hopefully become good friends and treasured companions.

Many young couples have the privilege of having two sets of parents with which to relate, as two families have merged. Even though the relationships are different, one thing does not change: God still requires honor and respect be given to our parents. It will take time and effort, but God will show you ways to honor them and he will then bless your marriage, giving you a long and satisfying life.

Have you talked to your parents today? This week? If not, give them a call, or better yet, pay them a visit together. You will bless them as they see you happily functioning in a godly marriage.

Lord, thank you for our parents. Help us to honor them with our words and actions.

THE LONG HAUL

Love...always endures.

1 CORINTHIANS 13:7 NCV

Shirley had dealt with a chronic illness for several years. Weakness, fatigue, pain, and limited mobility characterized her days. It had been a tough and frustrating time, especially because the doctors couldn't determine what was wrong. She wanted to go places and do fun things with her husband, Clint, but on many days, the physical ability to do those things just wasn't there. She was weary of the journey. It hurt her to know that she was impacting her husband's life in a negative way.

But here's the beautiful thing. Clint meant his wedding vows. He was in it for the long haul, for the sickness as well as the health. He knew the essence of real love. He knew it was a commitment that with God's help would enable him to persevere through the hardships with patience and tender care. He knew that in keeping his vows before God, he would be rewarded in this life and the one to come. God keeps his covenant with us, and he will see us through whatever trials come along as we keep our covenant with him.

What trials have you gone through as a couple? Have they drawn you closer to God and to each other?

Lord, help us to honor our wedding vows—through the tough days as well as the pleasant ones. Give us love that endures.

TIME MARCHES ON

Do not forget this one thing, dear friends: With the Lord a day is like a thousand years, and a thousand years are like a day.
2 PETER 3:8 NIV

When you find the right person, a mate who is the perfect fit for you, the passage of time seems irrelevant. The sense of security and comfort you experience softens the aging process. Whether you've been married weeks or years, the sense of togetherness makes the ever-changing situations and circumstances of life flow smoothly. Things that happened in your early-married years at times seem like yesterday. Time marches on, but treads softly.

Feeling safe in the knowledge that you are in the center of God's will for your marriage is a wonderful blessing. The striving is gone. Granted, there is work to be done in maintaining a good relationship, but the journey from the altar to eternity becomes a joyful one, filled with many of God's surprises.

How long have you been married? Does it seem like a short time or an eternity?

Father, you are the God of time. Thank you for bringing us together in your perfect timing. Keep us strong together for many years, until we stand face to face before you.

THE WAITING GAME

Be still before the Lord and wait patiently for him;
do not fret when people succeed in their ways,
when they carry out their wicked schemes.
PSALM 37:7 NIV

Most of us aren't good at playing the waiting game. We want what we want right now. If there's a problem, we want it fixed immediately. If we ask God for something, we expect an instant answer. In times of crisis, we are apt to look at others who are not necessarily serving God, and their lack of problems is troublesome to us. David, the Psalmist thought similarly: "For I envied the proud when I saw them prosper despite their wickedness" (Psalm 73:3 NLT).

God isn't punishing us by making us wait; in fact, he has a great purpose in it. God is busy transforming our characters: he's teaching us valuable lessons in trust, and forging a bond between us as we seek him together. If we don't see an immediate answer, we know that God is busily at work behind the scenes. Perhaps his dreams for us are bigger than our own and other pieces need to fall into place before the long-awaited answer is given. So be still. Encourage each other, and wait on God together.

Do you have trouble waiting on God? What areas in your life need to be perfected? List some of the lessons God may want you to learn.

Lord, teach us to wait on you. We know you have big things planned for our lives together.

THE CONTROL FACTOR

Whoever is slow to anger is better than the mighty,
and he who rules his spirit than he who takes a city.
PROVERBS 16:32 ESV

The desire to control has been an issue since the beginning of time. Wars have been fought; divorces have occurred; deaths have resulted from people vying for control. Marriage was created by God, not as a competition, but as a partnership. The battle to control has no place in marriage other than each partner developing self-control. Decisions, satisfactory to both, should be made by discussion, mutual agreement, and prayer.

God is our ultimate authority, and he is in charge. A good marriage operates from the framework where neither is struggling to control. Both are working together to accomplish the responsibilities set before them in an amicable fashion. The marriage benefits as the work is divided and decisions mutually made, always acknowledging God as the director. Be patient with each other and enjoy peace.

Are there issues in your marriage where you struggle for control? How best could you rectify those?

Father, we acknowledge that you are in charge of every facet of our marriage. Take control of every aspect and let us live each day for you.

PERSONALITY CLASHES

If possible, so far as it depends on you,
live peaceably with all.
ROMANS 12:18 ESV

People are unique individuals with distinct personalities. Occasionally you may meet someone who is difficult to get along with and you soon realize that your personalities don't automatically jive. It may take some work to develop and maintain such a relationship.

You may find that to be true in your marriage. Initially, you were attracted to your mate because of his or her good looks. Perhaps you discovered a talent or trait that was especially endearing. You learned you had common interests and shared similar values. Yet, even after all you knew, you undoubtedly discovered some new things after marriage—habits, personality quirks, and different ways of seeing things that cause occasional disagreements. What happened to the peace and joy you once experienced, and, more importantly, what is do be done? According to Scripture, look within. Ask God to reveal to you the ways you are contributing to the discord and open your eyes to your own difficult personality traits. Such a prayer will open the door for God to begin a transformation in your heart that will affect you both.

What are some of the personality differences between you and your mate? Ask God to reveal where each of you needs to change and to grant the grace to accept one another.

God, thank you for making us all different and yet giving us your love so we can live peaceably.

GETTING ALONG

Make every effort to live in peace with everyone.
HEBREWS 12:14 NIV

Marriage not only brings times of sweetness and flowers, but also times of disagreement and even strife. Once you are united in marriage and living under one roof, you soon discover that the two of you do not see eye to eye on everything. Decisions lie ahead, and your spouse's view may go against your grain and aggravate your sense of logic. Are you going to argue, each insisting on your own way, or are you going to compromise for the sake of peace? At times, even silence is wise as you both take the time to process your thoughts and ask God for guidance.

The goal is to have a peaceful home. Peace fosters growth both in your relationship to God and to each other. When new patterns of conflict resolution become a habit, disagreements won't be as frequent and peace will reign. The New Living Translation puts it this way: "Work at living in peace with everyone, and work at living a holy life, for those who are not holy will not see the Lord."

Does God's peace rule in your home? If not, what can you do differently?

Lord, thank you for the sweet peace that comes from knowing you and heeding your commands.

SMART PEOPLE

Those with good sense are slow to anger,
and it is their glory to overlook an offense.

PROVERBS 19:11 NRSV

Lisa amazed herself at how good she was at getting herself into messes. How many women could manage to get the car stuck between a concrete barrier and a piece of curbing? I mean, really stuck, with only an inch or two of maneuvering room. Back and forth, back and forth she inched in her effort to get out of the parking space. She cringed each time the tire scratched against the concrete, imagining the ugly marks that would be left there. She finally got the car out, but there was a knot in her stomach as she wondered how mad her husband, Tom, was going to be when he saw the tire.

To her surprise, Tom showed her mercy. He shrugged, "Everybody makes mistakes, honey. It's just a tire." He'd been praying about his quick temper, and keeping peace with his wife was one of his priorities. At that moment, her love for him grew. Tom truly put this Proverb's wisdom into practice and immediately experienced the benefits of his obedience.

Is overreaction or anger an issue in your marriage? How can you better manage your responses?

Lord, make us slow to anger and quick to forgive.

FAITHFUL IN PRAYER

Be joyful in hope, patient in affliction, faithful in prayer.
ROMANS 12:12 NIV

One of the most valuable gifts we have in our marriages is prayer. When we learn to trust in God and turn our problems over to him, there's an inexplicable joy and a sweet hope that comes, even when the circumstances haven't changed. Times of affliction are tough, especially when our spouse is affected. Our first inclination is to try to fix the problem and so often we can't. How wonderful to know the God who can! Continue to pray, even when you don't see the answer in front of you. And while you are waiting, ask the Lord what he wants you to learn from the situation.

There's a special sweetness that comes when couples pray together. A wonderful heritage is being crafted prayer by prayer, and one day will be looked back on with gratitude at the faithfulness of God. Hearts are bonded side by side.

Do you pray together as a couple? Take a moment to remember the answers to prayer you have received.

Father, thank you for the gift of praying together as a couple. Help us to hope in you and to be faithful in our prayers.

BEYOND THE LIST

Call to me and I will answer you and tell you great and unsearchable things you do not know.
JEREMIAH 33:3 NIV

Sometimes we wonder why God doesn't seem to be answering our prayers. Consider this: Have you really asked God for what you need? Maybe you've whined, agonized, fretted, or complained to other people, but simply neglected to ask God.

Prayer lists can help with this problem. Record your requests, your needs, your desires, and your big dreams, adding to it as needed. Use the list to guide your prayers and then record what God does in each situation. Believe God when he says, "I will answer them before they even call to me. While they are still talking about their needs, I will go ahead and answer their prayers" (Isaiah 65:24 NLT). Lists are helpful, but of course, God is not limited to them. He wants to do so much in our lives. Give each other the gift of being prayer partners. You'll never regret it.

Do you pray together? Do you pray daily for your spouse? Are you specific in your prayers and truly trusting God for an answer?

Lord, remind us to call out to you with our requests and needs. Thank you for always answering us.

NO FEAR OF BAD NEWS

She laughs without fear of the future.
PROVERBS 31:25 NLT

Trouble will come to every life and marriage. It's not "if"; it's "when." Remember the vows you made? "In sickness and in health, for better and for worse, for richer and for poorer, until death do us part." That is the bedrock of your marriage. From that platform, you will be held together through thick and thin by Jesus, as you trust him.

How can we prepare for the troubles that lie ahead? We certainly can't trouble-proof our lives, but we can build our faith by immersing ourselves in the Word of God, by spending time in prayer and trusting God's magnificent promises. There's an old saying: "Forewarned is forearmed." A wise couple is prepared—armed with the Word of God and ready for whatever comes.

Is prayer a big part of your marriage or is it put on the back shelf until trouble comes? Discuss the times when God has been with you through financial difficulties, health scares, or family problems.

Lord, thank you for being there during the troubled times of our lives and for always answering whenever we call on you.

AN OPEN PRAYER LINE

"This is the confidence we have in approaching God: that if we ask anything according to his will, he hears us."
JOHN 5:14 NIV

Have you ever tried to communicate with your spouse while their mind was elsewhere, and your words were unheard? Perhaps you asked your mate to pick up some coffee filters and creamer on the way home, but since no mental notes were made in the first place, it was forgotten. Or maybe there's something you want to ask, but you're nervous and afraid the request will cause conflict or won't be taken in the right way.

In contrast, you never have to worry about any of that when you come to God. You can be confident that whenever you approach him, he hears every word you say—even to the extent of knowing the unspoken requests that are too difficult for you to verbalize. Husbands and wives, do you have a request today? Ask in accordance with his will, and rest secure in the knowledge that you have been heard.

Is prayer a big part of your marriage? Are you confident that when you bring your needs to God, he really does hear you?

Lord, thank you for giving us the privilege of bringing our requests to you. We're grateful that you always hear us, and that the prayer line is never busy.

CHASE AFTER GOD

Seek the Lord while you can find him. Call on him now while he is near. Let the wicked change their ways and banish the very thought of doing wrong. Let them turn to the Lord that he may have mercy on them. Yes, turn to our God, for he will forgive generously.

ISAIAH 55:6-7 NLT

God wants to spend time with his children. He desires closeness—a deep heart connection. Have you ever thought about the fact that God's presence is near, but you're so busy with life that you are unaware? Perhaps you are oblivious to his invitation to intimacy with him. Can you imagine how much better our homes and marriages would be if we heeded that call. If we drew near to God as he draws near to us?

Let's seek the Lord. He is waiting to pour out his mercy and forgive our sin. Let's pursue him with the same zeal we had when we dated our spouses. Although it is beyond our understanding, we can be confident that the God who made the universe is waiting to spend time with us. He promises forgiveness and mercy in that place of fellowship. Pursue God together as a couple. A cord of three strands will never be broken.

Do you notice a deeper intimacy with your mate when you regularly spend time in God's presence? How can you carve out more time to spend with him?

Lord, put a desire in our hearts to chase after you. We're humbled that you want to spend time with us.

FIRST, RUN TO GOD

Look to the Lord and his strength; seek his face always.
1 CHRONICLES 16:11 NIV

Some of us continue to be slow learners even though we have been around the same block many times. Life offers us many opportunities to turn to God for answers, but often instead of first running to the Lord, we plan, we worry, we do foolish things as we forge ahead on our own. Then when all else fails, we go to God for help.

The stereotypical male driver prefers to drive miles and miles before admitting he needs help with directions. His ego just won't allow him to concede that he is lost! Similarly, instead of admitting our weakness and running to the throne of grace first as God invites us to do, we foolishly rely on our own wisdom. Husband, wife, remind each other to go to God with every need, every question, every problem. Let his wisdom and strength get you through. Why wait until there is a mess to clean up? First, run to God!

Do you and your spouse try to fix problems yourselves or do you look to God for the answers? Talk about a few of those situations you've encountered in the past.

Lord, help us to first pursue you for the answers and help that we need.

THE GOD PRIORITY

Without faith it is impossible to please God, because anyone who comes to him must believe that he exists and that he rewards those who earnestly seek him.

HEBREWS 11:6 NIV

Gretchen thought back over the last two years. Single for a long time, she had focused on her relationship with God because she knew it was more important that anything else. She became quite content. Even if she never married, God would be her husband. However, it wasn't long before Mike came into her life. He was everything she had always dreamed of in a mate. Gretchen believed Mike was God's gift to her because she made God her priority.

Married couples have dreams and goals in life. Some of them are small and some monumental, but none are as important as putting God first in your marriage. A successful marriage is sustained by faith in God alone. The rewards of contentment, joy, and peace in all circumstances become the hallmark of your life. If your dreams never come true, they have achieved the ultimate goal of eternal life through Christ!

Do you rely on God above all else? Do you put him first?

Lord, thank you that we don't need anything or anyone else besides you.

LENS OF LOVE

"First get rid of the log in your own eye; then you will see well enough to deal with the speck in your friend's eye."
LUKE 6:42 NLT

It's so easy to see the faults in others, and so difficult to see them in ourselves. That flawed focus can strain a relationship. But once we recognize our faults, we can look at our loved ones through a forgiving lens of love. Praying as a couple about our faults takes the focus off us and puts it on God— where our focus should be.

None of us are perfect. Let us dispense grace instead of grouching.

What steps can we take to help each other become more Christ-like? How can we be more accepting of each other's flaws?

Lord, give us the courage to deal with the flaws in our lives first before we focus on our sweetheart's imperfections. Help us to look at each other through a lens of love and acceptance instead of criticism.

REFLECTIONS OF CHRIST

"He who receives you receives Me, and he who receives Me receives Him who sent Me."

MATTHEW 10:40 NASB

Marriage is often compared to the relationship between the church and Christ, and we can learn some valuable lessons from Christ's example. When we accept each other with love and forgiveness, as Christ accepts his church, we receive a deeper understanding of what God has done for us, and we experience a better relationship with each other.

Learning to accept each other unequivocally also leads to a clearer understanding of our relationship with Jesus and of his relationship with God the Father. Our lives can become a reflection of that relationship. And what could be better than to have your spouse look at you and see a reflection of Christ?

What can our marriage teach us about our relationship with God? How does our relationship reflect God's unconditional love?

Father, help us to remember how you accept us so lovingly even though you know all of our shortcomings. Remind us to carry that lesson into our relationship so we receive each other with the same love, compassion, and forgiveness that you grant us.

OCTOBER

Be devoted to one another
in love. Honor one another
above yourselves.

ROMANS 12:10 NIV

WORK IN PROGRESS

You will say to me then, "Why does he still find fault? For who can resist his will?" But who are you, O man, to answer back to God? Will what is molded say to its molder, "Why have you made me like this?" Has the potter no right over the clay, to make out of the same lump one vessel for honorable use and another for dishonorable use?

ROMANS 9:19-21 ESV

If you've ever watched a potter at work, you know that a vase or bowl doesn't happen quickly. Time, patience, and a desire for quality smooth and shape the pottery. Sometimes, when there is a flaw, the potter starts over, but he doesn't throw the clay away. He knows the extra effort will make the final result a work of beauty and usefulness.

Our marriages are the same way. Our relationships are works in progress that take time and patience as two people learn to live together, and it's vital that God—the master potter—is the one in control. When there's a glitch or problem, it's time to make a fresh start not to throw away something precious.

What needs re-shaping in our marriage? How can we do that with patience and love?

God, mold our lives and our marriage into something special. Don't let us throw away the gift of what you've given us. Help us to accept flaws while still seeing the beauty of our relationship.

LIFE ADVENTURES

How blessed is the man whose strength is in You,
In whose heart are the highways to Zion!

PSALM 84:5 NASB

Marriage is an adventure. Adventures take us into unknown territories, and so do our relationships. Part of the fun in any adventure is having a companion along for the journey, and nothing could be better than experiencing joyful moments with a sweetheart.

However, adventures come with hazards and unexpected moments that threaten to wreck our trips. Life adventures deal with unexpected heartache, health problems, and financial difficulties. Where do we turn when life's trip takes a bad turn? Tour guides lead and advise travelers on their adventures, and we have the ultimate guide in God. When troubles disrupt the adventure, he sees clearly our path, and he will provide the necessary tools for the journey.

What are some adventures that we can do together for God? What have we learned from life adventure disruptions, and how can we use those moments to draw closer to each other?

Lord, we want our lives to be an adventure with you. Take us to the places where you want us to go, and remind us to come to you for help when difficulties arise on the journey.

THINKING OF YOU

God is my witness, how I long for you all with the affection of Christ Jesus.

PHILIPPIANS 1:8 NASB

Built into each of us is a craving for love and affection, and that longing is important in our relationships. God set the standard for perfect love, inspiring us with his example. But it's easy to get busy or preoccupied as responsibilities claim our attention. Forgetting to express affection creates a void in our marriages.

Marriage needs all kinds of affection. Physical touch is vital; hugs and kisses say, "You are the most special person on earth to me." And it's important to hear the words *I love you* each day. Try writing a quick note to leave by your spouse's morning coffee cup. Send flowers just because, or a text that says, "Thinking of you." As God beautifully shares his love with us, we can become extensions of his loving hands and heart and share that love with the partner he's given us.

How do you feel when your sweetheart is affectionate toward you? What can you do to be more loving to your spouse?

Father, thank you for the love you give us. Help us to fulfill the need for affection in our loved ones. Help us shower each other with so much love that our hearts overflow.

ETERNAL AUTHORITY

Even from eternity I am He,
And there is none who can deliver out of My hand.
    ISAIAH 43:13 NASB

Have you ever noticed that we have a tendency to want to be in charge? That can cause real conflict for our relationships especially if we refuse to compromise. Nobody likes being ruled or controlled, and dominance doesn't work in a marriage. When a spouse barks orders and rules with a heavy hand, resentment builds and love is squashed.

Fortunately, our controlling actions—when we've used authority in the wrong way—can be reversed with apologies and a willingness to let God lead. God's actions are irreversible and that is a blessing. Our best decisions are those made in accordance with his unchanging will, and those are choices that will never harm our marriages.

What kind of authority figure are you? Who makes the decisions at your house? How does that impact your spouse and your relationship?

Lord, remind us to base our marriage on love instead of control. Help us to remember that you are the true authority figure in our home, and that your actions last forever.

FORESIGHT

I know that You can do all things,
And that no purpose of Yours can be thwarted.
JOB 42:2 NASB

Part of being an authority figure is making decisions. Wouldn't it be wonderful if we could see the future before we made those choices? Unfortunately, we can't, and we have to live with the results of our actions. All of us have moments where we damage our relationships or the ones we love because of bad decisions.

How do we make decisions without foresight? How can we know God's will for our lives? We pray about it with our spouses, talk about it together, and if we are in accordance with his Word, then our decisions become much easier. God has perfect foresight, and his vision has purpose for all couples. Lives lived under God's authority are destined for success; that is true of marriages too.

How do you handle authority in your home? What can you do to make better decisions together as a couple?

Lord, we want you to be the ultimate authority for our home. Help us to make wise decisions based on our love for each other and for you.

BEST FRIENDS

A friend is always loyal,
and a brother is born to help in time of need.
PROVERBS 17:17 NLT

Have you ever been overwhelmed while working on something? Then someone said, "I really appreciate all your hard work on this," and complimented you on what you were doing. That encouragement took the drudgery out of the task. In our relationships, friendly and appreciative words from our spouses give us the jolt of encouragement that we need to make it through the day.

When talking about God as our friend, the Bible says that he loves us at all times, even when we mess up. He encourages us during hardships and when we are overwhelmed, and he loves us so much that he gave his life for us. What a role model of friendship for our marriages! Let us encourage and love each other, so that we can be loyal and dependable friends and partners.

How can you encourage your spouse? What makes you feel appreciated?

Father, thank you for being the perfect example of a true friend. Help me to be my spouse's best friend, and help me to show my appreciation every day.

WHAT YOU BRING

You are a chosen race, a royal priesthood, a holy nation, God's own people, in order that you may proclaim the mighty acts of him who called you out of darkness into his marvelous light.

1 PETER 2:9 NRSV

Each person is unique. He or she approaches life in his or her own one-of-a-kind way. Sometimes we find a person who is much like us. We refer to our mates as our "soul mates." But despite those feelings, God created us as different people and our perspective on things is completely ours. Think about Matthew, Mark, Luke, and John. They all wrote about the same events. But each wrote the story a little differently and included details that were important to him.

When we marry our soul mates we bring our uniqueness to the marriage. We may have the same values, which causes our actions and reactions to situations to be similar, but always in some way with our own touch. Our uniqueness compliments the uniqueness of our mates. Together in marriage, God has created a solid team to more effectively bring his light to the world.

How are you and your spouse alike? What makes each of you unique?

Lord, thank you for what each of us brings to this marriage.

STORMY WATERS

We also glory in our sufferings, because we know that suffering produces perseverance; perseverance, character; and character, hope. And hope does not put us to shame, because God's love has been poured out into our hearts through the Holy Spirit, who has been given to us.

ROMANS 5:3-5 NIV

Wouldn't it be nice if every marriage came equipped with a plan for smooth sailing? Instead, we encounter severe storms and rough waters as we face financial difficulties, health crisis situations, and relationship struggles. These moments can strengthen us or destroy us, and our attitudes influence the outcome as we face those challenges.

By asking God what he wants us to learn from those situations, we build perseverance and character to help us in future storms. As we see God's hand in our lives and marriages, we have confidence in his will for the years ahead. And when we ride out those challenges together as a couple, our love grows.

How do we react to challenges? How can we work together as a couple when stormy times arrive?

Lord, we know there will be challenges ahead for our marriage and our home. Help us to look to you for strength and direction. Use those moments to draw us closer to each other and to you.

CHEERFUL FOUNTAINS

A joyful heart makes a cheerful face,
but when the heart is sad, the spirit is broken.
PROVERBS 15:13 NASB

Have you ever noticed how our attitudes influence our homes? If we're tired and cranky, we become irritable, and then everyone is on edge. When circumstances break our hearts, sadness enters our homes and affects how we treat each other. When spirits are low, we have the chance to encourage our sweethearts and lift them up in prayer. The Bible says that when our hearts are merry, it's as good as medicine.

When we have joy in our hearts, we can't contain the cheerfulness, and that splashes into the lives of those we love. True joy is found in Jesus. It is an unexplainable joy that lasts even when times are hard. Is your spouse sad today? Does your sweetheart have a broken spirit? Bubble into their lives as a refreshing fountain of cheer and joy.

How does it affect your relationship when you're cheerful or when you are sad? What can you do to help each other?

Father, thank you for giving us joy in all circumstances. Help us bring cheer to each other when we are sad or hurt, and let happiness abound in our home.

UNDERSTANDING

As the heavens are higher than the earth, so are my ways higher than your ways, and my thoughts than your thoughts.
ISAIAH 55:9 NKJV

Have you and your spouse ever enjoyed God's handiwork in the sky? Blue skies and puffy white clouds are gorgeous. And there's something almost magical about a full moon and thousands of bright stars spread across the dark canopy of the sky. Those are the moments that make us understand what a big God we have.

Times like those are reminders that we shouldn't limit God when it comes to the dreams on our hearts. His dreams for us are always bigger than ours. If we'll listen to and understand his sweet whispers to us and follow through on those, we can achieve things as a couple that will be beyond our wildest expectations. He's equipped us with unique skills and life experiences, and it's such a joy to see the Lord use our spouse's life in a big way for God's glory.

Have you ever thought about what a big God we have? How do we limit him by looking at our resources instead of his?

Lord, help us to understand your ways. Thank you for being such an amazing God.

COMFORT DURING STRESS

May the God of hope fill you with all joy and peace as you trust in him, so that you may overflow with hope by the power of the Holy Spirit.

ROMANS 15:13 NIV

Marriage isn't for the faint of heart. As much as Hollywood romanticizes it, choosing to live with someone "for better or for worse" isn't always easy. The biggest fights often come during times of greatest stress—building or buying a home, having a baby, a new job, job loss, or health problems, to name a few.

Sometimes, we're so consumed with our circumstances that we forget God. Instead of going to him for peace and comfort, we look to our spouse to fill that need. If our sweetheart is also overwhelmed, there might be nothing left to give. Next time life is more than you can handle, go to God.

How does your spouse like to be comforted? In what ways can you go to God together but also comfort one another?

God, help us to come to you first when the daily pressures are too much, but also show us how to best comfort each other during these times. Open our eyes to each other's needs, and let our marriage be full of peace.

CANNONBALL COMMITMENT

I plead with you to give your bodies to God because of all he has done for you. Let them be a living and holy sacrifice—the kind he will find acceptable. This is truly the way to worship him.

ROMANS 12:1 NLT

Are you a toe dipper or a cannon baller in your marriage? There's a big difference in commitment level. A toe dipper holds back, making sure the water isn't too hot or cold. A cannon baller is all in, no matter what—full commitment.

God asks us to give ourselves in marriage the same way Jesus gave himself on the cross. He offered his whole life for each of us and asks us to do the same in our relationship with him and with each other. When you are a toe dipper, it's easier to walk away when the temperature isn't right, but cannon ballers are in, hot or cold. If you are still standing beside the pool, grab your spouse's hand and take a flying leap together.

Are there areas of your relationship where you hold back? What are some things you can do to show your spouse you are fully committed?

Lord, thank you for your full commitment to each of us. Help us to be fully invested in our marriage. Thank you for the covenant you made with us the day we said, "I do."

SCRAMBLED LINES

"The words you say will either acquit you or condemn you."
MATTHEW 12:37 NLT

In war, one of the first military strategies is to take out communication lines. By scrambling the communication between troops, the strength of the whole is weakened and becomes more vulnerable to the enemy. The same is true in marriage. Communication is the key to a healthy relationship.

Satan tries to block our communication lines. Have you had a moment in an argument where your spouse thought you said something you didn't really say or mean, or vice versa? It's a communication scramble. When lines get crossed and messages don't come through the way you intend, stay calm and try your best to help your spouse understand your real intention. Remember that no one reads minds; if you want your partner to know something, you must say it.

What are some times when you thought your spouse didn't understand what you were trying to say? How can you work to stop communication scrambles in the future?

Lord, please keep the lines of communication open between us. Please help us speak what's on our minds and to not place excessive expectations on each other. Open our ears to hear each other's words. Protect our marriage from Satan's schemes.

THE GREAT NEED

I am a friend to anyone who fears you—
anyone who obeys your commandments.
PSALM 119:63 NLT

Read the creation story in Genesis 1, and you will note that after each day of creation, "God saw that it was good." But as you continue to Genesis 2, you will find something that wasn't good. God looked at Adam and said, "It is not good for the man to be alone" (Genesis 2:18). God created a helper or companion for Adam—Eve.

God knew humanity's great need for companionship. In marriage, two are united as one: a constant companion. Your spouse is a friend who laughs with you, cries with you, and challenges you to be your best. In God's ultimate wisdom, he knew we needed one another. Take time to thank God for your lifetime companion and friend today.

When is the last time you had quality time with your spouse? What are some things you can do together that you both enjoy?

Almighty Father, thank you for the gift of companionship. Draw us closer to you and to each other. Weave us together in a way that only you can, and make us stronger.

COUPLES IN A CROWD

When he saw the crowds, he had compassion on them, because they were harassed and helpless, like sheep without a shepherd.
MATTHEW 9:36 NIV

Jesus loves people. As he rode into Jerusalem for the final time, he looked at the throngs of people who followed him. He saw individuals who were hurting because of unmet needs. But he was not sent to meet every physical need on the earth. With his crucifixion, he would meet the world's greatest need—eternal life.

Marriage involves two people, and we often look beyond our spouses to the crowds. Our compassion swells for the many who are hurting. However, our greatest opportunity to show God's love and compassion is not in a crowd, but at home. God intends for us to show great compassion in our marriages.

Are you sensitive to your spouse's needs and hurts? Do you need to reach out today and bless each other with a special measure of compassion and understanding?

Lord, thank you for your example of love and compassion toward the people you love. While we extend love to all people, bless us with that love for each other.

PEDESTALS

"Render true judgments, show kindness and mercy to one another, do not oppress the widow, the fatherless, the sojourner, or the poor, and let none of you devise evil against another in your heart."
ZECHARIAH 7:8-10 ESV

During courtship, our beloved can do no wrong. We put him or her on a pedestal and don't notice any shortcomings. Once we are married, we see each other at our worst as well as our best. Sometimes, we hang on to the perfection we saw during those courting days and refuse to allow our spouses to be human and fail once in a while.

While God knows our faults, his love sees no faults and he loves unconditionally. Showing God's love to your spouse by forgiving the small things helps your relationship grow and draws you closer to each other.

Can you recall a recent event that caused conflict between you and your spouse? Could it have been the result of one of you expecting perfection?

Lord, we know none of us are perfect, only you. As we fulfill your purpose for our marriage, help us to love each other through your Spirit living within us.

DANCES AND BURDENS

You should rather turn to forgive and comfort him, or he may be overwhelmed by excessive sorrow.
2 CORINTHIANS 2:7 ESV

Marriage brings times of extreme happiness and joy, but it also sees times that require comfort and understanding. Having a spouse means you have someone sharing good and bad times. When something wonderful happens in your life, having someone to do the happy dance with is a blessing. Your love connects you in a way that makes you feel that every joy is a shared dream.

Your spouse also provides comfort. When you have a bad day and feel overwhelmed, just sharing those feelings lightens the load. Your spouse is the person in this world who loves you more than anyone else. Naturally, he or she is the person from whom you would seek comfort.

Have you recently shared an accomplishment with your spouse? Has there been a time when you needed comfort and your spouse provided it? Take time to thank each other today.

Lord, thank you that marriage provides a lifelong best friend for sharing the journey. Help us remember to turn to each other for joy and comfort.

CHOSEN IN LOVE

*Put on then, as God's chosen ones, holy and beloved,
compassionate hearts, kindness, humility, meekness, and patience.*
COLOSSIANS 3:12 ESV

Doesn't it feel good to be chosen for something? Knowing God chose you to be his child is the ultimate feeling of love. A close second is knowing that your spouse chose you. Even though the world has beauty queens, body builders, technical geniuses, and more, you rose above them all. Feeling secure in that love makes you a better person, and you develop compassion not only for your spouse, but also for those around you.

A marriage strong in chosen love gives you the foundation to look at the world through eyes that empathize and reach out to others. Your marriage is not only a safe haven; it is a springboard to sharing God's love with others.

Think for a minute about the unconditional love between you and your spouse. When was the last time you reached out to others? Was that a result of the security of your marriage?

Lord, thank you for the security of marriage. Thank you that my spouse chose me. Most of all, thank you for choosing me as your forever child.

ONE IN TROUBLE

If we have troubles, it is for your comfort and salvation, and if we have comfort, you also have comfort. This helps you to accept patiently the same sufferings we have. Our hope for you is strong, knowing that you share in our sufferings and also in the comfort we receive.

2 CORINTHIANS 1:6-7 NCV

Mary came through the door at the end of the day and rushed straight to Jason's arms. She had unexpectedly lost her job, and the rejection and despair stung. As Jason wrapped his strong arms around her and spoke comforting words, her tears subsided, and the sense of tremendous loss shifted to one of changed direction.

Sharing sorrow, rejection, and other negative emotions is an opportunity for spouses to minister to each other and lend strength in weak moments. Wedding vows often mention becoming one. Difficult times are made a little easier because you are one with your spouse and you can draw needed strength.

Can you recall a time when the oneness of your marriage made things easier, better, or more fun? Discuss that time together and thank God for his marriage design.

Lord, thank you that the marriage bond includes sharing. Keep us one as we share troubles and comfort with one another.

SOLDIERS TOGETHER

Put on every piece of God's armor so you will be able to resist the enemy in the time of evil. Then after the battle you will still be standing firm.

EPHESIANS 6:13 NLT

Husbands and wives are soldiers together in the battle of life. In war and in marriage, it's vital to have someone by our side that we can count on when things get rough. When we have each other's backs, we complete each other and become more powerful than we could be alone.

When we come to the end of our lives and look back at our marriage, let us pray that we can say, "We have been faithful soldiers, and we survived and thrived. With prayer and God's help, we protected our home and our family, and we did it together."

What can you and your spouse do to become a team? How does it affect your marriage to know that you aren't fighting the battle of life alone?

Lord, life is a battle, and spiritual warfare can defeat our homes. Bind our hearts together and help us to work together to protect our marriage.

PURE INGREDIENTS

Clothe yourselves with the Lord Jesus Christ, and do not think about how to gratify the desires of the flesh.

ROMANS 13:14 NIV

One cup of sugar, two cups of self-rising flour, two eggs, and a quarter teaspoon of chicken manure. Wait, what? It was a good recipe, until. . . you know. No one would make a cake with chicken manure, not even the smallest amount. It would spread through the batter and ruin the whole cake.

In the same way, we cannot play with the integrity of our marriage. Even a hint of pornography or improper messages with someone of the opposite sex can destroy your relationship. One small slip is all Satan needs to weasel his way into your home and family. Don't let even the smallest amount of a bad ingredient be baked into your marriage.

What rules have you established as a couple to avoid compromising situations? Are there things you do as an individual that make your spouse uncomfortable?

God, protect our marriage. Open our eyes to the tricks Satan uses in an effort to sabotage our relationship. Help us to stand firm and keep our marriage bed holy.

GOD'S RICHES

"No one can serve two masters. Either you will hate the one and love the other, or you will be devoted to the one and despise the other. You cannot serve both God and money."

MATTHEW 6:24 NIV

Finances are listed as one of the top ten reasons people get divorced. Even without confessing a dangerous love of money, often a person's life is proof enough. Whether one spouse spends too much time at work, or the other has unmet expectations of how much money is provided, the focus is money.

Money is not inherently evil, but when love for money shifts your focus from God to your wealth, priorities change. The desire to increase that wealth takes over. God owns the cattle on a thousand hills, and all of your finances belong to him. Turn discussions of money into times of praise and thanksgiving for all God has done, and he will make your marriage all the richer for it.

What are your money expectations? How can you use your money to praise God together?

Lord, thank you for your blessings. Please support our family with the finances to meet our needs. Help us to stay focused on you, not money, and show us how to give back what you have given us.

SACRIFICIAL LOVE

You adulterers! Don't you realize that friendship with the world makes you an enemy of God? I say it again: If you want to be a friend of the world, you make yourself an enemy of God.

JAMES 4:4 NLT

If it feels good, do it. The world will encourage you to put yourself above all others. How many times have you heard, "I have to do what's right for me"? But the Bible tells Christians to live differently. "Don't be selfish . . . don't look out only for your own interests, but take an interest in others too" (Philippians 2:3-4).

In marriage, it is vital to put your spouse above yourself. If one is always looking out for the needs of the other, both have all needs met. Christ gave us the perfect example when he gave himself up for the church—the ultimate act of sacrificial love. Next time your needs want to battle for first place, take a deep breath and say, "After you!"

What are some ways to show your spouse you are choosing to put him or her first?

Lord, it's not always easy to put others first. You know better than anyone. Thank you for dying on the cross and putting our needs first. Help us to follow your loving example by putting each other before ourselves.

PRICE OF WEALTH

*Better is the little of the righteous
than the abundance of many wicked.*
PSALM 37:16 NASB

Have you and your spouse ever played the comparison game? It's easy to look at other couples with their fancy homes, sleek boats and cars, and exotic vacations, and end up a little (or a lot) envious. All of us like nice things, and we enjoy the ease and freedom that money brings. But sometimes, there is a price. Extravagance can come at the cost of time with our spouse. Other times, the quest for material things comes between us and God as church and time with him slip to the wayside.

Becoming physically rich and spiritually poor isn't worth it—and when the pursuit of wealth costs us a close-knit marriage, the price is too high. A wise husband and wife will learn that true riches and contentment come from an intimate relationship with God and with each other.

Have you and your spouse talked about money and what is important to you? What are some specific, nonmaterial gifts that make you wealthy as a couple?

Lord, remind us that our true wealth is found in each other and in you. Help us to realize that our marriage is a priceless gift, and make us content with what we have.

SUPPORTING ROLE

He who heeds discipline shows the way to life,
but whoever ignores correction leads others astray.
    PROVERBS 10:17 NIV

In almost every movie about marriage, the husband or wife has a friend who gives them relationship advice. In Hollywood terms, this is the "supporting role." That's a great title, because support is exactly what they do. There is one catch. What do they support?

Do they support the marriage, or a break-up over something that can be addressed with love? Husbands and wives need friends who give wise biblical counsel. When you are frustrated with your spouse and need to vent, seek advice from those who will point you to Christ. If a non-Christian friend gives advice against God's will, it could confuse and entangle you. Choose wisely when filling the supporting roles in your life.

Who are the people you go to when you need marriage advice? What qualifies that person to give you counsel?

Jesus, give us wisdom to surround ourselves with people who love us, love you, and will support our union. Open our ears to good advice, and give us discernment to know what advice doesn't follow the guidelines in your Word.

FINDING FLAWS

"For in the same way you judge others, you will be judged, and with the measure you use, it will be measured to you."

MATTHEW 7:2 NIV

Critique and criticism are two words with the same root but very different meanings. A critique is a detailed analysis of something. But a criticism highlights the faults in people and their actions. Criticism can kill a marriage.

Two imperfect people are going to have flaws and fights. But criticizing one another doesn't solve any problems. A critical person is actually one who lacks communication skills. If you have an issue you want to address, don't attack your spouse's character. Instead, address how a particular behavior makes you feel. And if your mate comes to you with a problem, listen with an open mind. You'll both be happier for it.

Is there an area in your marriage where you feel criticized? How can you work to communicate better?

God, open our eyes to our flaws. Help us to be forgiving with each other when we make mistakes. Mend our hurts and make us stronger.

A NEW WORLDVIEW

Suppose someone comes into your church meeting wearing nice clothes and a gold ring. At the same time a poor person comes in wearing old, dirty clothes. You show special attention to the one wearing nice clothes and say, "Please, sit here in this good seat." But you say to the poor person, "Stand over there," or, "Sit on the floor by my feet." What are you doing? You are making some people more important than others, and with evil thoughts you are deciding that one person is better.

JAMES 2:2-4 NCV

Marriage joins two households and two backgrounds. You may have grown up in a family that was very open and loving, while your spouse grew up in a home that looked at others by different standards. Merging two conflicting viewpoints means establishing a new way of relating to others.

Often, the way we look at others is personality-related. Some personalities find it easier to love everyone, while others are more closed off. As you learn how to live with each other based on your backgrounds, personalities, and other factors, remember that God's love within both of you should be the filter through which you view the world.

Do you see any prejudices in your lives as a couple? What can you do to overcome them?

Lord, like all people, not all Christians see the world in the same way. Help us see others through your eyes. Bless our marriage with the best of both individual views.

SUBMIT IN LOVE

Submit to one another out of reverence for Christ.
EPHESIANS 5:21 NIV

Submit. It's a word that often causes conflict between a husband and a wife. Yielding to the power and authority of another can be a difficult lesson especially if you supported yourself before you were married. But it is biblical to submit yourself to those in authority. The Bible specifically states that wives should submit themselves to the authority of their husbands.

For some, this is a very difficult thing to do. Perhaps changing the motivation for submitting would help. Those who grapple with this concept view it as a power struggle, but being submissive to your husband or wife allows you the opportunity to show your love and to deeply bless your spouse. Basing your submission on love and reverence for Christ allows worldly submission to your mate to become an act of worship to your Lord.

How do you feel about the concept of submission? Are there times when it is difficult? Do you find joy in fulfilling the biblical directive of submitting to your spouse?

Lord, most of all, make us submissive to you, and submission to each other will follow.

60/40

Be devoted to one another in love. Honor one another above yourselves.
ROMANS 12:10 NIV

In your marriage vows, you promised to love and honor your spouse for the rest of your lives. At the altar, when you were all dressed up and excited about becoming part of a married team, that felt reasonable. Once married life began, you learned how difficult it was to love and honor someone above yourself.

Some people think marriage should be a 50/50 deal. But God-fearing couples know that, in order to have a working, faithful marriage, it must be at least 60/40. Each of you must give more to the other. Yes, there will be times when you give more than you receive, but the same is true for your spouse. Each person must be willing to give more to the marriage every day by putting the spouse before his or her desires. This brings honor to the marriage and to God.

Have you thought about the give and take of marriage? Are you willing to give whatever is needed to honor your spouse as well as God?

Lord, thank you for my spouse. Show us ways that we can serve each other today.

BLESSED BY TRUST

*His pleasure is not in the strength of the horse,
nor his delight in the legs of the warrior;
the Lord delights in those who fear him,
who put their hope in his unfailing love.*

PSALM 147:10-11 NIV

God delights in each one of us when he feels our trust in him. His delight is even greater when he sees a marriage based on his love and a family that honors him as the head of the family. By putting God first, we have a solid foundation of love for God and for each other.

When you began your union at the altar, did you promise to love and fear God? Or did you discover his unfailing love and put your trust in him after your marriage began? Either way, as you travel this marriage journey, God is blessed when he feels your trust and sees evidence of you living out that trust.

Are there areas where you need to trust God more? Do you feel your trust in God as a couple has grown since you first put your faith in him?

Lord, thank you for never failing us. Strengthen us with your love day by day, and let our trust in you be a blessing.

CELEBRATING SUCCESS

Then I was constantly at his side.
I was filled with delight day after day,
rejoicing always in his presence,
rejoicing in his whole world and delighting in mankind.
PROVERBS 8:30-31 NIV

Marriage is a joining of two lives. Every hopeful part of those two lives becomes one: dreams, desires, and goals. As you work jointly toward goals you have set, either individually or as a couple, you realize that your delight comes not only in moving closer to your own dreams, but also in celebrating the successes of your spouse. Every accomplishment achieved, every dream realized, every goal met is cause for celebration.

All of us need someone to cheer us on, and spouses often fill that role. Most people are quick to give their spouses a word of encouragement, but sometimes it stops there. It is important to express your joy in the end result of the task. Genuine delight in the accomplishments of others brings true internal and external joy.

Have you delighted in the accomplishments of your spouse? Did you share those feelings? Spend a few minutes telling your spouse of your delight.

Lord, thank you for the shared joy of delighting in each other.

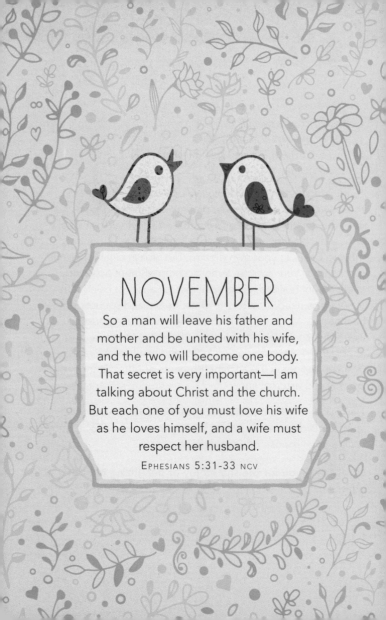

NOVEMBER

So a man will leave his father and
mother and be united with his wife,
and the two will become one body.
That secret is very important—I am
talking about Christ and the church.
But each one of you must love his wife
as he loves himself, and a wife must
respect her husband.

EPHESIANS 5:31-33 NCV

MR. & MRS. RELIABLE

He passed in front of Moses, proclaiming, "The Lord, the Lord, the compassionate and gracious God, slow to anger, abounding in love and faithfulness."

EXODUS 34:6 NIV

Reliability is an important trait for any couple. There's vast security in having someone who sticks with you. We experience perfect reliability with God, and from him we can learn qualities that will enhance our marriages. The first is compassion: caring about what touches the heart of our spouse. There is graciousness, the ability to dispense mercy when needed. A slow response to anger is another important trait that will benefit our relationships. Step back and take a deep breath when needed, but don't lash out in anger.

The final two traits that God shares with us in this verse are love and faithfulness. Those vows we took on our wedding day "to love and to cherish," and "until death do us part," were real promises. Let us also vow to always be the one our sweetheart can depend on, no matter what situation arises.

Do you feel secure in your marriage? What traits do you need to improve so that your spouse can depend on you?

Lord, I want my spouse to know that I am reliable until death. Help us to be gracious, compassionate, faithful, slow to anger, and to abound with love to each other every day.

CRUMBS AND TOOTHPASTE

"I can do nothing on my own. As I hear, I judge, and my judgment is just, because I seek not my own will but the will of him who sent me."

JOHN 5:30 ESV

One doesn't have to be married for long to realize that men and women are different. That can lead to conflict as we battle our pet peeves and our "I want it my way" mentalities. Whether it's squeezing the tube of toothpaste in the middle or leaving crumbs all over the countertop, little issues can take root in our hearts and create resentment. Sometimes, those differences are about more important issues such as our faith, families, and how we'll spend our money.

If we're wise, we'll realize that we can't fix these conflicts on our own. God, in his wisdom, can take our unique personalities and blend them together as one. When we listen to each other and seek God's will in all that we do, we are less judgmental of little differences that, once you think about them, aren't important.

How do you and your spouse handle pet peeves and differences? How can you do a better job of listening without judgment?

Father, please help us focus on what really matters in our marriage. Provide patience when needed and help us to seek your will for our home and our lives.

UNEQUALLY YOKED

Do not be yoked together with unbelievers. For what do righteousness and wickedness have in common? Or what fellowship can light have with darkness?

2 CORINTHIANS 6:14 NIV

If you are married to a non-Christian, are you doomed for divorce? It's a question many believers ask after struggling to get a non-believing spouse to understand their relationship with Christ. The short answer is no. You are not doomed. But God, in his ultimate wisdom, knows it is better when two believers unite because a marriage centered on God is a strong one.

If your spouse isn't a believer, don't give up. Draw close to the Lord in your personal relationship with him. Show Jesus through your attitude and actions. Pray for your mate to know Christ. Many people have been introduced to Jesus through their spouses; yours just might be next.

Why do you think some unequally yoked marriages don't survive? How can you ensure the survival of your blessed union?

God, please draw near to us. Help us both to know you more. If one of us doesn't understand the incredible gift of salvation, open our eyes to see your will. Make us stronger together.

CHOCOLATE OR STRAWBERRY?

There is neither Jew nor Greek, there is neither slave nor free, there is no male and female, for you are all one in Christ Jesus.
GALATIANS 3:28 ESV

You like your coffee light. She likes it dark. Broccoli is one of your favorite veggies, but he can't even handle the smell of it cooking. You love Mexican, but she could eat Chinese every day of the week. Husbands and wives are going to have differences of opinion; it's normal.

More than likely, you were drawn to those differences in your spouse because he or she had something you didn't have. But sometimes, you are distracted by how dissimilar you are. Instead of focusing on your differences, focus on traits you share—like your love for Christ. Most likely, where you have a weakness, your partner has a strength. Thank God for the way your strong and weak points work together to make you one.

What are some of the ways you and your spouse are very different? How do those differences work together to make you better?

Lord, thank you for our differences. Help us to focus on what's truly important and not get caught up in our unique traits. Use those areas to make us stronger together.

WITHOUT A RUDDER

*A man without self-control is like
a city broken into and left without walls.*

PROVERBS 25:28 ESV

When sailing a boat, one needs a sail, a rudder, and a good breeze. Imagine trying to sail to a particular destination by relying only on the wind to get there, with no way to steer. Sometimes the wind blows one way, then another, and sometimes not at all. You can't depend on it.

Trying to steer your marriage based on emotion creates the same problem. Emotion is like the wind. Sometimes you're up, sometimes down, and sometimes you're indifferent. Trying to reach a particular destination in your relationship by relying solely on emotion is nearly impossible. God is the most reliable rudder for your marriage, so let him guide you safely to shore. Don't get caught out on the water in the middle of a storm without him.

What are some areas where you struggle with allowing emotion to control you in your marriage?

Heavenly Father, please guide our relation"ship" where you would have us to go. Help us to use self-control when it comes to emotions, and to show grace to each other when we don't.

UPROOTING BITTERNESS

In your anger do not sin. Do not let the sun go down while you are still angry, and do not give the devil a foothold.
EPHESIANS 4:26-27 ESV

Most of us began our newlywed days with starry-eyed visions of future, euphoric days. Indeed, many days are full of joy, but there are also days of rip-roaring anger, where steam rises from our ears. Sometimes, it is an important problem, but often the silliest issues set us off. Anger can be deadly in a marriage if we let it take root, and we allow bitterness to set in.

God cautions us against bitterness when he tells us to patch up divisions before the sun goes down. He knows that anger festers and grows when we don't deal with it, and that allows the devil to creep into our marriages, creating discord in a holy union that God put together. The words "I'm sorry," and, "I was wrong; will you forgive me?" are sometimes hard to say, but they are invaluable in protecting and preserving our homes and marriages.

What's the best way to handle anger? Why do we have trouble forgiving our spouses when they've made us angry?

Lord, next time I get angry at my spouse, remind me to forgive just as you've forgiven me. Uproot any bitterness between us. Make our pillows uncomfortable until we've taken care of any conflict between us.

FLIERS AND BASES

Let us consider how to stir up one another to love and good works.
HEBREWS 10:24 ESV

Have you ever watched the cheerleaders at a football game? They shout, jump, scream, and dance for their teams. The most exciting cheer to watch is the human pyramid. The girl on the top usually stands on one leg and holds the other high to the gasps and cheers of watching fans. While she is pretty amazing, how did she get there? She climbed on the backs of her teammates.

Every top flier needs a base. Husbands and wives work as support systems. Sometimes you are the flier, and sometimes you are the base. When your spouse is standing with arms stretched high to achieve a dream, get down on your knees to provide support. Marriage is a team effort!

What are your God-given dreams? What can you do to encourage and support each other?

God, thank you for placing dreams in our hearts. Help us to see each other's goals and to work together to achieve them. As we work to be successful, may we always do everything for your glory.

SEMPER FIDELIS

*Only fear the Lord and serve him faithfully with all your heart.
For consider what great things he has done for you.*
1 SAMUEL 12:24 ESV

Semper Fi! or *Always Faithful!* The Marines adopted this Latin phrase, shortened from *semper fidelis,* in 1883. This branch of service is known for being tough and for leaving no man behind. You may not be a member of the armed forces, but you can adopt a motto like this for your marriage.

Being faithful means remembering you and your spouse are on the same team. Every marriage has its skirmishes, but when you are in the heat of battle, remember to be faithful. Don't bring up past mistakes and don't attack your spouse's character. Husbands and wives know each other's shortcomings. Being faithful means not preying on the weaknesses of your mate. Remember, you serve the same God and are on the same team. *Semper Fi!*

What does being faithful mean to each of you? How can you show more loyalty in the heat of a battle?

Lord, you taught us the true meaning of being faithful. You will never leave us or forsake us. Help us to treat each other the same way you treat us, and to be faithful in all things.

LIGHT IN A DARK ROOM

The unfolding of your words gives light;
it gives understanding to the simple.
PSALM 119:130 NASB

Have you and your spouse ever been in a situation where you didn't know what to do? You struggled with the decision. You agonized over it. And then a loving friend said, "Well, if you did… then all of the pieces would fall into place." And suddenly, their wise words made an impossible situation become possible.

It's much like being in a dark room during a power outage. You can't see where the furniture is or if there are things on the floor that will trip you. But when the lights come back on, you see clearly. That's what this verse depicts. When God says something to us, it's like having light come into a dark room— and it's so clear and simple that everyone can understand it. Do you and your spouse need to understand what to do in a situation? Ask God to put his spotlight on the words he has for you.

Can you think of a time when God has helped you through his Word to understand what to do in a situation? How did that cast light on the solution?

Dear Father, when we come to you in the dark places of our lives, shine the light of your Word into our hearts and give us wisdom.

NO ROOM FOR PRIDE

Love the Lord, all you his saints!
The Lord preserves the faithful
but abundantly repays the one who acts in pride.
PSALM 31:23 ESV

"No, thanks, I don't need help."

"I can do it alone. Just go away."

When we make statements like these, we let pride and self-control come between us and our partners. Declaring that you want to handle things on your own can take you down a very lonely path. Marriage doesn't have room for pride or selfishness. God gave you to each other so that you could share your problems, build each other up, and serve him together for the rest of your lives. When you allow pride, selfishness, control, and other issues to get in the way, you sacrifice the closeness God intended.

Change your self-centered, declarative statements to, "Yes, I would love your help," or, "Thank you; let's do this together." It will strengthen your marriage, please the God who created marriage, and help you grow closer to each other.

Have you recently let "me" bump the "us" out of your marriage? Do you know why? How can you and your spouse prevent this in the future?

Father, thank you for marriage. Because you brought us together, we don't ever have to struggle to do anything on our own. We are a team.

LEAVING YOUR COMFORT ZONE

As He was going along by the Sea of Galilee, He saw Simon and Andrew, the brother of Simon, casting a net in the sea; for they were fishermen. And Jesus said to them, "Follow Me, and I will make you become fishers of men." Immediately they left their nets and followed him.

MARK 1:16-18 NASB

Some of us enter marriage with the hope that we're going to set down deep roots. We crave constancy and its security, and there's nothing wrong with that. However, it usually doesn't take long for us to discover that life and marriage are full of changes. If we're going to deal well with that, we have to be flexible—especially when it comes to serving God.

Sometimes, God asks us to be flexible, perhaps to leave our comfort zones or give up a dream that we've had on our hearts. His dreams are always bigger and better, and it builds an amazing bond in a marriage when we are flexible enough to follow God as a couple.

How can you and your spouse be more flexible about serving God? Can you think of a time or two when he changed your plans? How did that affect your marriage?

Lord, we want to follow you. Help us to be flexible in allowing you to change our plans to the bigger, better ones that you have for us.

CRUNCHING ON ICE

Love is patient.

1 Corinthians 13:4 NCV

Martin and Glenda were enjoying an evening of television when Martin began crunching his ice. Crunching ice annoyed Glenda to the point of major irritation. Glenda chose to deal with Martin's ice crunching in a gentle and kind way. Instead of yelling and reminding Martin that his ice crunching made her skin crawl, Glenda simply gathered her things and headed to another room. Before she reached the door, Martin realized what was happening. "Honey, please come back," he said. "I know I am running you out of the room. I'm sorry. You are so patient; thank you."

Married love transcends the little irritations of life. It goes beyond frustration and responds to those habits with love. When we marry, we marry the whole person. The seemingly perfect man or woman we fell in love with turns out to be imperfect, as we all are. A godly spouse will focus on the positive and find ways for love to grow. That love will not be sidetracked by small, irritating distractions.

Are there little things about your spouse you find irritating? Have a good laugh about them together.

Lord, thank you that we did not let small things divert us from this wonderful union. Help us to transcend little irritations, and continue to grow our love.

COVERED WITH LOVE

*Most important of all, continue to show deep love for each other,
for love covers a multitude of sins.*
1 PETER 4:8 NLT

Sometimes husbands and wives do stupid things. We forget birthdays and anniversaries. We say thoughtless things—usually without intending to hurt our spouses, but damage is still done. We get busy and forget to express our thanks for the countless little (and not so little) tasks that our partners do for us each day. If you feel stuck in that cycle, it doesn't have to stay that way. When we truly love each other, we can make a conscious effort to become the loving husband or wife that our sweetheart deserves.

Jesus provided the perfect example of love. He delights in spending time with us. He adores us so much that he gave his life for us, and he takes joy in giving us the desires of our hearts. We can't reach the perfection of God's love, but when we go out of our way to show our love, it's amazing how that will cover a multitude of sins.

What could you do today to show your spouse the depths of your love? Ask each other about what makes you feel loved.

Father, thank you so much for your amazing gift of love. We're grateful that even when we mess up, love can smooth the way in our relationships. Show us how to love like you.

MAGIC WORDS

"Therefore what God has joined together, let no one separate."
MARK 10:9 NIV

Marriage is a sacred bond, ordained by God. It is a precious promise between a man and a woman: a lifelong vow that should be protected at all costs. But our wedding vows aren't magical words that make protection happen. We need to focus careful thought and attention on our marriages, and we need to be proactive about any negative influences that could creep in and crack our bonds. Without care, other people (including family members), outside influences, wandering eyes, and the like can impact our marriages and homes.

The God of the universe joined you and your spouse. Wedding vows aren't magic words, but your sacred union is better than magic. Shouldn't you both put forth the utmost effort to keep the world from destroying this priceless and irreplaceable gift? Work together to be a united front, keep your guard up, and work hard to keep the fire of your love burning.

What could cause division in your marriage? What steps can you take to protect your God-given relationship?

Father, thank you for uniting our lives in marriage. It is a sacred, priceless gift; help us to protect it at all costs.

A LOVE THAT ENDURES

Give thanks to the Lord, for he is good;
his love endures forever.

PSALM 118:1 NIV

Most wedding vows include some type of forever phrase, and all imply that the pledge we make to our spouses is binding. Once we commit ourselves to someone in marriage, the expectation is that we will keep our promises. God's everlasting love is a perfect promise. Once he enters our lives, we are his forever. We sin and we make mistakes, but his love for us never wavers. Thanks to Christ's sacrifice, he looks at us as if we never got off the path and loves us just the same.

Married love should be the same way. We love our spouses because they are God's gift to us. We know from the beginning that our mates are not perfect. However, we also love them with a forever love—a love that grows, forgives, and endures. In our wedding vows, we promised forever love, and with God's help, we can keep that promise.

Have you talked about the forever love that you share?
Thank each other for times when love endured difficulty.

Lord, we know we are not perfect, yet you love us unconditionally. Thank you for this enduring love. Help us to follow your example in our marriage.

THE BENEFITS OF GENEROSITY

One who is gracious to a poor man lends to the LORD,
and He will repay him for his good deed.
PROVERBS 19:17 NASB

A wise young person realizes, long before their wedding vows, that the character and qualities of a person are far more important than outward appearance. Compassion and generosity are two of the best qualities to have in a partner.

We are blessed beyond measure through the gift of Christ. Yes, we often deal with hardships, health issues, or financial problems, but we don't have to look far to see that we can bless someone else. That can be extra special when done as husband and wife. God says that when we help a poor man, it is the same as lending to God. He will repay us for the good deed. There's an extra bonus too: when we help other people together, it binds our hearts even closer.

Can you remember a time when your spouse's generosity touched you? What are small acts you can do together to help your neighbors?

Lord, you've been beyond generous to us. Give us hearts that are touched by the needs of others and help us serve you together.

TRUSTING TOGETHER

Those who know the LORD trust him,
because he will not leave those who come to him.
PSALM 9:10 NCV

Every couple faces challenges. They may be about our health, jobs, or relationships. Some problems are financial; some of our dilemmas are caused by time or the lack of it. Our biggest problem when we face life's challenges is that we think we need to solve them on our own. You are a team that God has joined together. Together you face times of trouble. And together you can support each other and pray together.

The Lord has promised not to abandon those who seek him. In prayer, you may receive revelations that will help overcome obstacles, or you may not obtain the solution you seek. Healing may not be the answer, a new job may or may not appear, but rest in the knowledge that the Lord knows you, loves you, and has your best at heart. Trusting God together will strengthen your faith.

Do you go to God together in prayer when facing life's obstacles? What is the biggest challenge each of you face right now? Can you trust the Lord to handle problems?

Father in heaven, sometimes life is so hard. Our difficulties are overwhelming and it's hard to see the way out. Please help us to trust. Thank you for loving us.

A WORTHY PRINCIPLE

Each of you should give what you have decided in your heart to give. You shouldn't give if you don't want to. You shouldn't give because you are forced to. God loves a cheerful giver.

2 CORINTHIANS 9:7 NIRV

Tom and Heather were just out of their teens when they married. Money was tight, their rented house was in a shabby part of town, and they both had minimum-wage jobs. Mostly they lived on love. Some months it was touch-and-go with paying the bills, but they decided to adhere to the biblical principal of tithing. Each paycheck they calculated the ten percent they would put in the collection plate.

Fast forward twelve years to find them with two lovely children and a newly purchased house. Heather was a stay-at-home mom, and Tom now held a good position in a local company with a promotion looming. Looking at their finances, they realized they weren't tithing any longer. That figure seemed so much larger than when they first started out. They weren't sure they could afford to give that much. They had bills to pay! After talking it out, Tom and Heather decided to start tithing again. It was hard at first. They had to cut back. But tithing meant they were part of helping the hungry, seeing to the needs of the community, and supporting missionaries. They saw how that was much more deserving of their money.

Have you decided what you will give? Are you deliberate about it? Can you call yourselves cheerful givers?

Lord, you have given us so much in addition to your love. Help us to be grateful. Put in our hearts a happiness to give back to you a portion of the abundance you have given us.

SHARING DIFFICULTIES

May the righteous be glad and rejoice before God;
may they be happy and joyful.

PSALM 68:3 NIV

We all have grumpy moods. Things get on our nerves or don't go our way and everyone around us knows to watch out. We might be sick, worried, or just plain bored with our life. Life in the Spirit is meant to be so much more—rich, full, free from petty arguments and disagreements. One of the things you can do in your marriage is build up your spouse when you see them struggling. You are a team. When one is having trouble, the other can hold them up.

In the midst of trials, you may not feel like rejoicing. You are not glad for your situation. But one interesting promise that God has made us is that we can be happy in him. Choosing to praise the Lord in all circumstances will bring about a glad and happy spirit. Rejoicing in all the Lord has done for you can lift the burden of depressive situations in front of us. Share your burdens and face your difficulties together.

Can you go to your spouse when they are feeling down? Do you see yourself offering help and prayer in heavy situations? Can you count on each other in times of need, or do you keep everything to yourself?

Father God, we want to rejoice in you but sometimes we fail. Remind us of your blessings in our lives. Help us to lean on each other in times of trouble.

TOP NEEDS

I am jealous for you with the jealousy of God himself. I promised you as a pure bride to one husband—Christ.
2 CORINTHIANS 11:2 NLT

Remember back to when the two of you were in that euphoric season of falling in love? Nothing was too good for your sweetheart. You would go out of your way to show your love. It might have been love notes, long walks, favorite meals, or treats. When was the last time you made an effort to make your husband or wife feel special?

Studies have shown that the top needs for men and women are different. Women need affection, conversation, and honesty. Men need sexual fulfillment, recreational companionship, and domestic support. Understanding what your partner needs is the first step in meeting those needs. A solid, mature marriage depends on each person feeling cherished by the other. Show love to your sweetheart in ways they can understand.

Do you show your love for your husband or wife? Have you ever asked them if you meet their needs? Do you feel secure in your marriage?

Lord, help us to love one another with a pure love. We want our love to deepen and grow. Keep uncertainty from our relationship. Thank you for joining us together.

ACCEPTABLE WORDS

*Let the words of my mouth and the meditation of my heart
be acceptable to you,
O Lord, my rock and my redeemer.*
PSALM 19:14 ESV

Sometimes it seems that the only safe place is home. Outside the warm circle of marriage we can be bombarded by verbal abuse, disrespect, put-downs, and blasphemy. Speak joy and life into your spouse, don't tear them down when you talk to them. Purpose to build them up with your words. It has been proven that respect, courtesy, and loving encouragement from one's husband or wife will have a marked change for the better in the relationship.

God wants your marriage to be strengthened. The words we speak have consequences. Do we purpose to build our loved one up, or do we shame them with rudeness and contempt? An interesting thing happens when we praise our spouse whether they deserve it or not: our hearts change for the better!

Do we speak with love and compassion to each other? Do we let irritations show with put downs and derision? Can we agree to speak purposefully to each other with love?

Dear Jesus, help us to speak with love to each other. We desire to build each other up and to be encouraging. Thank you for bringing us closer each day.

CULTIVATE THANKFULNESS

Be thankful in all circumstances, for this is God's will for you who belong to Christ Jesus.
1 Thessalonians 5:18 NLT

We must read this verse carefully. "This is God's will for you" does not refer to all of life's circumstances, but to the important attitude we must cultivate in all circumstances: thankfulness. Being thankful is a heart issue, not a circumstantial one. We can't always change our circumstances, but we can always choose to be thankful to God.

Are you unhappy with where you are in life? Dissatisfied with your job? Stressed by an unfair boss? Tired of making one more meal, changing one more diaper? Cultivating a habit of being thankful in, not for, all things is liberating. A thankful heart is not a prisoner to life's curve balls. As the apostle Paul says, you belong to Christ Jesus, and we can always be thankful in that assurance.

What can you be thankful for today? Make a list with your spouse.

Dear Jesus, we have not always been thankful in all circumstances, but we want that to change. Help us to be thankful today, all day, in spite of difficulty, simply because we belong to you. Absolutely nothing compares to that!

GIVING UP BEING RIGHT

Do everything without complaining and arguing, so that no one can criticize you. Live clean, innocent lives as children of God, shining like bright lights in a world full of crooked and perverse people.

PHILIPPIANS 2:14-15 NLT

The challenge to being a good witness is often giving up our right to be right. We want to show Christ's way of life to a lost world. When we sit in darkness and someone lights a match in a corner, our vision is drawn to it. In the same way, you can shine in darkness with a calm demeanor and composure in the midst of an intense or trying moment. Your opponent might think, "What does that person have that I don't?"

We are citizens in God's kingdom when we draw others to the light of Jesus. It only takes a moment to put water on a small flame, extinguishing it before it becomes an uncontrollable inferno. In the same way, we can extinguish quarrels by letting go and remaining calm.

Do you struggle to let go of your right to win an argument? Will you ask the Lord to help you in this area? Brainstorm together the ways to extinguish arguments early.

Lord, help us to be kind and restrained in the heat of the moment. Help us answer accusations with love and turn the environment upside down. Let us become more like you each day.

OFFERING THE OLIVE BRANCH

*How good and pleasant it is
when God's people live together in unity!*
PSALM 133:1 NIV

An hour into your visit, you realize you haven't heard a sound from the children. "Uh oh! We better go take a look!" You rush into the other room, only to find them intent on a focused board game. What a pleasant surprise!

The neighbor, who misunderstood your intentions at the PTA meeting last week, now avoids looking at you in the grocery store. You decide to extend an olive branch and grab ingredients for homemade brownies. Later, you deliver the brownies to their door, along with a note of apology for something you know you didn't do. The neighbor may accept the gift well, or not. Regardless, you have done your part in opening the door, and making restoration in your relationship. Unity with acquaintances, friends, and family takes work, patience, and a good dose of God's grace, but what a reward it is!

Do you enjoy the pleasantries of life with God's people? Can you think of a time you offered an olive branch or when someone offered one to you?

Father, when we're tempted to lash out or promote ourselves, give us your grace and strength to offer peace.

TIMES OF SEPARATION

Remembering your tears, I long to see you so that I may be filled with joy.

2 TIMOTHY 1:4 HCSB

Have you and your spouse ever been separated for a while by circumstances? Perhaps it was a work trip, or one of you needed to travel to help a relative. Whatever the situation was, you may have felt uneasy with the parting. There was a longing to be together, a feeling of incompletion. It's like you were missing a limb—an integral part of yourself.

When you married, God joined you from two people into one. It's a mystery, but a wonderful one! It is easy to drift apart during times of separation. Try to keep communication open: call or text often. If the parted time is extended, send a card or letter. Share updates with your spouse. Perhaps you could Skype or Face Time. Think about what a joyful day it will be when you are united, and celebrate your reunion when it comes.

Are you good at keeping in touch with your spouse when you are apart? Can you try to keep each other informed about how you feel and what you experience? Do you have a plan for supporting each other in times of separation?

Lord, when we are apart, help us to stay in touch with each other. Don't let a parting create emptiness between us. Remind us to treat each other with affection, and keep our love fresh and alive.

GLAD FOR TODAY

This is the day that the Lord has made;
let us rejoice and be glad in it.
PSALM 118:24 ESV

We celebrate birthdays and anniversaries with special plans involving favorite foods, activities, and the like. To mark the day sometimes gifts or cards are exchanged. What about celebrating *today* as if it were a gift? Well, it is!

When we marry, we assume that we will have many, many years together, but this is not always the case. Some of us may be called home sooner than expected. Learn to celebrate together each day. Rejoice in your oneness. Surprise one another occasionally with a card or special meal. Make memories together. Enjoy the journey that is marriage. Be glad for today!

Are you aware of each day as it passes? Do you take your spouse for granted? Can you surprise one another with special plans once in a while?

Father in heaven, help us to enjoy each day you give us. Allow us to appreciate each other and find new ways to show our love. We want to rejoice in you.

THE MAGIC WORDS

How can we thank God enough for you in return for all the joy we have in the presence of our God because of you?

1 Thessalonians 3:9 NIV

Do you use the words *please* and *thank you* when talking to each other? Don't assume your husband or wife knows that you are grateful for the things they do for you—tell them! Make it a habit to use these simple and polite words in your conversations with each other. We teach the "magic" words to our children at an early age, but somehow when talking to the most important person in the world to us, we drop them.

Gratitude and politeness expressed to each other goes a long way. It doesn't matter if your spouse takes out the garbage all the time, they will still appreciate a simple thank you. As you get up from the table, be sure to say *thank you* for the meal. It might have been hot dogs, but your partner took the time to make it for you. Sharing gratitude shows respect for your spouse's time and efforts.

Can you endeavor to show respect to each other by saying "please" and "thank you"? Will you make it a habit? Can you do this without keeping score?

Lord, showing gratitude and respect for each other is such a small thing we often forget to do. Help us remember to do this. Make us appreciative for all we do for each other. Please help us to pay attention to all the things you do for us.

HIS FAITHFULNESS

As for me, I shall sing of your strength;
Yes, I shall joyfully sing of your lovingkindness in the morning,
for you have been my stronghold and a refuge in the day of my
distress.

PSALM 59:16 NASB

Bill and Kathy had been struggling for months. Both of them had lost their jobs. They'd sent out resume after resume without success. Meals had consisted of whatever they could buy cheapest at the grocery store. They'd stretched their pennies until there were very few pennies left. And, yes, there were days when they wondered if they'd be homeless, if they'd make it through this hard time.

But something else happened as the days stretched out through their trial. They experienced God's provision as bags of food unexpectedly showed up on their doorstep and their bills were miraculously paid. Their faith and their prayer life together had been enhanced as they saw firsthand how God had been their refuge and their strength. They learned to worship him in the valley. And when Thanksgiving Day rolled around—even though only one of them had received a job offer—they were able to sing, "Great is Thy Faithfulness" with heartfelt thanks for a God who had given lovingkindness every morning and who'd provided all that they needed.

Are you experiencing financial challenges? What are you being taught through this?

Father, help us to worship you in good times and in bad. Thank you for being our stronghold.

BLESSING OF HOSPITALITY

Whenever we have the opportunity, we should do good to everyone—especially to those in the family of faith.
GALATIANS 6:10 NLT

Your neighbor has a plumbing problem and you don't know which end of a screw driver to hold. You probably can't help much there. But while they wait for the plumbing to be fixed, you could invite them over for a meal or let them use your shower. Look for opportunities to be of help when you can. Listen to those around you. We tend to live in our own private bubbles. When you start up a friendship with another couple, you have a chance to model Christ in your lives. Show them the love of God through kindness.

Don't know your neighbors? Plan a block party for the 4th of July. Go mow your lawn when the neighbor is mowing theirs. Offer the elderly couple across the street a loaf of homemade bread. Give away some tomatoes from your garden. Go Christmas caroling. There are so many ways to show kindness. Let it become second nature.

How can you get to know your neighbors? Do you know which ones are believers? Is your house known for hospitality?

Dear Lord, help us step out of our comfort zones and get to know the people around us. Give us wisdom to discern the needs of our neighbors. Give us the blessing of hospitality.

SHOWING MERCY

Whoever has the world's goods, and sees his brother in need and closes his heart against him, how does the love of God abide in him? Little children, let us not love with word or with tongue, but in deed and truth.

1 John 3:17-18 NASB

Nearly every day we hear about hungry children, abused women, and countries ravaged by war. Our neighborhoods are full of needs: an elderly widow can't take care of her yard, the people across the street have a daughter with cerebral palsy, your sister just had a baby. God's love in us gives us empathy for those in need.

What can you do as a couple to show compassion to the needs around you? You can use these opportunities to spend time together! Volunteer to do a neighbor's yard work, cook a meal for the neighbors, discuss and decide on a monetary donation you can make for a non-profit organization. When you work as a team you not only accomplish more, but you share experiences and concerns. You and the recipients of your kindness will be blessed.

How can you show mercy to those around you? Can you think of ways the two of you can help? How can working together also benefit you as a couple?

Jesus, help us to be sensitive to the needs around us. We have been blessed by you and desire to share ourselves and our resources. Make our hearts tender to help others.

DECEMBER

Oh come, let us sing to the Lord;
let us make a joyful noise to the
rock of our salvation! Let us come
into his presence with thanksgiving;
let us make a joyful noise to him
with songs of praise!

PSALM 95:1-2 ESV

FORBEARANCE

Love... always trusts, always hopes.
1 Corinthians 13:7 NCV

Are they ever going to learn? How many times do we need go over this? Every family deals with such questions. Spouses want to believe the best of their partners, but waiting to see it happen can try their patience. Unconditional love is a learned quality. It develops as we please the Lord and acknowledge our need for his love. His love is the key to forbearance. In our old nature, we cannot love each other without conditions and stipulations.

When we become frustrated and impatient, we must continually remind ourselves that the source of patience lives in us. Think of how God's forbearance, tolerance, and unbelievable love is expressed to us, through Christ and our daily lives.

Have you ever been late, or kept someone waiting? Have you struggled to overcome an annoying habit? How can you remind yourself of God's patience in your life?

Lord, thank you for your patience with us. Forgive us for not being patient with others. Thank you for continuing to bear with us, and by your grace and mercy, help us extend those to others.

BLESSED THROUGH RESPECT

"Honor your father and mother. Love your neighbor as yourself."
MATTHEW 19:19 NLT

Perhaps you are out with the guys, and they start talking unkindly about their wives or making comments about other women. Maybe girls' night turns into complaint night. Respect doesn't only apply when you are with your spouse. It means representing and protecting your spouse even when you are with others. Your neighbors, coworkers, and friends are watching. Your children need to see you respect each other, so they respect you and their future spouses.

Speak kindly, encourage, and value each other. Let your spouse know how important he or she is to you. This will bless your spouse, your relationship, and your home, and it will honor the Lord.

Why is respect so important in a relationship? If you are in a situation like the ones above, what can you do to honor and respect your spouse? What are ways you can show respect for each other this week?

Lord, give us hearts that want to respect each other. When situations can take us down the wrong path, put a check in our spirit, so we do not disrespect one another. Remind us that we not only represent our spouse, but also you.

THE TEAM ON THE FIELD

We are both God's workers. And you are God's field, God's building.
1 Corinthians 3:9 ESV

It is easy to focus on personal needs and wants rather than the needs and dreams of others. However, marriage is a team sport, and a team player is willing to serve others and help them fulfill their potential.

What an honor and responsibility to live what we believe in ordinary, daily tasks. We are the team on the field, living out our Christian marriage before a watching world that is desperate to see authentic love that gives and serves. That love is only possible when we love and honor our Servant King and allow him to live through us.

In your marriage, are you on the same team when conflict arises? Are you serving one another in such a way that your children, family, and friends sit up and take notice? Have you ever tried to out-serve one another? Give it a try today.

Lord, it is so easy to think of ourselves and our personal needs first, but you came to serve, not to be served. Give us that attitude as we choose to love and honor you and each other.

CONSULTING THE LORD

Trust in the Lord with all your heart
and do not lean on your own understanding.
PROVERBS 3:5 NASB

Thinking about the future is exciting and terrifying. Many wonderful possibilities lie ahead, but many unknowns do too. When we seek the Lord's direction in daily decisions, not just big ones, we learn how to trust him.

How wonderful to know that the creator of the universe delights in unfolding his plans for us! Let us acknowledge his lordship in our lives and consult him in all events.

What big decisions do you need to spend less time worrying about and more time trusting the Lord? Remind each other of the Lord's faithfulness in past decisions as a way of encouraging one another about the future.

Lord, we want to include you in all of our decisions. Forgive us for forgetting to bring everything to you. You have been faithful to us in the past, and we know that we can trust you with our future.

SLEEP ON IT

> *Don't sin by letting anger control you.*
> *Think about it overnight and remain silent.*
> PSALM 4:4 NLT

Wise husbands and wives learn to think before speaking in the heat of a disagreement. We can prevent many wounds if we remember that the Lord is present and listening. Sharp words hurt and break not just your spouse's heart but the Lord's heart as well.

If we can agree that it would be better to table the discussion and sleep on it, we may find that the problem looks different in morning's light. By being quiet for a time, we avoid saying things that we may regret, and it gives the Lord opportunity to speak to us about the situation.

How would some past conflicts look different if you had been quiet overnight? Are you able to look back and laugh at quarrels that seemed important at the time? Talk about how you can help each other process anger.

Lord, you know that conflict can bring anger. Help us to remember that we don't want to break your heart or each other's by giving in to sin. Help us quiet our thoughts and emotions and seek your face.

COMPLEMENTARY

We are God's handiwork, created in Christ Jesus to do good works,
which God prepared in advance for us to do.
EPHESIANS 2:10 NIV

You liked the same food, the same movies, the same music. The list went on and on. You could talk for hours. At least, that's how it was when you were dating. Now, differences seem to have multiplied. How can two people who love each other so much be so different?

You are different because God created you that way. The challenge is to live and love in a way that allows for the uniqueness of each person as you walk in harmony. The Lord has a plan for each life, and when you walk in his ways, your lives complement each other and bring him great glory.

How can you complement your differences in practical ways? What has God called you to do currently that is allowing your unique walk with the Lord to bless your spouse and others?

Lord, sometimes our uniqueness is a problem, and we try to change each other. You knew exactly what you were doing when you created each of us and brought us together. Grant us obedient and willing hearts, and let us help each other fulfill our potential for you and your glory.

HOLDING THE MIRROR

Better is open rebuke than love that is concealed.
Faithful are the wounds of a friend,
but deceitful are the kisses of an enemy.
PROVERBS 27:5-6 NASB

Did you ever get home from an event only to find that you had something sticking to a tooth or a zipper partially undone? Why didn't somebody tell me? We long for friends that will save us from embarrassment, and often that friend is a spouse.

A real friend goes deeper than superficial appearance issues. We need spouses who will gently hold up the mirror so that we can see our weaknesses, poor habits, and spiritual blind spots. This kind of communication takes skill and time, and both partners must agree to give and take with a gracious spirit, wanting the best for each other.

Can you help each other see a fault without hurt feelings or defensiveness? Begin by confessing a problematic "log in your own eye" before addressing a "speck" in your spouse's eye.

Lord, we want to be the friends that can hold the mirror for each other. Help us gently address problem areas without hurting one another.

TEAM HUDDLE

*Let us aim for harmony in the church and try to build
each other up.*
ROMANS 14:19 NLT

Watch any sports event, and you'll see the team in a
huddle reviewing the game plan. At the end of the huddle,
there is usually a cheer. There is a sense of purpose,
camaraderie, and excitement about working toward a
common goal. Throughout the game there are some rough
spots, but there are many times of accomplishment celebrated
by the entire team.

You and your spouse are a team. There are plenty of
huddles (and hopefully cuddles) to discuss your life's strategy.
Being a team adds to the sense of family unity. You can discuss
differences of opinion but the outcome will be what is best
for the family team. Being part of that makes you feel like you
belong and are one. Three cheers for your family team today!

*Do you have a strong family team strategy or do you need
to work on that?*

Lord, we want you to be head of our family team. Show us
the best plan and guide us to implement that plan without
faltering.

CHORAL METHODS

Live in harmony with each other.
ROMANS 12:16 NLT

For a choir to sound its best, all must sing their parts and make every effort to blend their voices. One person being too loud, off key, or out of tempo warps the resulting sound. Everyone must be open to correction and change. With so many chances for mistakes, why not just sing alone? With hard work, a choir creates beauty. No one can create the richness and depth of a choir on their own.

Our lives can also be richer and fuller when we learn to cooperate with each other and reach out to others. We can choose to be hardheaded and unreachable, or we can hold our opinions with an open hand and consider different ways of looking at the world. Harmony in relationships happens more easily when we understand that we don't always have the answers or get our own way.

How are you stretching yourselves to include different kinds of people in your lives? Are you living in harmony enough with each other to be able to offer yourselves to those in need?

Lord, in your wisdom you created unique people to inhabit your world. Give us your sight to view ourselves, each other, and the people around us with grace and compassion.

REFRESHING WATER

With joy you will drink deeply from the fountain of salvation.
PSALM 12:3 NLT

Can you remember a day of yard work or outdoor games when you forgot to take a drink along? Can you also remember the sensation of having that thirst satisfied with a tall, cold glass of water? What a relief to feel your body rehydrate.

Daily life, with its cares and responsibilities, can drain the joy and happiness out of us. As believers, we have refreshment that the world doesn't have or understand. Christ provides all that we need for life in himself. He is our shepherd, redeemer, counselor, rock, fortress, righteousness, light, peace, wisdom… the list goes on. When we come in out of the heat and pressures of life and drink deeply by spending time with our Savior, we find the refreshment we need.

Have you developed an individual quiet time and place to be with the Lord so that you can be refreshed? Do you also have worship time together?

Lord, when it's all said and done, and everything is stripped away, what really matters is you. Help us to enjoy you and your presence and to experience you in deep and meaningful ways both individually and together.

GOD FROM ETERNITY

"No one can undo what I have done."
ISAIAH 43:13 NLT

Try to think of a metaphorical comparison for this verse. For example, if someone squeezes the toothpaste out of the tube, who can effectively put it back? Is anyone more powerful than God? Scripture says there was no god formed before him, and there will be none after him. Apart from him there is no savior. God is God, and we are not. Therefore, we must come under his authority.

We have two options. We either choose to believe, or not. There are no other choices. If we choose to believe, then we should commit to that choice. Religions outside of Christianity require work for salvation, but for Christians, this means Jesus died in vain. Christianity requires simple acceptance of what God, through his Son, Jesus, accomplished on the cross. As for works? We offer them to honor him.

Do you believe that God is from eternity, and that he has the ultimate last word in your life? Will you step willingly under God's sovereign authority? Talk with your spouse about what you struggle to give to God, be they gifts or worries.

Father God, we believe in you as sovereign, creator and authority in every area in our lives. We accept your good authority over us, and rest in your goodness and provision.

ROOTED IN CHRIST

Blessed is the man who trusts in the LORD,
and whose hope is the LORD.
For he shall be like a tree planted by the waters,
which spreads out its roots by the river,
and will not fear when heat comes;
But its leaf will be green, and will not be anxious
in the year of drought,
nor will cease from yielding fruit.

JEREMIAH 17:7-8 NKJV

When you were little and everything seemed right with the world, trust was easy. As you grew, times became much more confusing. We all have fond memories of the early days of marriage when young love flourished. Later, debates and differences ensued, and you wondered if this marriage was a mistake. It didn't help when it seemed there were more bills at the end of the day than money in the bank, more chores than hands, or more harsh words than kind ones.

Perhaps you wonder if God is still the God you thought he was. Through pain and discouragement, you continue to grow when you are rooted in Christ. Be supporting branches for each other, and dig into God's Word and promises together.

Does fear creep in at uncertain times? When the winds of life blow, are your roots deep enough to keep you to keep you grounded? Talk with each other about your fears.

Lord, when life gets hard, our trust in you can be shaken. Today, we choose life, to trust in you and not be anxious. Help our marriage and spiritual roots to grow deep, and flourish for your glory.

EVERLASTING AND UNFAILING

"I have loved you with an everlasting love;
I have drawn you with unfailing kindness."
JEREMIAH 31:3 NIV

In this verse, God is speaking to the children of Israel, calling them back from captivity under the Egyptians. His love and kindness gave them the choice to serve him, or not. We often see our lives in comparison to the children of Israel.

When life grows dark, and we see the evidences of our sin, God is calling out to us. His kindness leads us to repentance. He wants the very best for us. To be at peace within our own soul and with our maker, no matter our circumstances, is a great gift. When we take time to understand what *everlasting* means, and then add his love to the equation, we are blown away by his generosity.

Do you ever ask, "Who am I, that God should love me eternally?" Can you believe that he is drawing you with unshakable kindness? What evidence is there of that love in your life?

Father, thank you for always pursuing us with generous kindness. Help us wrap our minds around the truth of your eternal love and your plans for our lives.

POURING SALT IN A WOUND

It is time to forgive and comfort him. Otherwise he may be overcome by discouragement.

2 Corinthians 2:7 ESV

In this letter to the church of Corinth, Paul instructs that the reprimand for a grievance shouldn't be too severe. Kicking someone when they are down is dirty fighting, bordering on revenge. Pouring salt in a wound doesn't help anyone.

Those who play judge and jury are struggling to take the place of God. Instead, we need to turn, forgive, and comfort. When we continue to add insult to injury, we misrepresent who God is. The other person becomes overwhelmed, traumatized by the excessive chastisement. God gave us the power to forgive each other; use that gift to his glory.

Do you find yourself wanting to hurt each other by handing out more punishment than the sin required? If either of you needs forgiveness, seek and give it now.

Lord, please help us treat others the way we want to be treated—with fairness and grace. Help us to ask forgiveness from those we've hurt. We ask your forgiveness for hurting others in our zeal for righteousness.

SHARPENING IRON

Iron sharpens iron, so one man sharpens another.
PROVERBS 27:17 NASB

Most of us have a true desire to serve God, but it's easy to slip along the way, to lose sight of our goal to live for him. That's where having a spouse who also loves God is such a huge gift—because you can help each other with encouragement, accountability, and a commitment to work together to become who God wants you to be.

If we aren't where we need to be spiritually, we can be a deterrent to our spouses instead of a blessing. We can't help sharpen someone else if we haven't worked to become sharp ourselves. When iron sharpens iron, there has to be the touch of someone's hands for the sharpening process. That's where God comes in, and a wise couple will say, "Lord, sharpen us so that we can help sharpen each other."

How can you help sharpen each other? Are you where you need to be spiritually?

Dear Father, we don't want to be halfhearted Christians. Help us work together as a team to encourage each other in our faith and to keep one another accountable.

PRAYER OF BLESSING

He took them in His arms and began blessing them, laying His hands on them.

MARK 10:16 NASB

Mary's pastor was at the end of a terminal illness. He'd been like a dad to her for many years, loving her, praying for her, and giving wise counsel. During Mary's last visit to his home before his death, he pulled Mary close for a hug, and then he laid his hand on her head and prayed a prayer of blessing over her, asking God to keep her and her husband's faith strong and flourishing. He asked for God's touch on her life and supply an abundance of blessings through the years. That tender moment made Mary feel so loved.

What if we did that as husbands and wives? What if we gathered our sweethearts close to our hearts and prayed for them, asking God to bless every area of their lives? Today would be a good time for the two of you to sit down and make a list of ways you want God to bless your spouse.

How would you like for God to bless your spouse? How do you think it will impact him or her to experience your prayer of blessing?

Lord, help me to dispense blessings instead of hurt or heartaches. Bless our home and bind our hearts together in tenderness.

PLACE OF PEACE

*"And you, my child, will be called a prophet of the Most High;
for you will go on before the Lord to prepare the way for him,
because of the tender mercy of our God, by which the rising sun
will come to us from heaven."*
LUKE 1:76, 78 NIV

Wade had a hard day at work. On the way home, he had
a flat tire and it seemed everywhere he turned there was
another problem. But as he walked across the driveway and
into the house, he knew his day was about to change. Heather
would have the house straight, a home-cooked meal on the
table, and she'd be ready with a hug and kiss. Home was his
haven and he could count on that.

Every marriage has calm places. Recognizing how to help
your mate feel peaceful is a tremendous gift. God has done
that for all of us. When we arrive in heaven, we will find a place
of peace that has been prepared in advance. We don't know
exactly what it will be like, but from the Biblical description it is
definitely going to be worth the wait!

*What and where is your sweet place of peace? How can
you create that for your mate?*

**Lord, thank you for the gift of each other. Show us how we
can honor one another each day.**

UNLIMITED FORGIVENESS

"He arose and came to his father. But when he was still a great way off, his father saw him and had compassion, and ran and fell on his neck and kissed him."

LUKE 15:20 NKJV

As much as we don't want to do it, all of us mess up from time to time. When that happens, we usually hurt the one we love, sometimes causing extreme damage to our relationship in the process. When you're the one who has been hurt, that can be hard. You know that God says to forgive, but how are you supposed to do that? The story of the prodigal son gives us some good guidelines. The son had it great at home and his father loved him. But he broke his father's heart when he left, and he suffered horrible consequences as a result of his rebellion. He hit bottom.

But you know what? When the prodigal came to his senses and returned home, his father didn't meet him with, "You hurt me! How could you do that?" He ran to him, grabbing him in his arms, and hugging him with tenderness. What if we loved each other like that? What if we forgave like that?

Do you have a hard time forgiving your spouse? How can you learn to forgive like God does?

Lord, give us hearts that are tender. Help us to forgive our spouses like you forgive us.

GENTLE RAIN

Let my teaching fall on you like rain; let my speech settle like dew. Let my words fall like rain on tender grass, like gentle showers on young plants.

DEUTERONOMY 32:2 NLT

Have you ever lived in an area that experienced drought? The dirt is so dry it cracks. The grass is brown and the flowers curl up as if hiding from the heat and sun. It is difficult to plant anything because the soil is so hard. Rain is much-anticipated, but if it comes down in fast torrents, it runs off instead of soaking into the dirt where it is needed. The best scenario always arrives when a gentle rain comes that soaks into the ground slowly.

That's how God wants his words to fall into our souls and marriages. Like the gentle rain that leaves behind tender soil and plants, his words can refresh our hearts, providing wisdom, warnings when necessary, inspiration, and encouragement. Let's not have hard hearts when God wants to speak with us; let's be like the tender grass and young plants that soak up every drop.

Is your heart tender toward God? Do you and your spouse desire the refreshing rain of God's presence in your home?

Lord, let your words fall on us like rain on tender grass. Let us soak up each one of them and let them refresh our souls.

370

FIXED THOUGHTS

Fix your thoughts on what is true, and honorable, and right, and pure, and lovely, and admirable. Think about things that are excellent and worthy of praise.

PHILIPPIANS 4:8 NLT

Temptation is a real enemy of our marriages and it can have a devastating effect on our homes. Whether it's a glance at someone who isn't our spouse, hours on Internet sites where our eyes shouldn't be, or temptations with gambling, alcohol, or some other substance, those moments leave us vulnerable and can cause severe damage to our relationships.

That's where we need to be proactive as couples, where we need to set up areas of accountability. Let's determine that we will "fix our thoughts on what is true, and honorable, and right, and pure, and lovely, and admirable" as it says in this verse. If our attention is captured by those things, we won't have time or the inclination to stray into areas that could harm our precious relationship with each other.

Have you struggled with temptation? How can you help each other with that?

Lord, help us to keep our eyes fixed firmly on you. Keep us from temptations that will harm our marriage.

IMPORTANT INSTRUCTIONS

All Scripture is given by inspiration of God, and is profitable for doctrine, for reproof, for correction, for instruction in righteousness.
2 Timothy 3:16 NKJV

Henry and his buddy took on the project of putting his new grill together. They tossed the instructions back in the box as Henry said, "We don't need that!" Several hours later, the grill was assembled—well, other than the three pieces that were left over. Three evidently important pieces, since the grill wouldn't work. After several attempts to fix it, they did something unusual, they read the directions. And they discovered that the leftover pieces should have been installed at the beginning.

We laugh at those two guys, but don't we do the same things spiritually? The instructions (God's Word) are just sitting there waiting for us to get the directions that we need for our lives. Let's not have to go back and fix things in our marriage that could have been avoided if we'd just read God's instructions and followed them to begin with.

Can you remember a time when you didn't follow God's instructions? What were the implications and how can you do better in the future?

Dear Lord, help us to always read and follow the instructions in your Word. Don't let us mess up because we didn't read them.

HIDDEN WORD

Your word I have hidden in my heart,
that I might not sin against you.
PSALM 119:11 NKJV

Michael had been struggling for several weeks. His company had hired a new receptionist, Mandy: a stunning young brunette. Michael loved his wife and he'd meant his wedding vows, his pledge to love only her. But just a few days after she was hired, Mandy started coming on to Michael, flirting and making excuses to call him or to bring things to his office. Days turned into weeks, and Michael was starting to think about yielding to the temptation. But just as Mandy sashayed into his office one morning, the verse from 1 Corinthians 10:13 about God helping us escape from temptation came to mind. Conviction immediately slammed into Michael's soul—conviction brought by a verse that he had learned as a child. Truth that had been hidden in his heart until he needed it. That afternoon, he changed his course.

It would benefit us as husbands and wives to hide God's Word in our hearts. Those precious truths will serve as safeguards for our homes and our marriages in coming years.

Can you remember a time when a Bible verse arrived in
your memory just as it was needed? Start learning some
new verses together.

Father, please keep us from sinning against you and each
other. When tempted, convict us through your Word.

A SWEET GIFT

*"But I, with shouts of grateful praise, will sacrifice to you.
What I have vowed I will make good. I will say, 'Salvation comes
from the Lord.'"*

JONAH 2:9 NIV

The missionary's slideshow from the orphanage in Africa was touching, but when he told how someone had given bottles of soft drinks to the children there and it was such a special treat that they made it last for a couple of days, it moved Cliff and Tracy to tears. They vowed that day that those children and the staff of the home would have the gift of a soft drink for Christmas that year.

They honored that vow, not just for that year, but for many years to come. It was their favorite Christmas gift to give, and they wiped away tears when the missionary sent a picture of everyone enjoying their soft drinks. It was a true joy for Cliff and Tracy to give, but it was also a reminder of another gift that had been freely given to them—God's sweet gift of salvation. What vows could you make as a couple to share the sweetness of Jesus with a world that needs to experience his love?

How could you and your spouse vow to serve God? Have you thanked God lately for his gift of salvation?

Lord, we praise you for being an amazing God. Help us vow to serve you more.

SPIRITUAL TRADITIONS

Stand firm and hold to the traditions that you were taught by us, either by our spoken word or by our letter.

2 THESSALONIANS 2:15 ESV

Traditions are a great thing. Those kinds of memories bind our hearts together whether it's bike rides down the beach, particular foods that you serve because Grandma used to make them, or having blueberry muffins by candlelight for the first day of school. But those traditions are even better when they impact our faith. Maybe you read the Christmas story together on Christmas Eve, perhaps you pray together on New Year's Eve asking for God's blessings for the year ahead, or you write a letter to your son about what it means to be a man of God, or you mark all of your family's favorite Bible verses in the gift of a Bible for a newborn.

The important thing is that we pay attention to those words, letters, and events that have shaped us as Christians and as husbands and wives. Those will help us stand firm in our faith and strengthen our marriages and our homes.

What spiritual traditions do you have together? What new traditions could you implement?

Father, thank you for the elements of faith that were planted in us. Help us to stand firm in our faith and in our marriage.

THE GIFT OF MARRIAGE

"A new commandment I give to you, that you love one another: just as I have loved you, you also are to love one another."
JOHN 13:34 ESV

The most precious gift ever given was found in a stable in Bethlehem—perfect love wrapped in swaddling clothes. A gift given with no strings attached, with no price for us to pay. Love just freely offered, ours for the taking. What a perfect example of the kind of love we should have in our marriages.

Christmas is a good time to stop and reflect on how much God has given to us and to think about the love revealed through that tiny babe in a manger. The child grew up, taught us how to live and then died for us. Long before this event, at the beginning of time, God created the wonderful and mysterious union we call marriage as a way to show his love and grace to the world. Held in such high esteem, God describes its relationship to that of Christ and the Church. It's a beautiful institution birthed in God's heart. Do we see it as that? Do we love like that?

How can you reflect God's love each day in your marriage? Will you be intentional today in loving your spouse like Jesus loves?

Lord, thank you for showing us what perfect love is. Help us to love each other as you love us.

WELL EQUIPPED

All Scripture is God-breathed and is useful for teaching, rebuking, correcting and training in righteousness, so that the servant of God may be thoroughly equipped for every good work.

2 TIMOTHY 3:16-17 NIV

Nathan is a contractor. Every morning before he leaves for the jobsite, he loads his truck with the tools and supplies he'll need for work that day. Some days he doesn't plan well, and he gets to the site and discovers he doesn't have his drill or the galvanized nails that he needs to complete the work. It costs him time, aggravation, and money when he has to stop what he's doing and either go home for what he needs or make a trip to the building supply store.

God wants us to be thoroughly equipped for life, and as husbands and wives, we need to avail ourselves of the God-breathed teaching that is offered in his Word. We'll save ourselves from aggravation, regrets, and correction from God. Let's make it a goal as a couple to spend time together in his Word so that we are equipped for whatever God asks us to do.

Do you spend time together in God's Word? How can that equip you for life as a couple?

Lord, make us sensitive to your Word. Supply our marriage with the tools that we need to become well-equipped servants for you.

THE WORD

The word of God is alive and active. Sharper than any double-edged sword, it penetrates even to dividing soul and spirit, joints and marrow; it judges the thoughts and attitudes of the heart.

HEBREWS 4:12 NIV

Most of us want to be the best spouses we can be. But for that to happen, God has to smooth away the imperfections. He has to cut out the things in our hearts that shouldn't be there. He has to get through all the muck until he reaches our hearts and souls. He doesn't just judge our actions, he judges our thoughts and attitudes as well.

That's where God's Word comes in. The Bible isn't an old book to be left on a shelf or on the coffee table collecting dust. The words in it are alive, and if we'll read them with the right heart attitudes, those verses can seep into our souls, replacing the messed-up things there with pure and clean thoughts and a heart that wants to please and honor God. Reading his Word together as a couple will provide a strong bond that won't be easily broken, and as we see each other striving to please God, it will deepen the love that is already there.

Do you read God's Word with the right attitude? How will that affect your marriage?

Lord, show us the treasures in your Word and make our hearts receptive to the things you need to change in us.

CONSIDER THE CREATOR

When I consider Your heavens, the work of Your fingers, the moon and the stars, which you have ordained, what is man that You are mindful of him, and the son of man that You visit him?

PSALM 8:3-4 NKJV

Mark and Marie sat on the beach while on vacation. The stars glowed and the sky looked like a giant canopy. The waves rolled in to the shore with powerful whooshes and then crept peacefully back to sea. As the couple sat there in companionable silence, a mama deer and her two babies wandered down the beach. Mark took a look around him—a really good look—as he soaked in the majesty of God's creation.

Mark felt so small as he realized what a big God we have. And as he sat there and thought about all of that, his eyes stopped on one of God's other stunning designs—his beautiful and compassionate wife. Mark reached out for her hand and then he said, "I was just sitting here thinking about God's amazing creation, and how you are his best one by far."

When's the last time you stopped to think about God's creation? When's the last time you admired the magnificent spouse he created for you?

Lord, you are an amazing designer. Thank you for creating my spouse. It's so unbelievable that you, who created the world, know who we are, and still you are willing to spend time with us.

RULE FOLLOWERS

Joyful are people of integrity, who follow the instructions of the
LORD.
Joyful are those who obey his laws and search for him with all their
hearts.
PSALM 119:1-2 NLT

Some people are rule followers. For them, a rule is a rule
and there is no question about whether or not to follow it.
Other people have a harder time following the rules. But no
matter if it is hard or easy for you, rules are there for us to have
parameters by which to play games, drive cars, live life, and
so much more. When others know you are a rule-follower, they
know you can be trusted and that you will do the right thing.

Trustworthiness is of supreme importance in marriage.
When you promise to love, honor, and cherish, you are also
promising to trust your mate, even if the exact word is not in
your vows. You are becoming one in every way with another
individual, and you are committing to being trustworthy. Both
of you will find tremendous peace and joy in knowing the
other can be trusted.

Are there areas where you find it difficult to trust your
mate? Resolve those issues today.

Lord, thank you that we are able to fully trust you. Help us
to be trustworthy in our marriage today and every day that
follows.

BUILDING ON
THE FOUNDATION

*"From the beginning I told you what would happen in the end.
A long time ago I told you things that have not yet happened.
When I plan something, it happens. What I want to do, I will do."*
ISAIAH 46:10 NCV

From the time of Adam and Eve, God planned marriage to
be a union. You can trust your marriage has twined the two of
you into one. It may have been love at first sight, or perhaps
you slowly got to know each other and friendship became
romance. It doesn't matter; God had plans for you. He formed
the foundation of your love. Build upon that foundation.

If you are newlyweds, you may wonder if you will have
children. If you are new parents, you may wonder what college
your child will go to. Older parents may wonder about empty
nests. Whatever stage you are in, it is normal to question what
the future holds. Enjoy the present. God will take care of you
no matter what the future holds.

*Are you missing out on the present in your marriage? Are
you so busy worrying about the future you are failing to
pay attention to your spouse? How can you make each day
important?*

**God, help us slow down and live in the present. Let us put
our trust of the future in your hands. Please give us the
wisdom we need each day and keep us from worry.**

DEDICATED TO GOD

What can I offer the LORD for all he has done for me?
I will lift up the cup of salvation and praise the LORD's name for
saving me.
I will keep my promises to the LORD in the presence of all his people.

PSALM 116:12-14 NLT

Alan and Grace had special plans for New Year's Eve. They'd planned an evening at home with just the two of them. They had a candlelight dinner in the dining room. They watched favorite old movies, popped popcorn, and laughed together. And as midnight approached, they knelt beside their sofa for what had been their tradition since their first year of marriage. They prayed together, thanking God for keeping them through the year that was ending, for being there for the hard times, and for his many blessings.

And then they prayed for the year ahead, asking God to help them be faithful to him and to each other, asking him to smooth the path before them, give strength where needed, and bless them so they could bless others. They kissed when the clock struck midnight, and began a new year that had been dedicated to God.

How can you honor your vows to God and each other?
Have you established a tradition for New Year's Eve?
Perhaps it could involve some time together in prayer.

Lord, we commit to serving you and loving each other as we begin a new year together. May all that we set out to do be saturated in prayer and Godly wisdom. Thank you for your continued blessing on our marriage and family.